Taki Abdul Redha Al Abduwani

The Value and Development of Soft Skills

D1742287

Taki Abdul Redha Al Abduwani

The Value and Development of Soft Skills

The case for Sultanate of Oman

LAP LAMBERT Academic Publishing

Impressum/Imprint (nur für Deutschland/ only for Germany)
Bibliografische Information der Deutschen Nationalbibliothek: Die Deutsche Nationalbibliothek
verzeichnet diese Publikation in der Deutschen Nationalbibliografie; detaillierte bibliografische
Daten sind im Internet über http://dnb.d-nb.de abrufbar.
Alle in diesem Buch genannten Marken und Produktnamen unterliegen warenzeichen-, marken-
oder patentrechtlichem Schutz bzw. sind Warenzeichen oder eingetragene Warenzeichen der
jeweiligen Inhaber. Die Wiedergabe von Marken, Produktnamen, Gebrauchsnamen,
Handelsnamen, Warenbezeichnungen u.s.w. in diesem Werk berechtigt auch ohne besondere
Kennzeichnung nicht zu der Annahme, dass solche Namen im Sinne der Warenzeichen- und
Markenschutzgesetzgebung als frei zu betrachten wären und daher von jedermann benutzt
werden dürften.

Coverbild: www.ingimage.com

Verlag: LAP LAMBERT Academic Publishing AG & Co. KG
Dudweiler Landstr. 99, 66123 Saarbrücken, Deutschland
Telefon +49 681 3720-310, Telefax +49 681 3720-3109
Email: info@lap-publishing.com

Herstellung in Deutschland:
Schaltungsdienst Lange o.H.G., Berlin
Books on Demand GmbH, Norderstedt
Reha GmbH, Saarbrücken
Amazon Distribution GmbH, Leipzig
ISBN: 978-3-8383-8622-5

Imprint (only for USA, GB)
Bibliographic information published by the Deutsche Nationalbibliothek: The Deutsche
Nationalbibliothek lists this publication in the Deutsche Nationalbibliografie; detailed
bibliographic data are available in the Internet at http://dnb.d-nb.de.
Any brand names and product names mentioned in this book are subject to trademark, brand
or patent protection and are trademarks or registered trademarks of their respective holders.
The use of brand names, product names, common names, trade names, product descriptions
etc. even without a particular marking in this works is in no way to be construed to mean that
such names may be regarded as unrestricted in respect of trademark and brand protection
legislation and could thus be used by anyone.

Cover image: www.ingimage.com

Publisher: LAP LAMBERT Academic Publishing AG & Co. KG
Dudweiler Landstr. 99, 66123 Saarbrücken, Germany
Phone +49 681 3720-310, Fax +49 681 3720-3109
Email: info@lap-publishing.com

Printed in the U.S.A.
Printed in the U.K. by (see last page)
ISBN: 978-3-8383-8622-5

Table of contents

Chapter 4 Research Methodology

Chapter 5 Soft Skill Orientation of the sample institutions

Chapter 6 Assessment of Soft Skills and distance travelled

Preface

The objective of the study is to assess the role of soft skills in human capital theory and explain the differences in soft skill acquisition in Oman across different activities and skill groups. Being quasi-experimental, the research design includes not only quantitative analysis but also qualitative case studies and in-depth narratives so as to showcase the relevance and relative contribution of soft skills as contrast to hard skills in improvement of human capital.

The research questions relate to: what are the different soft skills, how they can be categorised and measured and how differences in their endowment can be explained in the skill groups in given institutional setups, besides identifying the different sources of acquisition and impact of various intervention programmes like training, coaching and mentoring. The questions bring out not only the topical relevance of soft skills but also the growing emphasis on them in the work environment. The objectives have been to measure soft skills through an index in different skill groups in banks and oil companies; to assess the distance travelled and to assess the interaction between hard and soft skills through a human capital index in the performance of the employees. The hypotheses perceive variability in endowment of situational as contrast to personal and interpersonal skills (wherein soft skills are categorised into personal, interpersonal and situational, comprising of 31 sub-skills), the association between soft and hard outcomes and distance travelled and the performance of the reference groups.

The analysis shows that the oil companies place a lower degree of emphasis on soft skill development when compared to the banks owing to technical requirements. The soft skill index for the senior managers would be higher in the banks when compared to the oil companies. The difference will shoot up as a result of intervention programmes, indicating the benefits of effective training and development policy in the banks. Adoption of best practices needs analysis, case study approach and positive interactions between the trainers and the trainees which prove as important factors in upskilling. Since the reference group is drawn from the intervention sample, the difference in the soft skill index emphasises development pattern that is taking place. The impact of intervention is shown as greater in the case of senior managers especially in the banks when compared to the junior managers. It appears that the approach to soft skill enhancement is biased towards the senior managers in the banks who utilise the intervention facilities to the maximum extent possible when compared to the junior managers.

When the bank and the oil company scores are averaged for the regression analysis, the relative contribution of hard and soft skills to performance shows that the senior managers are able to realise a higher level of soft skill enhancement when compared to the junior managers (the soft skill coefficient being higher than the hard skill coefficient in the post-training scenario).

In respect of improvement in human capital stock index, the bank senior managers realise higher scores in soft skill when compared to hard skills, whereas in the oil companies, the contribution of soft skill to the index is lower. Though soft skills are important, the analysis shows that hard skills dominate and only in Bank A the senior managers realise a higher contribution of soft skill than the hard skills.

The observation that skills are developed not only in the workplace but also in other institutional setups like family, school and college negates the signalling approach to educational planning (where the emphasis is only on the workplace) and reinforce the prevalence of human capital theory, especially its soft component. Soft skills not only empower the higher education institutions and workforce in advancing career development and personal growth, they also create new opportunities and go beyond money motivation. The importance of experiential learning is brought out by concentrating on narratives.

Though there are many studies on human capital theory and empirical studies on soft skill development and measurement are very much limited in their focus, the present study attempts to bridge the knowledge gap in the understanding of soft skills in workplaces across different avocations and skill groups. The construction of the skill wheel and the soft skill index along with distance travelled and human capital index showcases the growing importance of soft skills, the exposition of which rests with the present study.

CHAPTER

1

Knowledge economy, human capital and development

1.1 Introduction

The purpose of this study is to evaluate the strategy of higher education in achieving the long-term objectives of soft skill development in Oman. The research questions revolve around: what is the role of higher education in economic development; what is the role of human capital (hard and soft skills); why the study of human capital is important in evolving strategies of higher education in the promotion of soft skills; why human capital theory is a better alternative than market signalling or screening in espousing the cause of soft skills; what is the role of higher education institutions in skill development and what is the role of human capital in education development in Oman.

Since human capital is the stock of knowledge, skills and abilities, which can help employees increase productivity and performance at work, it may be interesting to know how far it has been able to contribute to economic development vis-à-vis other types of capital. There have been many studies on this aspect (dealing with hard or technical skills) but our interest is not only to assess the relative contribution of the hard skill components but also to document the presence and need for soft skills in an emerging economy like Oman. This study contributes to the need for soft skills at the learning stage and at the workplace to be enabled by experiential learning.

The chapter is structured as follows. Section 1.2 explains the author's interest in the study. Section 1.3 discusses the role of education in knowledge development and some trends in higher education. Section 1.4 assesses the contribution of human capital and higher education in economic development. As education is represented by investment in human capital in the growth process, its significant contribution has been of critical study; especially with respect to returns on its investment vis-à-vis other forms of capital. Section 1.5 provides a background of Oman and examines the status of higher education there and characterises some of the major issues faced by higher education institutions in the region. Section 1.6 concludes emphasising the importance of human capital development in improving a country's competency and competitiveness.

1.2 Interest in the study

With a global economy comes opportunity and competition. As the Dean of a private college in Oman, I help my students meet that challenge through a curriculum and culture that embraces innovation. Our programmes incorporate masters and bachelors degrees in business, computing and accounts focused on innovation management and entrepreneurship. Our faculty is committed to both outstanding teaching and providing an opportunity for students to be trained. The flexible undergraduate curriculum that we have implemented allows every student to customise the programme to achieve his or her goals. We have launched an initiative to support first-year students during that critical transition from high school to college through foundation courses. The primary objective of our education is to provide the students with the skills required for the workplace so that they can be competitive and be responsible citizens. However, knowledge and skills alone do not suffice. The important thing is attitudes and I feel that neglect of this component in the education system is responsible for many of the ills in society. We have to respond to this increased awareness, by exploring and experimenting in our own individual and creative ways. We need to take some responsibility for the condition of the student and for the direction he or she is heading and we should take absolute responsibility for our own behaviour and actions.

From this perspective as an education administrator, I have been involved in higher education in Oman since many years and I am instrumental in devising ways and means for development of higher education in the region and for the growth of private sector participation in tertiary education. Education in Oman has received importance only in recent times. As a Dean, I have participated in many national and international workshops and conferences on higher education and felt the necessity to recognise the critical role of human capital in educational planning and development. I have noticed that not only among students but also among workers in many institutions, the attitude to creative thinking is missing which has prompted me to undertake studies relating to human capital. Also, I found that human capital was equated with only education qualification resulting in the lack of awareness on attitudinal change toward innovativeness. With the research methodology training I had during my graduate degree, I began to browse literature on human capital and came out with interesting ideas on the softer side of human capital. I realised that what the students and workers lack is soft skills and hence I must equip myself with grounding in the theory of soft skills so that I can develop teaching methodologies for my students to excel in soft skills which is more important than hard skills. The interest in soft skills invariably enabled me to assess education as to its contribution to knowledge economy and sustainable development. The culmination of this interest was the undertaking of the present study.

1.3 Education and knowledge economy

What is the purpose of education? Is it to enhance quality of life and/or to generate competency towards competitive economic advantage? The achievement of the first or second objective will be determined by the focus on knowledge acquisition as distinct from its commercialisation. In the past, education was not considered a basic need and it was the prerogative of a select few. It was only after the scientific revolution in the seventeenth century that interest in education became apparent leading to growth of many disciplines and institutions to provide it. It was after the Second World War that interest in higher education became prominent towards enabling competitive advantage, besides lifelong learning.

The word 'education' is derived from the Greek word 'educt', which means 'to bring out or enlighten'. Since education expressed in terms of knowledge has become the most enlightened factor of production, attention has been given to systematise education as an important input in the production process (Weitzman, 1998). Knowledge is defined as the ability to transform the existing resources to the advantage of the user. It helps not only to generate new wealth through innovations, but also in creating many knowledge-based opportunities (Bell, 1973; Drucker, 1969; Lane, 1966). The supply of knowledge includes different types of education, which help to generate new ideas and also refine human behaviour and habits required for lifelong learning and research and development (Stehr, 2001).

UNESCO Commission (2000) emphasises changing the aim of education from narrow instrumental one to one which embraces a broad view of learning to know, to do and to live together. For Avicenna (1993), education must aim at the formation of a personality complete in body, mind and character. In examining new roles for higher education, we need to contend if the new functions contribute to the broad aims of education. Knowledge as a factor of production has not been recognised as such owing to its special characteristics like being a public good. It is seldom quantified or priced, sometimes codified, but is more frequently tacit and implicit. In OECD countries more than 50 percent of GDP has been based on the production and distribution of knowledge (Bardo and Evans, 2006). The two main mechanisms of knowledge accumulation are specialisation in knowledge commodities and trade in goods and factors of production which generate new sources of technological inputs (Grossman and Helpman, 1991; Hargreaves, 2000; Lucas, 1993; Romer, 1990). With the growth of information and communication technology resulting in knowledge-based economy, the role of knowledge has to focus much on technical and business education which has led to its importance in higher education. As a result of this change, Anderson (2008) has commented that in the transition to a knowledge economy, apart from the focus on information technology, higher education has to emphasise abilities and skills of thinking about how to think and learning about how to learn. This calls for a redesigning of the skill

3

endowment of individuals orienting towards the job market. In other words, in the 'learning society', knowledge management assumes a vital role and hence the national educational systems have to be restructured in order to encompass the features of knowledge economy.

The creation and development of knowledge may be considered to be purposive given the nature of competition among different countries to lead in technology development (Lucas, 1993). When Higher education institutions (HEIs) which play a crucial role in knowledge generation make it value-free, a balance between social and commercial benefits has to be struck (Barnett, 2000). This leads to education for sustainable development which involves changing objectives of higher education in different cultures over time (Williams, 1973). The changing nature of knowledge and new methods of knowledge production demand creation of expert teams of scientists and policy makers with practical know-how, who can influence the larger society in adopting the new patterns of not only the education systems but also to restructure the societal framework towards nation building process. In this, education has become a major input in the process of development, much more than physical or natural capital (Gibbons et al., 1994).

1.4 Role of human capital in economic development

As knowledge is embedded in human capital, education and economic development become interrelated and exhibit worker quality and skills and how these affect the level and growth of productivity. There is evidence that productivity increase takes place through human capital, wherein education becomes productivity–enhancing rather than a device that individuals use to signal their ability (Porter, 1990). Sianesi and van Reenen (2000) point out that the increase in school enrolment rates by one percentage point leads to an increase of 1-2 percentage points in per capita GDP. As contrasted to this human capital flow, an increase in human capital stock (additional year of secondary education) leads to over one percentage point faster growth each year not only in OECD countries but also in the developing countries (Sianesi and van Reenen, 2000).

According to the neo-classical theory, a one-off permanent increase in the human capital stock (average years of education) is associated with a one-off increase in productivity (Becker, 1993; Johnes, 2006). It may be possible for emerging economies to catch up with the advanced countries by adopting the latter's educational technology. As per the new growth theory, a one-off permanent increase in the human capital stock is associated with a permanent increase in productivity through increasing returns to knowledge (Cortright, 2001; Gundlach, 2001). The new theory lays importance on knowledge generation and its distribution as a factor in endogenous development (Johnes, 2006). Large investments in human capital have resulted in better economic progress and higher efficiency in the use of labour force and wealth distribution.

However, education, apart from investment in human capital is considered as social investment toward achieving a higher level of economic growth but also greater equity in wealth distribution. In the sociological view, education enables meritocratic social mobility through selection and screening. However, lengthening of average schooling time may lead to social inequalities and wage differentials corresponding to different levels of education (Thurow, 1996). When the opportunity cost of studying shows an increase, there has to be an increased demand for higher education, sometimes concurrent with a decline in job opportunities of particular educational levels (Turner, 1992).

Psacharopoulus and Woodhall (1985) suggest that investment in human capital has higher rates of return than in physical capital. If we branch out human capital into knowledge capital, it may have a prominent role to play when compared to physical capital. Increase in productivity as a result of growth in higher education takes place not only in urban areas and industry but also in agriculture (Becker, 1993). However, employers adhere to a set of beliefs which values explicitly educational attainment in the selection of employees. Further, they conceive the problem in terms of minimum levels of education suitable for different types of employment. What is emphasised in recent times is the soft component of human capital as necessary for successful careers and continued education. If this is so, there may be lesser returns for over-educated people when compared to those with modest attainments in particular jobs (Anderson and Heyneman, 2005). Since globalisation is a discursive as well as a material practice (Edwards and Usher, 2000), HEIs in Oman which follow the UK or USA educational pattern, would experience this type of competitiveness so as to affect the pace of education development.

Human capital theory indicates that labour market earnings increase for individuals with more education because educational institutions increase the productive skills of students (Becker, 1993). The theory has been applied to education in explaining investment decisions in higher education and on-the-job training where the generic skills are developed. Investment in education occurs only if the expected returns compare favourably against existing alternatives, such as full-time employment. The key assumption of human capital theory is that "schooling raises earnings and productivity mainly by providing knowledge, skills and a way of analysing problems" (Becker, 1993, p.19). Human capital theory combines investment in education, labour market earnings of students and the very process of classroom learning into an amalgam of knowledge development. Herein lies the critical role of its soft component.

Moja (2002) contends that higher education is able to contribute to economic development by making available by creating knowledge and by transferring it across regions. The globalisation process has led to an unprecedented demand for access to higher education while at the same time most governments are unwilling or unable to provide the necessary support to public institutions

5

(Power, 2000). Higher education has the capability of strengthening the transfer system in improving the employability of students. Mobility of students and faculty across borders and greater use of information and communication technology enable learning process to assume critical value (Altbach, 2002). Internationalisation of education refers to specific policies and initiatives undertaken to deal with these global trends and include policies relating to recruitment of foreign students and faculties besides collaboration with foreign academic institutions and establishment of branch campuses abroad. In view of this, the importance of knowledge development and the changes in education systems and training methods to achieve this, increased investment becomes the prerogative in the globalised era.

Important fallout of globalisation has been privatisation of educational services and improvement in their quality. As education contributes substantially to a country's GDP (10 percent in USA and the fifth largest service export in 2000), commercialisation and commoditisation of education has resulted in its being more globalised. Further, the slow withdrawal of government from the social sector puts higher education in the hands of private sector in an increasing scale (Power, 2000). Globalisation and growth of private sector participation in education development have enabled higher education to have many roles, the important one being intrinsic (Robeyns, 2006), wherein a person may value knowing something for the sake of the knowledge. Education also has an instrumental role in terms of both personal development and collective responsibility besides catering to both economic and non-economic ends. The instrumental personal role helps a person to find a job to the less vulnerable on the labour market, to be better informed as a consumer and to be more able to find information on opportunities. The instrumental economic role may be collective such as if a large percentage of population is illiterate; the market for books and newspapers becomes automatically limited. With regard to non-economic role, the personal level enables access to information, knowledgeable about health issues and communicates with the outside world. At the collective level, the non-instrumental role enables people to live in a society peacefully in spite of having different views of life leading to a tolerant society (Robeyns, 2006).

The above roles of education can be conceptualised in different typologies (Robeyns, 2006) like education as human capital, education as human right and education as human capability. As per human capital approach, skills and knowledge acquired through education become an important part of a person's income generating abilities. The hard or technical skills denote the extrinsic value of human capital, whereas soft skills indicate its intrinsic values. However, the intrinsic importance of education, besides personal and collective social roles has not been given due recognition so far. Education as a human right stresses that education should be guaranteed to all because of its intrinsic importance and this conceptualisation becomes exclusive government-focused. According to the capability concept, human functions become the constitutive elements of living, wherein being healthy and educated or holding a job or being part of a family and having friendships are functions which are in the nature of outcomes, whereas capabilities are real opportunities to achieve valuable states of being and doing. This approach enables evaluate people's wellbeing such as inequality and poverty and may be used as an alternative to social-cost benefit analysis. Education at once becomes intrinsic and instrumental besides being interdisciplinary (Robeyns, 2006). However, in the corporate world human rights are evaluated in terms of legal rights only and human capabilities are impaired by judicial and political decisions.

The human capital approach in emphasising on investment in education and training to realise increase in productivity becomes both instrumental and economic in the monetised world. Since soft skills are personal, their acquisition depends on the knowledge base on the one hand and the efforts of HEIs and workplaces in imparting the skills to students and workers on the other. Different industries have different skills requirements for their jobs, which the HEIs have to deliver. In the continuing learning process, the workplaces take up skill development activities where the HEIs left and equip their workers in the requisite soft skills. Hard skill requirement is fixed, but not that of soft skill and since the competency level of a worker depends both on the hard and soft skills, when hard skill is no longer in a position to be improved, the focus in the workplace is mainly on soft skill development. When the global perspective is considered, the strategy of education development has to strive to achieve competitive advantage. In countries like Oman which are still developing in their education field, globalisation has impacted on the emergence of globalised education with which the citizens can hope to compete with others in a competent way.

1.5 Higher education in Oman

Oman is the second largest Gulf Cooperation Council (GCC) state in terms of area after Saudi Arabia and is composed of varying topographical areas consisting of desert plains, valleys and mountains with scanty rainfall except the southern region which receives monsoon rains. Oman was predominantly an agricultural country specialising in the manufacture of traditional artefacts like pottery, copper work, weaving and silverware before the discovery of oil in 1962. The social infrastructure was weak with very few educational institutions and hospitals. Many Omanis migrated to other countries to sustain their livelihood. After 1970, when oil became the major source of growth, the government launched successive development schemes to modernise the country. Today, Oman has evolved into a middle income country, with its nominal per capita income level of US $20,000 (CIA, 2009). It has a population of about 3.4 million with a workforce of about one million. Of this, 40 percent are expatriates (MONE, 2009).

We can also consider the human development index, which takes into account life expectancy, education and per capita income levels (with equal weights) that brackets Oman as middle level

7

with a rank of 53 out of 179 countries in 2008 (UNDP, 2008), showing an improvement over 2003 when it was ranked 79 (UNDP, 2005). Countries with high per capita income also have a higher human development index and Oman has been showing progress in human development also. Oil revenue has been financing improvements in major social and economic infrastructures like schools, colleges, hospitals, roads, communications and construction. However, given its very low oil reserves to current production ratio, the necessity arises to broaden the Omani economic base and hence the attractions of developing a knowledge-based economy so that long-term sustainability can be established. This becomes pertinent when the illiteracy level was at around 20 percent according to 2003 census (MONE, 2003).

Towards long-term development, the government has launched Vision 2020 with the objective of complete literacy by the end of seventh plan in 2010. To achieve this, the government has increased its spending on education upto about five percent of GDP recently (MONE, 2008a). The share of primary education in total government expenditure has been 36 percent, secondary education having 47 percent share leaving less than 10 percent share to tertiary education (UNDP, 2007). The importance given to tertiary education is grossly inadequate when compared to many advanced and also developing countries. It should be noted here that it is not mere reallocation of resources to tertiary education that will improve its status; rather it has to be through a balanced development of all levels of education. This requires additional investment in human capital which will facilitate substantial increase in science and technology (S&T) and research and development (R&D) intensity in many sectors. If manpower demand by these sectors will be a function of the existing level of technology and the quality of human capital required in particular sectors, as and when technology intensity increases the nature of manpower demand by firms will also change. Higher education involves increased investment coupled with increased productivity and innovativeness. The level of technical progress would be incorporated in the human capital endowment (Becker, 1993).

Currently, the proportion of unskilled and semiskilled labour force in Oman is about 75 percent, showing little variation over the past decade (MONE, 2008a). Through what is called as Omanisation process, the government is trying to replace expatriate workers with local workforce wherein targeted increased level of localisation in many sectors is to be achieved. The growing demand for technical manpower in the oil and non-oil sectors then will have to be matched with the supply. Towards this, many HEIs have been established to educate and train the youth.

The Arab Regional Conference on Higher Education (1998) has realised the importance of the contribution of higher education to local development. One of the main targets of the strategy has been to make HEIs prompt the students to undertake community service on the lines of UNESCO's (2003) novel programme called the UNILIT (UNIversity Students for LITeracy). The concept is based on the idea that "each one teach one" which presupposes that each university student enrolled in UNILIT will raise at least one person per year out of the darkness of illiteracy. The hope is that by the time a student has graduated from university, he or she would have contributed to eradicating the illiteracy of at least four individuals. This initiative is particularly important in the Arab region where illiteracy rates remain some of the highest in the world. But it is also an attempt to connect grassroots literacy programmes and HEIs in an effort to achieve sustainable human development. University-community partnership allows universities to extend their commitment to educate and to provide educational services at different levels of learning (UNESCO, 2003). In this, the focus of the innovative programmes is on the buildup of soft skills not only for lifelong learning but for better employability too.

In Oman, there are ten publicly-run colleges and a state-administered Sultan Qaboos University besides 25 private colleges and four private universities as a result of which the contribution of higher education has been marked in respect of enrolment and improvement in literacy. However, the challenges faced by these institutions are many and include absence of a clear comprehensive educational philosophy and the education system has failed to introduce consistent training programmes especially in soft skills and create partnership with the business community in better utilising the skills and efficiencies of the graduates. It is very clear that there is a gap between the society's present and future needs for education and the plans for further expansion in education system (Wagiran, 2008).

The importance given to educational development in the country is of recent origin. The proportion of population obtaining higher education is less than eight percent but has to double if the necessary content of S&T personnel for knowledge development has to be obtained. The changing industrialisation scenario in the country demands generation of appropriate skilled and technical personnel which the HEIs have to supply in the respective fields. If Oman has to compete with other countries in achieving educational standards and productivity increases, human capital policy to be adopted depends on focus on soft skills. From this perspective, it is essential that the country assesses the stock of human capital and willingness for innovativeness in synthesising the above aspects towards increase in competency and governance. Some of these objectives have been spelt out by the Seventh Five Year Development Plan (MONE, 2008b) and looking at the progress made especially in the recent years, it may be said that the achievement in respect of enrolment in higher education has been high but the focus on S&T and soft skills has been weak, given the country's dependence on technology imports.

1.6 Conclusion

The disparity in educational attainment and in productivity between the developing and advanced countries lays in differential knowledge generation and use. HEIs have been spearheading knowledge creation and transfer through various strategies in the globalised era. Investment in human capital has showcased the critical role of education in economic development and trade in human resources through strategic alliances has resulted in diffusion of knowledge and innovativeness. For a country like Oman which has initiated universal education with an emphasis on knowledge-based economy, higher education has a daunting role to play in generating workforce towards achieving global competitive advantage. In this, emphasis on the soft component of human capital becomes crucial. Since the contribution of human capital to economic growth is well established we would like to disaggregate human capital into hard and soft components to evaluate how the development of the latter will speed up the process of knowledge development. The HEIs have the responsibility to develop the soft skills of students so that they would be competitive at the workplace. HEIs in Oman have to concentrate on the development of soft component of human capital through partnership programmes for better employability of students.

In understanding the role of education in economic development, the status of educational planning within that of economic planning requires to be assessed, for it is the nature of educational planning that impact on the quality of higher education. Chapter two critically assesses the different aspects of educational planning along with its approaches to bring in the relevance of human capital theory in inducing strategic directions in education development.

CHAPTER

2

Educational planning and strategies of Human Capital development

2.1 Introduction

The first chapter stressed the importance of human capital in knowledge development and this chapter examines the role of human capital in educational planning. While human capital itself is an approach to economic development, approaches to human capital development focus on training to improve business, technical and soft skills of employees. As Foss (2008) points out, development of human capital takes place through a continuously supportive process which stimulates and empowers individuals to acquire knowledge, values, skills and understanding they require at the workplace. In the past, education was considered as a consumption good, in that its primary function was one of facilitating lifelong learning (European Commission, 1995). Hence, the approach to educational planning has to focus on both lifelong learning and acquisition of knowledge and sustainable education development results. The chapter reviews literature on educational planning and human capital development, with special emphasis on measurement of human capital and how it can be augmented through soft skill teaching and training at institutional level or workplace.

The chapter is structured as follows. Section 2.2 reviews different approaches to educational planning. While section 2.2.1 critiques the human capital approach, other approaches are discussed in section 2.2.2. Section 2.2.3 critically examines the different approaches and establishes the relevance of human capital approach and discusses the strategies of higher education within the framework of human capital approach. Measurement of human capital is briefed in section 2.3 and section 2.4 discusses the strategies of human capital development which involve training and soft skill acquisition. Section 2.5 concludes justifying the human capital approach as a better instrument in educational planning.

11

2.2 Approaches to educational planning

Educational planning aims at tuning education standards to the demands of globalisation in achieving the multiple goals of growth and development. It focuses on the importance of forecasting and the advantages of qualitative indicators in addition to quantitative aspects toward establishing a viable developmental plan. The relevance of decentralised decision making and implementation process involve interactive and rational planning models. Planning involves application of systematic analysis toward education development that meets the needs of the society. It establishes relationship between general planning mechanisms and educational policy (OECD, 1980). Educational planning (within the ambit of general planning) is concerned primarily with future development and embodies the skills of anticipating, influencing and controlling the nature and direction of the change. It deals with the consequences of active intervention which will change the present into something better in the future. Further, it is closely linked not only with policy making but also with decision making and determines appropriate goals and prepares for the change. The overall strategy has to be concerned with sequence, consistency and probability (Forojalla, 1993).

The approaches to educational planning emphasise on development of human resources along with other resources so that the planning goals are realised. The screening approach was mooted by Arrow (1973) and others, while the signalling approach was enunciated by Spence (1973). Becker (1975) commented on the human capital approach and also on credentialism. Lazear (1977) and Gullason (1989) consider the consumption value of education. This approach is similar to the social demand approach wherein willingness to pay emerges as the sole criterion for individual demand for education. Webster (1970) reviews demand for places, manpower requirements and rate of return approaches to educational planning. Forojalla's (1993) approaches cover the nature of human resources, social demand and manpower requirements. We propose to integrate all these approaches and group these under four function-oriented approaches so that the treatment becomes comprehensive for comparison. In addition to human capital approach, other approaches of willingness to pay, screening and manpower requirements will be examined as to their relevance to augment educational development.

2.2.1 Human capital approach

Knowledge is an inherent part of human capital development and involves knowing about facts and collecting information to do something. In continuation of section 1.3, issues like know-what, know-why, know-how and know-who can be considered as different stages of knowledge development (OECD, 2000). 'Know-what' refers to knowledge about facts and is close to the process of information capable of being broken down into bits and communicated as data. 'Know-why', which is crucial for technological development, refers to scientific knowledge of principles and laws of nature in the human mind and society. Production and reproduction of 'know-why' is often managed by specialised institutions like research laboratories. 'Know-how' is the ability to do something and is related to the skills of production workers and the ability to perform actions more generally. The sharing of know-how creates networks and when networks are formed between research teams and laboratories, 'know-who' assumes information about 'who know-what' and 'who know-how to do what' (OECD, 2000). Know-how and know-who are basically tacit knowledge and therefore difficult to quantify and measure. Know-what and know-why are easily codifiable while know-how and know-who indicates learning process that involves social practices. Know-who is socially embedded knowledge which is difficult to be transferred through formal channels of information (OECD, 2000). Promotion of skills and learning capabilities to exploit the above aspects of knowledge leads to up-gradation of human capital through formal education, continuous and lifelong learning and training to match labour supply and demand in terms of skill requirements.

The concept of human capital was first proposed by Jacob Mincer (1958), later developed by Theodore Schultz (1961) and Gary Becker (1962). According to them, human capital is the stock of valued skills, knowledge and insights, controlled by an individual wherein the attributes become valuable in the economic context. This stock may yield labour and management services or entrepreneurship. Human capital plays a part similar to that of physical capital like machinery or factories been defined as the knowledge, competency, attributes and skills embodied in individuals facilitating the creation of personal, social and economic well-being (OECD, 2001a). It is intangible and hence estimates of its stock are constructed indirectly. It is embodied in individuals and cannot be disposed of or sold to others. It consists of hard component which is the cognisable technical skill and also the non-cognisable soft skill which is personalised. According to OECD (2001b), investment in human capital becomes critical to develop both these components. Investment in human capital fosters technological change and in turn is affected by modern knowledge and technology changes. Innate ability, acquired knowledge through formal education and competency acquired through training on the job are the components of human capital (Blundell et al., 1999).

Human capital has been treated as a stock of assets yielding future cash flows. However, it could be substitutable by other forms of capital, especially in a neo-classical set-up. In modern endogenous growth theory, where technical change takes place within an organisation, human capital acts upon other factors and facilitates growth of indigenous technology, as well being augmented in the process. Human capital may be industry or firm specific, referring to skills or knowledge useful only to a single trade or employer and general, useful to all employers (Becker, 1993). According to Collins (1971), this approach is similar to technical-function analysis wherein

13

education augments economic productivity directly. It is formal education which provides the necessary specific or general skills required for highly skilled jobs, accounting for increase in educational attainment. Technological progress changes the skill requirements for jobs continuously. Human resources have been contributing to creation of wealth in many countries and hence this approach toward educational planning emphasises the contribution of human capital to economic development. The present study is interested more in training and human capital development at the workplace.

2.2.2 Other approaches

The second approach to educational planning considers that what is important is the intrinsic or consumption value of education (Alstadsaeter, 2004; Forojalla, 1993; Webster, 1970). The approach is to be distinguished from the social demand approach wherein anticipated future demand for education from students and parents is estimated as stemming from private investment (Williams, 1974). Because it is demand-oriented, it can be construed that education fulfils the consumption aspect more than investment. The consumption approach indicates the role of non-pecuniary returns to education focusing on the willingness of individuals to pay for different levels of education. This suggests that instead of maximising lifetime income, the individual tries to maximise lifetime utility from education (Oosterbeek and van Ophem, 2000). While lower levels of education can be termed as consumption 'bads', higher levels constitute consumption 'goods'. When human capital and consumption approaches are combined, Kodde and Ritzen (1984) find that the demand for education will be greater than in human capital approach, owing to direct utility gain through consumption demand.

The third approach centres on the so-called screening model (Arrow, 1973), which assumes that education has no inherent social value. Instead, the system provides a method of sorting students through a filtering process. By this method, the most able students are placed in the most difficult and best remunerated jobs. In this approach, output of the system is assessed through ranking, where the quality of the ranking is based on the capacity to perform high quality jobs. Education may act as a signal or a device for unobservable ability wherein firms sort out information about ability from education and students choose a particular educational level to signal their ability to potential employers (Bedard, 2001). The signalling model predicts a higher high school dropout rate in region that contains a university whereas the human capital model predicts no difference at all (Quiggin, 1999). However, under signalling, education certifies which people would have greater ability but it does not tell in what way that occurs, because schooling may not significantly reinforce that ability in any direct manner (Sakamoto and Kim, 2006). Though education may be associated with productivity, it may not directly cause it. Rather, the association between education and productivity stems from the individual's ability and trainability (Sakamoto and Kim, 2006). As education may be the primary screening device which employers value most, it certifies who requires lower training cost based on the ability and trainability. Changing the distribution of education may change who gets the better jobs but distribution of wages may not be affected. Hence, according to this model, education has little to do with equalisation of wage distribution and reduction of poverty.

The concept of 'credentialism', similar to that of screening, indicates that the degrees earned by the students convey information about their abilities and capacities. This suggests that the earnings of graduates will exceed those of high schoolers not because productivity of the college graduates is raised, but because more productive students move over to colleges (Becker, 1993). However, when the employers consider only the certificate of the prospective candidates, they tend to focus on getting the most qualified personnel resulting in less qualified people not being selected for the jobs, even though they may be eligible for the same. This process, if continued, may lead to mismatch between qualification and wages owing to supply-demand divergences and may result in 'over-education' or 'under-employment' situations. The difference between screening and credentialism is that while employers hire workers with credentials, the required credentials have little or nothing to do with any direct skills and actual earning capacity, whereas under screening, workers with credentials will be more productive than those without credentials.

It has been observed that higher education students have at least some interest in the labour market outlook when they choose education (de Grip and Heijke, 1998). As a remedy for the poor match between the educational system and the labour market, the manpower requirement approach was initiated by OECD in the 1960s (van Eijs, 1994). In this, planning begins once GDP target growth is fixed and manpower requirements in various occupations and educational qualifications required for these occupations are determined. According to International Labour Organisation (Forojalla, 1993), there are 45 occupational categories under four classes of university degree or equivalent; secondary education with one-three years of training following higher school certificate; secondary plus technical training for one or two years at certificate level but below a diploma and full primary education plus practical training. Labour requirements, when compared with flow of graduates will provide the required training needs which will enable the actualisation of GDP target. However, the matching process in the labour market becomes problematic and hence the approach has to be more flexible to take into account the reliability of forecasts. Under this approach, there has to be a match between education and labour market (Dekker et al., 1993), wherein labour market data are incorporated in many information products for vocational and educational purposes.

Further study becomes a way to avoid unemployment and a higher degree will increase the opportunities in the labour market. The employers who demand labour have to know about the nature of workforce to fill up the vacancies in that the workers will have the specific knowledge and skills towards achieving increased productivity. Manpower development becomes the building stock for enhancement of human resources through formal education and training (Abegaz, 1994). The assumption of educational attainment determining productivity (human capital theory) is relaxed under this approach since the matching process is concerned with allocation of workers with different educational backgrounds over jobs in which different skills are required (de Grip and Heijke, 1998). Where there is a mismatch between the acquired and required skill level of the workers, this indicates the existence of under or over-education of the workers.

2.2.3 A critique of the approaches

Educational planning has become an important tool in generating different educational attainment levels not only to match the manpower requirements but also in the enhancement of productive capacity of the organisation and the economy. Therefore, investment in education has to yield a rate of return such that investment is justified as in any other sector. If investment in education is expended just for its consumption without any impact on the returns, the country's overall investment programme becomes less productive. The willingness to pay for education is justified only when education returns it back. Though education can be considered as a lifelong learning process, unless it yields adequate earning capacity, the learning process will be flawed or dependent on subsidisation by others. We construe that the investment component of education has much to contribute to development over that of the consumption component.

As regards screening, the approach in rejecting the association of education (beyond a certain point) to higher productivity maintains that increasing the number of people in higher education will result in lower standards and the usefulness of academic achievement will stand reduced. As contrast to human capital theory, education has little to do with productivity or equity and in regards to the poor people, screening will diminish their disadvantage against those where wealth and birth status make higher education easier. Under signalling, even though employers may initially lack information on the productive abilities of the workers they hire, they will acquire the information in due course of time. If education does not improve productivity and identifies productive workers only, then it will become less related with earnings as job experience accumulates. We may construe that when education becomes an effective screen, the better educated will become more productive and will earn more even after the employers acquire more information. When there is emphasis on worker productivity, the signalling component of the return to education becomes small.

If credentialism is the rule, the required credentials will have little or nothing to do with the actual productivity on the job. The screening approach contends that workers with credentials are more productive than those without credentials. However, the human capital theory explains more of the variance in outcomes such as wages and earnings than screening.

The relationship between human capital and growth suggests that increase in productivity becomes the major factor in innovation and competitiveness. Hence, increase in the quantity and quality of the human capital stock gains momentum as recommended by the Lisbon strategy in 2000. The OECD *Jobs Study* (OECD, 1994) emphasised investment in human capital and extension of lifelong education.   Psacharopoulos and Patrinos (2002) have compared returns on education for three decades for many countries with estimates on both private and social returns. The annual rate of return on upper secondary education averaged 16.4 percent for women and 14.9 percent for men in 1995 when compared to 13.6 percent returns to business capital in European Union (OECD, 1998). Above the threshold level, every year of schooling and one percent increase in investment in human capital contributes to 0.6 percent of GNP (Lleras, 2004). At the micro level, there is evidence that education attainment and soft skill development are primary determinants of individual income and labour market status. It has been observed that an additional year of schooling increases wages by around six percent in the European countries like Italy and can increase up to nine percent in cases of under-regulated labour market. A year of training (including soft skills) increases wages as much as by five percent (Fuente and Ciccone, 2002).

Countries which had devoted a sizeable portion of their GDP (say around six percent in each on health and education) have witnessed rapid growth of skill formation and augmentation of human capital (OECD, 2006). Further, an increased share of expenditure on higher and tertiary education has ushered in the knowledge-based economy. It can be argued that growth in knowledge complements basic factors of production in improving their productivity and enhancing their acquired competitive advantage. In countries where investment in education has been below the desired level (such as in Africa), technological achievement and productivity growth have been slow. Because of this, not only has the rate of effective utilisation of the basic factors slowed down, but their integration with other factors has become less efficient.

One of the main critiques of human capital approach relates to the lack of substitution among various groups of workers and it may be that fixed coefficients of employment forecast may fail to consider the impact of technology on the skill up-gradation of different groups and the need for predictions may be a source of error. The best way will be to relax some of the assumptions of human capital theory like educational background only as determining productivity. It can be argued that individual's productivity will be closely related to the quality of the matching process between education and the job. It has been reported that the returns on training in soft or fundamental skills are higher when compared to that on business or technical skills (Woodhall, 2001). As school enrolment rates increase, average incomes may stagnate with increasing

17

unemployment rate. By improving the quality of education, it may be possible to endow human capital, both in its hard and soft components with an orientation toward lifelong learning thus transforming the firms into learning organisations. The present study is concerned with the organisations that improve the quality of human capital through specific interventions.

2.3 Measurement of human capital

Measurement of human capital will indicate not only its contribution in the production process, but also its role vis-à-vis other resources. The different measures of human capital include cost-based, income-based and educational-based measures (OECD, 1998). Inputs into the human capital production process including cost of bringing up and educating people form the basis for the cost-based approach. The investment cost of education would include the opportunity cost of wages foregone while studying, while future returns will indicate the difference in the income stream accruing to persons with higher qualification. In the income-based approach, earnings of individuals will be influenced by acquired skills and education. In the education approach, human capital is based on literacy rates, enrolment rates and mean years of schooling. Defined differently, human capital may be considered as the present value of expected future returns or as the accumulated sum of past investment or as a sum of individual's capabilities expressed in some common unit of account.

Early measures of human capital were more concerned with demonstrating the country's wealth in terms of monetary value of both human and physical capital (Bassanini and Scarpetta, 2001). Later on, human capital became a variable to explain economic growth and a potential policy instrument. Human capital contributed to economic growth at the macro level and produced spillovers toward enhanced development of individual capacity (Le et al., 2005). Measurement of human capital may have limitations contributed by changes in technology, socio-economic conditions, changes in schooling and changes in work ethics (Murray, 2005). When human capital envelops soft skills, it has to consider not only educational attainment but different levels of soft skill development also, which may have a larger say in productivity increase.

Mulligan and Sala-i-Martin's (1995) labour income-based measure attempts to obtain an index value rather than a monetary value of human capital. One of the advantages of this measure is that by netting out the effect of physical capital, variation in quality and relevance of schooling across time and space are pinpointed. Further, the elasticity of substitution across workers can vary and the method does not assume equal amounts of skills on workers with equal amounts of schooling. However, the model may fail when wages vary for reasons other than changes in the marginal value of human capital. The assumption of zero-schooling workers are identical always and everywhere and that different levels of schooling are perfect substitutes is open for debate. The

18

model neglects the contribution of informal schooling, on-the-job training and health in concentrating only on formal schooling.

Jeong modified Mulligan and Sala-i-Martin's model by considering the industrial labourer as classified by ILO rather than no schooling labour as *numeraire*. According to Jeong (2002), industrial labourers who supply their physical effort with little skill are more comparable than other types of workers. In this case, human capital can be defined as the ratio of aggregate labour income to the average income of the industrial labourer. It may be added here that industrial labourers have the same human capital across countries and contribution to human capital will be proportional to wage rates. According to this, rich countries have two to three times more value of human capital when compared to poor countries.

The estimated rate of return could be grossly overestimated because individuals differ in education and other characteristics. Becker's (1993) empirical analysis suggests a strong correlation between ability and education. Even granting for adjustments in differential ability like rank in class, IQ, parents' education, personality, communication ability, motivation and family upbringing, it can be proved that private rate of return would be more than 10 percent and there would be a marked earnings differential between college and high school graduates (Becker, 1993). Further, relationship between investment in education and on-the-job and vocational training, health and other human capital would also affect earning differentials. The gain from college education can vary depending upon urban or rural status, graduate or dropout status, race and sex even within a given demographic group.

The human capital theory explains interpersonal and interregional earnings differentials, the relationship between age and earnings and effect of specialisation on skill. Specific investments are expended for hiring costs to execute training and because of this unemployment may be greater among unskilled than skilled workers. College students on the whole tend to be more able than high schoolers but gains from college education will vary amongst different groups. Thus, the concept is relevant not only to micro investment in education, on-the-job training and other skills and knowledge by individuals and firms but also in understanding macro changes in inequality, economic growth, unemployment and foreign trade.

Following Mulligan and Sala-i-Martin (1995), we can measure the value of human capital as ratio of aggregate labour income to the wage of the uneducated. To support this argument we will have to assume that wages need not change for reasons other than changes in human capital and uneducated may be perfect substitutes for other labourers. In the aggregate production function, production depends on total human capital and non-human capital in the economy (Mulligan and Sala-i-Martin, 1995). This is similar to the model proposed by Lucas (1988) where the concept of capital is broadened to include human capital also, as contrasted to attribution of growth to existing stock of human capital which generates innovations and improves a country's ability to imitate and adapt new technology.

Human capital is related to labour force and as such includes all productive aspects of education, on-the-job training, physical and mental fitness and the quality of matching process between workers and firms (Murphy and Saleh-Isfahani, 2003). Because different people have different skills, it may not be possible to simply add all human beings to compute human capital. People who are more productive have to be given a larger rate. According to Jorgenson and Fraumeni (1992), a machine's productivity is instrumental in its quantitative performance whereas human capital has to be quality-adjusted sum of the labour input. For example, employing a zero-schooling worker (base) implies that the productivity and wage for other educational qualifications may differ across different environments owing to changes in aggregate stocks of physical and human capital and other inputs. In other words, individual productivity depends not only on the individual stock of capital but also on the available stock of other inputs. The author aggregates the level of skill of every individual by computing the stock of human capital of all workers with certain years of schooling and move over different educational attainment status of the labour force aged 25 to 65 years with the following categories (ILO, 1972):

0. No schooling
1. 0-4 years of elementary school
2. 5-8 years of elementary school
3. 1-3 years of high school
4. High school graduate
5. 1-3 years of college
6. College graduate or more.

In our analysis in chapter seven on estimating changes in the quality of human capital stock, we will be adopting a similar yardstick to measure changes in the quality of human capital stock, wherein the baseline will be that of high schooler. Human capital computed using earnings per person may show a very strong correlation with labour income and skill formation (Jeong, 2002). Of the above categories, wage for each category has to be taken to be the average weekly earnings as against earnings of those with no schooling.

Mulligan and Sala-i-Martin (1995) have constructed measures of human capital in the US for six census years. They assign different weights for different workers because of the fact that schooling in different places under different times has different qualities. Further, different types and quantities of schooling have different relevance in different places over a period of time. The important contribution of the authors lies in allowing for variable weights to capture the schooling quality and its relevance. The benchmark is a zero-schooling worker and the measure of income requires the assumption of perfect elasticity between zero-schooling workers and the rest. Since labour income incorporates both human and physical capital, higher physical capital would mean higher labour income. If labour income is divided by wage of a zero-schooling worker, the effect of physical capital can be separated. Human capital has been found to be positively related to average years of schooling, It is found that efficiency was increasing in US schooling though the phase at which the wages rose with schooling varied over time (Mulligan and Sala-i-Martin, 1995). However, there have been cases where some states in the US had low human capital stock for higher schooling. Movements in the relative productivities of different workers showed that in 1980s human capital growth was larger than that of schooling. This leads us to the different strategies to be adopted to develop human capital so that not only productivity levels but also the knowledge endowment of the society can be improved.

2.4 Human capital development through soft skills

Measurement of human capital and its critical role in the labour market induces the organisations to employ quality labour input for competitive advantage. In this context, it is soft skill formation techniques that assume criticality in improving the quality of human capital. We will define soft skills and establish their growing importance in this section, while its classification is explained in the next chapter. Soft skills refer to the cluster of personality traits, social graces, language proficiency, personal habits and teamwork. Since the focus of the study is on soft skills, we shall consider this aspect in some detail. Though the concept of soft skills is of recent origin, it was Dale Carnegie who spearheaded its crucial significance in his 1936 book 'How to win friends and influence people' and set the motion for soft skill training and development. Even today Dale Carnegie training system is practised world over in order to improve skill endowments. Where skill shortage is witnessed, it is more so in the case of soft skills and the employers will be very happy to have 'aesthetic labour' that could look and do right. In modern-day business courses, soft skill component like personal development, effective communication and leadership qualities and problem solving skills are incorporated into the curriculum so that when the students come out of their graduation, they will possess the necessary soft skills the companies look for. Soft skills not only empower hard skills and create new opportunities, but also help to advance personal development and ethics in professionalism. Stasz et al. (1996) and Fleischer and Dressner (2002) have emphasised the importance of soft skills for new recruits and in any workplace and how employees progress after the initial appointment.

The term 'soft skill' has two origins according to Simpson (2006). The first originated from employers identifying the need for non-traditional skills which relate to the individual and how they interact with others. Owing to the changing nature of business and industry where soft skills play a dominant role and when unemployed people have to be inducted into employment, the target groups

21

have to be identified with specific skills which are different from hard skills (Dash, 2001; Gorman, 2000). The interventions of the European Social Fund (ESF) projects in assessing the progress made by beneficiaries in not being defined by hard targets gave credence to the emergence of soft skills through the distance travelled measure

According to Simpson (2006), soft skill is an ability or competence, either inherent or acquired which can be repeatedly performed. It is a skill which can be verified and assessed through its performance only and can be demonstrated, learnt, taught, trained or coached but acquired only by performing them and can be improved through reputation and practice. Moss and Tilly (2001) view soft skills "as skills, abilities and traits that pertain to personality, attitude and behaviour rather than to formal or technical knowledge". These skills refer to a person's psychological traits, social graces and other behavioural patterns like motivation, communication, team spirit and self-confidence. The importance of the soft skills emerges from the demand by employers looking into non-technical skills in the individuals which facilitate interaction with others (Schick, 2000). The other reason for their emergence is the need for soft outcomes where the progress of the individuals is described as 'distance travelled'. In the absence of soft skills people get fired when they do not show for work or show up late. Even if they show up they are not ready to work because they are either sleepy or hung over. They may be improperly dressed, hostile to supervisors, disobeying direct orders, lacking in production and being rude to customers (Fan et al., 2005).

Of the two approaches of sustainability in soft skill endowment (Hillmer, 2007), the stand-alone model of skill development uses the approach of training and providing opportunities to develop soft skills through specific courses that are carefully planned for this purpose. Embedding soft skills in the teaching and learning activities across the curriculum or workplaces is the precinct of another model. Each element of soft plan skills is spelled out in the learning outcomes and then translated into the instructional. This is followed by implementing several teaching and learning activities. Employees are assessed as to the progress they make in theoretical knowledge, know-how (in which circumstances to use specific knowledge or adopt specific attitudes), show-how (the ability to use knowledge and skills or adopt specific attitudes) and demonstration in work. Toward achieving this, they develop competencies at the workplace as suggested by Maguire and Hogan (2004) through acquiring interpersonal, personal, business and technical skills required to work effectively with others. The next chapter will discuss the soft skill methodology in detail.

2.5 Conclusion

Since education and economic development are closely associated, educational planning has to function as an instrument in achieving improvement in productivity, with due importance shown to non-economic aspects. A knowledge-based economy has to turnout scientists capable of innovating

22

and human capital theory becomes relevant in this case. The higher the level of education and more technical the training, productivity will be higher. Higher productivity levels along with higher educational attainment will lead to innovativeness, thus resulting in competitive advantage for the country.

Under willingness to pay approach, education is termed as consumption rather than investment and under manpower requirements approach, the chances are that the planning mechanism will be influenced by politicians and bureaucrats and delineation of workers appropriate for specific jobs may be problematic. Though screening identifies productive workers, when credentialism creeps in, the association between educational attainment and worker productivity is impaired. Hence the human capital approach which has been empirically validated in many countries forecasts investment in education so as to get returns from economic development. The soft component of human capital may be difficult to be learned unlike that of its hard component. However, it may be developed through different learning methods like experiential learning. Also, through training it may be possible to develop soft skills and this has to be the focus of higher education in validating the human capital theory. The next chapter will introduce the concept of soft skills and explain how they can be measured. The chapter develops a methodology to assess the prevalence of different soft skills, exemplifying their importance in human capital theory and economic development.

Acquisition and assessment of soft skills:
A literature review

3.1 Introduction

If human capital is important in explaining a country's growth and development, soft skills become crucial in assessing workers' employability in the service-oriented economies. This chapter poses questions like what are soft skills, how they can be measured and what is their contribution to increasing productivity? It continues the discussion of chapter two into developing the soft skill methodology and its assessment. The literature reviews concentrate on the significance of soft skills, their measurement and assessment and sources of their acquisition and the efficacy of training programmes. The chapter is structured such that section 3.2 conceptualises and groups soft skills into three basic skills based on literature review. Section 3.3 reviews the empirical significance of soft skills, while section 3.4 reviews measurement and assessment through the skill wheel and distance travelled concepts. Section 3.5 presents a review of different sources of soft skill acquisition, emphasising the relevance of Kolb's learning theory at the workplace. Section 3.6 critiques the soft skill enhancement techniques like training, while section 3.7 concludes. Through the literature review, the chapter develops the soft skill measurement method which is used for both general and reference group analyses in latter chapters.

3.2 Conceptualisation of soft skills

The concept of soft skills introduced in the last chapter has been grouped under personal development, basic work skills and core work skills (Moss and Tilly, 1995). Personal development involves such developments as motivation and feelings of responsibility, self awareness, confidence and self esteem, recognition of prior skills, personal and career aspirations, concentration and engagement, fitness and health, recognition of rights and responsibilities. The basic work skills include reliability and punctuality, personal appearance and presentation, team working, completion of work, relationship with others, basic literacy and numeracy and ability to complete forms and CVs. The core work skills include communication, advanced numeracy, proficiency in information and communication technology, reasoning, planning and prioritising, interpersonal skills and problem solving skills (SELD, 2006).

Considering the importance of personal traits in critical assessment of an individual's soft skills, personal soft skills may be placed at the top. The behavioural patterns are captured by the way the person communicates with others and hence communication assumes the next important role. Interpersonal skills closely follow those of communication. Once these three groups of skills are developed, team work which is a must in organisations becomes facilitative. Finally, the problem solving skills identify a person's capacity and competency in realising the set objectives of the organisation. Soft skills have been grouped under five broad categories by Motah (2007) and Simpson (2006).

Table 3.1: Different types of soft skills

Personal	Interpersonal	Communication	Teamwork	Problem solving
Appearance & Personal Hygiene Attendance & Punctuality Positive attitude Motivation Numeracy Langauge IT Skills Enterprise Emotional intelligence Assertiveness Self-Confidence Self-esteem	Respondability Listening capacity Recognition Rights awareness Responsibilities Respectability Customer relationship	Oral Non-verbal Verbal Social Business Marketing of ideas Presentation	Teamwork Negotiation Learning Reliability Work ethics Leadership Authority Conflict management	Goal setting Planning & organisation Decision making Problem analysis Creative thinking Time management

What matters is the individual's personal development and interpersonal relations in a given situation which determine the effectiveness of particular skills in employability or lifelong learning. Hence, the multitude of above soft skills may be grouped under three major skill areas, namely personal, interpersonal and situational so as to be amenable for comparison and easy measurement. Acquisition of the respective soft skill enhances attributes and behavioural patterns related to personal, interpersonal and situational development. Though there are many groupings of soft skills like, personal, interpersonal, leadership, problem solving, communication, presentation and so on, they refer to either personal, interpersonal or situational aspects or a combination of them. That is, the objective of acquiring soft skills is to develop personal attributes and how an individual interacts with others and how one performs in a given situation. The grouping of different skills under the three broad categories specifies the entire gamut of personal, interpersonal and situational aspects of skill development. The groupings have been accomplished based on the existing studies like Moss and Tilly (1995), Simpson (2006) and Motah (2007) and the insight gained by the pilot survey.

1. Personal soft skills are intrapersonal skills that lead to personal development and include

- Responsibility- assuming responsibility in workplace
- Motivation- being positively motivated to take up that responsibility
- Punctuality- maintaining timeliness and being punctual in work
- Mentoring- attitude that results from experience
- Self-confidence- building self assertiveness and confidence
- Language- proficiency in literacy and numeracy
- Innovativeness- being innovative in thinking and action
- Enterprising- being enterprising in action
- Self-management- the ability to identify the self in terms of achievement

Intrapersonal skills are defined as those skills individuals need to possess and perfect in order to manage themselves and as a prerequisite to interpersonal skills. These skills are concerned with lessening internal conflict; understanding how one handles external experience internally and coming to terms with one's qualities, limitations and potential. People with high intrapersonal scores tend to know and feel good about themselves and think positive about what they are doing in their lives, besides having high emotional intelligence (Goleman, 1995). High intrapersonal scores indicate people who can express their feelings confidently, without being aggressive toward other people. Acquisition of one or a combination of the above nine qualities enhances the personal development of an individual and helps in achieving the goal of higher competency levels. It may be pointed out here that employers usually look to link soft skills with improving the competency level of the employees that has direct bearing on productivity increase in the organisation.

2. Interpersonal skills are required for smooth interaction between co-workers on the one hand and with customers on the other and include

- Analysis- the ability to analyse the issues on hand resulting from interactions
- Creative thinking- the ability to think critically and creatively so as to effect good analysis
- Team work- ability to work in a team for successful results
- Recognition- the ability to recognise merit in others and appreciate
- Diverse capacity- the ability to act in diverse capacities so as to derive the interpersonal synergy effect
- Leadership- the ability to lead others successfully in work-related and other activities
- Decision making- the capacity to make effective decisions and implement them
- Conflict management- the capacity to manage crises and effectively deal with them
- Communication- the ability to effectively communicate, orally and written and also the ability of presentation
- Respect- respect shown to others which is an essential listening quality

Though acquisition of the interpersonal skills is more complex and challenging, the process of interacting with others may be facilitated smoothly once the personal attributes are fulfilled. If personal skills any be acquired by training, mentoring or experience, interpersonal skills can also be acquired by these methods besides experience and teamwork.

3. Situational skills are those skills that have relevance in given situation and may be firm or individual specific. These may be a combination of various personal and interpersonal skills applied to specific situations and hence exhibit characteristics of situational analysis.

- Goal setting- the ability to set objectives for successful performance in given situation.
- Planning- planning and organisation capability in realising the goals.
- Cooperation- ability to cooperate with each other in the interaction process
- Negotiation- ability to negotiate effectively for realisation of the goals.
- Reliance- ability to trust others in the realisation of goals
- Authority- the ability to convince others on consensus in achieving the goals
- Effectiveness- proficiency in effectively dealing with any situation.
- Problem solving- ability to solve problems when they arise and also to foresee how potential problem can be solved.
- Learning- the ability to learn from situational analysis leading to life-long learning
- Adaptability- the ability to adapt to a given situation in solving the problems
- Time management- the ability to allocate time in such a way as to maximise its utility in the given situation.
- Empathy- ability to empathise with a situation so that proper emotionl bondage is created

In the assessment of the various soft skills, we use a scoring system in the numerical scale to elicit the response. The response of the participants would be one of: strongly disagree, disagree, neutral, agree or strongly agree and for convenience of comparison we have converted all the responses into actual scores in the Likert scale 1-5 so that they are continuous and indicate the relative importance of particular skills. A score of less than one will indicate low intensity and skills which are yet be mastered and a score of above four, indicating mastery of the skills. A score between one and four will then indicate some mastery of the skills

3.3 Empirical evidence on the significance of soft skills

Employers are concerned with desirable levels of motivation, reliability and flexibility, wherein the nature of the outcomes would indicate how far they are employing the right people. ECOTEC (1998) explored issues on qualitative outcomes achieved on innovative training and employment projects between 1995 and 1997 to demonstrate the evidence of transferable skills and abilities to both employers and employees. Moss and Tilly (1995) identified interaction and motivation skills as important indicators to employers. They found that interaction skills are the most important qualification in retail business while motivation and hard skills are important in auto parts and insurance. Only in public sector, hard skills seemed to be important. The requirements for both hard and soft skills have been rising over the years; while 50 percent of employers report a growing need for hard skills, 43 percent report the need for soft skills (Moss and Tilly, 1995).

The result of the entry study on 3,464 new students in Malaysia of the 2003-04 academic session showed that the students' soft skills were moderately high on a four-point scale (Konting et al., 2005) in lifelong learning, information management, moral and professional ethics as well as in teamwork. There was a significant difference on the mastery level of soft skills among students of different entering qualifications and programmes of study. However, there was no significant difference between their soft skills mastery level according to their gender and their level of involvement in sports.

The National Employers Skills Survey (2003) identified 17 percent vacancies in the sample industries at the time of survey. In eight percent of the firms, vacancies were difficult to be filled and four percent of the units reported skill shortage vacancies. The reasons for hard-to-fill vacancies were applicants not having required skills or attitudes, lack of qualification and work experience, competition from other employers and remote location. The reasons for skill gaps have been lack of experience, lack of motivation against the staff, not keeping up with change, high staff turnover and recruitment problems (NESS, 2003). The areas where the employees lacked soft skills have been communication (28 percent), customer handling (25 percent), teamwork (24 percent) and problem solving (22 percent). The result of skill shortages have been on increased workload, customer service difficulties, loss of business, delayed new products, increased operating costs, quality standard problems and difficulties in introducing new working practices (NESS, 2003). The response to skill gaps have been to provide for the training, reallocation of work, change in working practices and introduction of new motivational programmes. The training programmes included management, supervision, training in languages, training in new technology, health and safety and job specific programmes (NESS, 2003).

Heckman and Rubinstein (2001) cite the case of General Educational Development (GED) programme in the US to demonstrate the importance of soft skills in determining earnings and educational attainment. The GED is a degree equivalent to high school for those who do not have official high school diplomas. The GED recipients have similar levels of cognitive skills like regular high school graduates, but they receive lower wages in the labour market. The reason for this is accorded to lack of non-cognitive skills. The GEDs were more likely to engage in different types of illegal behaviour, to be quarrelsome at work and have more trouble in holding stable employment than the average school drop-out and high schoolers (Atkinsons and Williams, 2003).

The 2000 study by the Institute for Employment Studies on measuring soft outcomes had the objective of assisting organisations receiving European Social Fund (ESF), funded by the Hackney Strategic Partnership (HSP). Tools are devised to assess factors relating to an individual's life skills, health and well being, many directed to employability. The tools may be establishment specific and hence the different groupings mentioned above have to be geared to the needs of the particular establishment. The assessment tools used by the HSP were paper based written questionnaires, computer software questionnaires, games and web-based assessments. The assessment may be self administered or facilitated by a tutor. Self-administered assessment requires high levels of individual motivation and it is hard to check the validity, besides slipping of consistency. It may be pointed out that self assessment is a skill in itself which requires self awareness. Facilitated assessment entails higher cost and staff time but may offer more validity and consistency.

In the US, the Report of The Secretary's Commission on Achieving Necessary skills (SCANS, 1991) identified the skills required for employment and proposed levels of proficiency in them. In a highly decentralised school system oriented to general education such as in the US, curriculum development and assessment provide students with broad skills needed for the workplace. In the system are present a core of academic skills, higher order thinking skills, adapting to change supported by problem-solving abilities, creativity, decision-making, learning how to learn, interpersonal skills and dealing with diversity. In England, the original list of core skills included communication, problem solving, personal skills, numeracy, information technology and competence in a foreign language (Stephens and Hamblin, 2006). These skills were to be integrated into instruction for students in the 16-19 year age group and were framed primarily as entry level skills for the workforce though did not form part of a lifelong learning agenda. The employability skills are academic skills that provide the basic foundations to obtain, keep and progress on a job and achieve the best results. Hence, personal management strategies have to focus on skills, attitudes and behaviour besides teamwork skills to achieve the best results (Stephens and Hamblin, 2006). A recent development in Canada is the introduction of the Employability Skills Toolkit for the Self-Managing Learner. In Europe, the Definition and Selection of Competencies project of OECD (Salganik et al., 1999) investigated the effectiveness of education systems using a broader range of indicators including curricular competencies and human capital indicators The project recognised that the competencies had to apply to school and work settings but equally to life situations beyond those areas.

In support of soft skills training programmes, Winter (2004) lists the advantages of incorporating such training in all aspects of curriculum development. The students may be assigned to motivated teams to work together in completing the task. The trainees may be allowed to act as managers once in a while so that they can learn how to be managed by managing others. In every area of the intervention, appropriate workplace discipline has to be insisted upon and the participants have to be provided with many opportunities in acquainting with successful people. In order to help the workers to develop their jobs, support services have to be provided like child care, transportation and others.

In the past, soft skill training programmes have measured their success through their attainment of hard quantifiable outputs like gaining a formal or publicly recognised qualification, number of participants getting jobs and number of participants completing a course (Balgobin et al., 2004). However, obtaining a qualification is not an indicator of employment and there may be other skills which the employers value more. Soft skills result in soft outcomes such as achievement in terms of interpersonal skills, teamwork, problem solving, motivation and confidence, punctuality and reliability which improves the employability of the worker (Carneiro and Heckman, 2003). Though it is hard to measure soft outcomes owing to subjectivity and qualitative assessments, attempts have been made to quantify some traits like punctuality and good attendance records though others like confidence may be difficult to quantify (Balgobin et al., 2004).

Discussions on skills are focused mainly on cognitive-ability. Becker (1964) compared human capital models with cognitive-ability models of earnings completely ignoring the non-cognitive skills. Spence (1974) emphasised the signalling aspect of education, interpreted as a cognitive skill. The neglect of non-cognitive skills has been due to the lack of any reliable measure of them (Heckman and Rubinstein, 2001). Whereas for cognitive skill the dominant general intelligence factor is adopted as the test, no single factor has emerged on non-cognitive skills owing to diversity of traits subsumed under this category. Job stability, consistency and dependability have been more valued by employers (Klein et al., 1991). Carneiro et al. (2006) feel that because education policy can more easily influence non-cognitive skills than cognitive skills, educational interventions targeted at problem groups will be effective only if soft skill formation is emphasised.

3.4 Soft skill measurement and assessment

This section reviews works on soft skill measurement through the skill wheel and soft skill assessment through the analysis of distance travelled. While the skill wheel profiles the changes that are effected in the skill profile of the individuals, the distance travelled concept illustrates the improvement in the skill endowment of the individuals owing to intervention programmes.

3.4.1 The skill wheel

The HSP profile divides the soft skills into three components – 'how you feel', 'how you look' and 'how you perform' (Balgobin et al., 2004). Authority, motivation, confidence and self esteem skills are included under 'how you feel'. 'How you look' comprise of what you wear, first impressions, non-verbal communication and personal hygiene. Under 'how you perform', attendance, being on time, time management, working with others and communication are included. We have modified the HSP profile as follows

- Feeling: motivation, confidence, authority and self esteem.

- Appearance: what you wear, first impressions, personal hygiene and non-verbal communication
- Performance: attendance and punctuality, language, attitude, presentation and communication, time management, working with others (interpersonal), teamwork and problem solving

In the fourth chapter, we derive the skill wheel which profiles the skills listed in the previous section. We summarise the HSP method of showing different aspects of soft skills in the following diagram and graph.

Figure 3.1: Profile of soft skills according to score circles

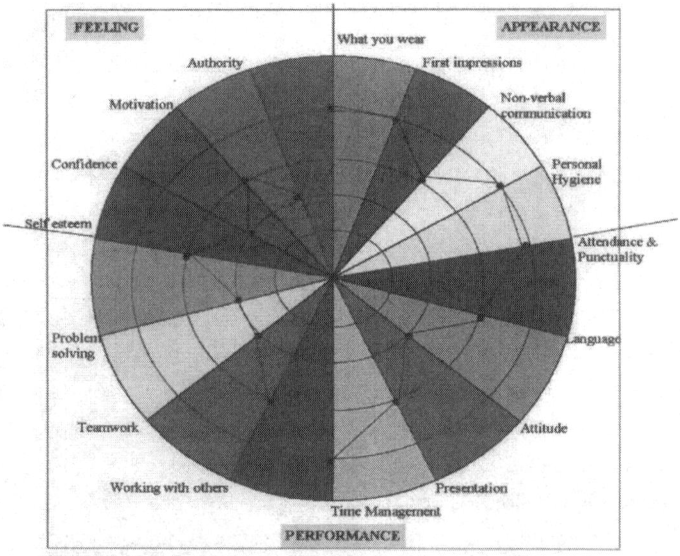

Notes: centre of the circle, score = 0; first circle, score = 1; second circle, score =2;
Third circle, score = 3; fourth circle, score = 4; outer circle, score = 5
Source: adapted from Balgobin et al., 2004.

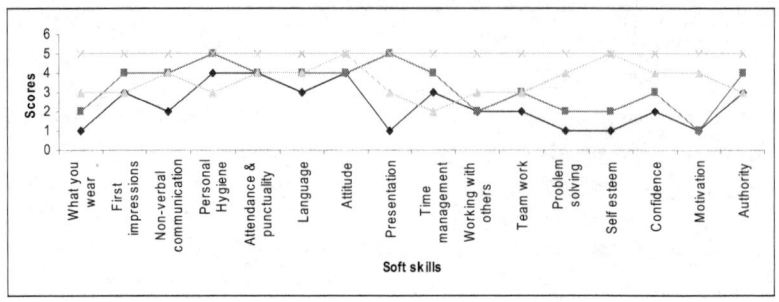

The five divisions of the profile circle indicate scores in the 1-5 scale. If the employee scores nil in all the skills, then his score will be at the centre of the circle meaning nil. When the score is on the first inner circle line, the score will be equal to one. When the performance is evaluated as on the second inner circle line, the score will be equal to two and so on. An employee who performs such that he or she is awarded a score of five in all the skills, then the employee's scoring will be positioned on the outer circle line. If the scoring is different for different skills, the midpoint of the respective skill cones and the entire profile will join the midpoints which will result in a line which will be a circle if there are equal scores for soft skills or a line of different curvature when the scores will be different for different soft skills. In the diagram we have presented the soft skill profile of a typical case wherein all the score points are joined by a line. If the maximum score is five for all the soft skills, the actual score points will indicate the distance from the maximum. If we can measure the soft skill performance of an employee like this before and after an intervention the *ex post* profile diagram will show the distance travelled by the employee.

Figure 3.2 plots the hypothetical scores of four employees in all the soft skills wherein series four indicates the performance of an employee who has scored maximum five in all the soft skills. As contrast to this upper limit, the lower limit will be the horizontal axis line indicating zero values (which may not be encountered, otherwise a case of non-employability) in all the soft skills. Between these upper and lower limits we can have any number of series depending on the number of employees taken in the focus group. If this graph would indicate *ex ante* performance, the exposed graph will indicate the distance travelled in improving not only personal but also organisational performance by the employees because of the intervention.

The objective of any intervention programme will be to improve one particular or many soft skills depending on the job requirements and the employer's expectations. Otherwise the concerned programme is not justified. If after intervention, the curvature of one or some soft skills is elongated in the skill wheel (Figure 3.1), that shows the distance travelled in that particular soft skill. Depending upon the time lapse and the change in the curvature, the rate of growth in specific soft skill may be calculated and the soft skill index constructed. There may be some skills if mastered thoroughly will help the employee personally and professionally. There may be some soft skills which are yet to be mastered and the employee has to identify which, if mastered would help in his or her personal or professional development (Butcher and Marsden, 2004). Soft skill development has been assessed in terms of distance travelled in the skill wheel and by the quantum of increase in the skill index.

3.4.2. Distance travelled

To measure the distance travelled by the employee some kind of scale will be needed and the workers will have to be positioned on that scale in order to record the progress. 'Distance travelled' indicates the growth in the performance of the individual because of intervention which has to be assessed in terms of achievement of personal goals like leadership and self-esteem and organisational goals like increase in productivity or image (Lloyd and OSullivan, 2003). If hard skills describe how far an employee has professional knowledge, soft skills explain the effectiveness with which this knowledge is translated into achievement of goals. Even if the progress is personal to the employee, a baseline will be required to demonstrate the progress (Dewson et al., 2000a). If an employee is rated as low on the scale, it could mean that he or she will have low self esteem and motivation.

The important thing to note is that when there is an intervention (new appointment, training, promotion, award or obtaining a higher degree while on job) it will impact on the employee so that there may be progress in the different soft skills. Progress in achieving hard skills may facilitate fixing of the relative skill in particular areas and further progress can be made with reference to standard practice (Balgobin et al., 2004). As skills develop, the assessment tool reflects the progress through movement along a scale and the scores will indicate the distance travelled. The scores which measure the progress can be awarded based on scales like Likert scale which measures a range of responses from say one to five in the ordinal scale.

The distance travelled in any soft skills depends on the efficacy of particular intervention. If the intervention is only to improve (say) communication skills, the post-intervention curvature should show a big change in respect of that particular soft skill without others undergoing a change. If there is change in other skills, we call this as spill-over effect. For example, an intervention in leadership skills may have spill-over effect on all other soft skills, improving their scores after intervention. An intervention in communication skill may not have any spill-over effect on others if the objective is narrowed down only to communication.

Frequent interventions have the objective of augmenting soft skills and where a particular job requires all the three groups of skills mentioned above, more than one intervention tool becomes necessary. In such instances, to measure the distance travelled, the timeframe will be different (say, one work cycle or one year as the case may be) and hence the construction of the soft skill index will be in terms of period analysis. Let us say the objective of the intervention is to achieve improvement in the particular skill in the short term. Depending on the stage of operations, the soft skill assessment will also have a short term. If the intervention has the immediate objective of improving the communication skill of a particular skill group, the assessment analysis will have to be carried out immediately after the intervention. On the other hand, if the objective is cultivation of leadership qualities over a period of time say, one or two years, in that case, final assessment will be after that time lapse, though there can be intermediate assessments.

Soft skills generate soft outcomes and the indicators of these soft outcomes measure distance travelled which shows the degree of employability of the participant (Dewson et al., 2000a; Lloyd and O'Sullivan, 2003). Hard outcomes imply transfer to a preferred place or division, promotion, foreign visits, participation in seminars, publication of papers, appointment as a coach or mentor, awards, incentives, membership in committees, in-charge responsibility, obtaining new qualifications and being given more responsibility and accountability, which are easily quantifiable. On the other hand, soft outcomes are qualitative and indicate the progress toward achievement of the hard outcomes. Some of the soft outcomes are better work, personal and situational skills. Soft indicators signify improved time keeping, effective team building, improved communication and presentation skills, low sickness and absence from work, positive attitude and so on. These indicators will in turn improve the hard outcomes and the employee in achieving his/her employability and integration in the labour market realises 'distance travelled' (Dewson et al., 2000a). Soft outcomes will vary according to the prior skill and the target groups.

In our study, distance travelled is measured as improvement in the particular skill score after the intervention when compared to pre-training scenario in chapter six. The skill wheel indicates the changes in scores before and after intervention. The indicators are measured by aggregating the scores in the numerical scale 1-5. Since aggregation of the ordinal values will be subject to comparison inadequacies, we have assigned values one to five in respect of soft skill scores depending on the response so that the values will be amenable for comparison.

For particular skill group like junior or senior manager, in a given timeframe there may be one or more interventions (formal or informal) enveloping one or more soft skills. For example, junior managers may be subject to more than one intervention in a given timeframe to acquire or improve many core skills, whereas the senior managers may require only one or nil intervention. The number of interventions required may depend upon the existing soft skill profile (Figure 3.1) of the particular skill group and the budget. Since any intervention has its own cost, if adequate returns are not forthcoming, the firm may not initiate such programmes.

3.5 Sources of soft skill acquisition

This section reviews literature on different sources of soft skill acquisition like family, school, higher education institutions and workplace. Skills are affected by personal actions and environment. Innate abilities may be personal and hereditary; also, soft skills may be acquired from different sources. Whereas learning hard skills generally has a definite timeframe, learning soft skills is flexible and reinforces the productive element of hard skills (Heckman et al., 2006). The environment may indicate aspects of self-study, training and experiential learning at the workplace, besides the influence of family, school and higher education institutions (Becker and Tomes, 1986). Skills have a multiplier effect, in that acquisition of one skill leads to the formation of other skills (Cunha et al., 2005). In every stage of skill formation, investment in human capital takes place and if investment continues throughout, it ensures good return and complements the augmentation of further skills and increase in productivity. This section is in two parts, dealing with the role of family, school and higher education institutions and highlighting the role of experiential learning at the workplace. A separate section on the role of higher education institutions in the sample region is discussed in chapter eight. The reference group analysis in the seventh chapter documents findings on the different sources of soft skill acquisition.

3.5.1 Family, school and higher education institutions

Learning can be both formal and informal and soft skill acquisition through formal learning may be by attending training courses or being taught in the classroom. Informal learning is mainly from family, friends, experience and observing the environment. Since effective skill formation is a life cycle process as pointed out by Heckman et al. (2006), soft skill acquisition and enhancement starts early in life. Skills inculcated in early childhood determine the nature of adult life. Family's role can be seen in taking initiatives, being frugal besides adherence to basic ethics, obedience, taking responsibility and experiencing role plays (Clark, 1993). In a New Zealand study (NZME, 2005), the influence of the family in children's achievement at school and elsewhere was documented wherein collaboration between parents and teachers was critical for child development. In the UK, family influence on children's sports (Kay, 2004), verbal communication (Buck et al., 2002) and decision making (Mantle et al., 2007) illustrate the influence of family in early childhood growth. Studies by Peters (2007) and Michael (2004) point out the crucial role of family in the development of young students especially linked to their social and emotional development.

The findings of the National Longitudinal Survey of Youth confirm the importance of family in acquisition of quality skills by an individual. In this study, it was shown that access to family material resources and exposure to values and social networks determined the scores on aptitude tests (Guzman and Jekielek, 2004). Moss and Tilly (2001) point out the influence of family in inculcating leadership qualities in the students which is further reinforced at the school level. Dhuey and Lipscomb (2008) opine that soft skill foundation at the school stage especially in leadership qualities determine the latter day wage differentials. The example of role models in teaching and training of students is illustrated by Schurink et al. (2006), wherein the activities focus on the guiding and growing of soft skills under difficult situations. Role plays add authenticity to the development of particular skill. Where there is low level of education attainment, the same may be compensated by high level of personal development.

Family management enables acquisition of such skills which later may prove useful in the workplace. As Evans and Kersh (2004) point out, such soft skills have tacit dimensions and hence their value is not easily revealed, unless adequately documented by the training activities. At the college level, teaching of the value of education and its expectation steers the students toward ethics and lifelong learning with self esteem and problem solving skills as has been pointed out by Tinto (1993). Measures to improve the ability of the students to use observational techniques and analyse skill performance enhances their future ability to demonstrate the employability skills in better way and in this skill formation happens intergenerationally also according to Carneiro et al. (2006).

At an early stage, family income determines the nature of investment in human capital and subsequent investments decide the efficacy of soft skill development. As skill begets skill, it leads to what is called 'self-productivity' and investment in human capital complements that (Carneiro and Heckman, 2003). In this, credit constraints have had impact on the education and soft skill attainment (Heckman and Lochner, 2000). According to them, there is a close relationship between schooling, ability and family income. It has been observed that differences in skill attainment by family income reflect the role played by ability differences. While it may be demonstrated that lower family income results in lower level of education attainment (hard skills), at times, other family influences could improve soft skills.

At the college level, presentation, teamwork, counselling, ideastorming and respectability qualities are being imparted to the students and are assessed by appropriate ratings (Cunha et al., 2005), wherein the scores reflect the soft skill embedded in each stage of teaching or training or observation as the case may be. Recently, the growing number of corporate scandals has necessitated the inculcation of business ethics into the students (Bunker and Wakefield, 2004). While many are conversant with hard skills, it requires ethical capability to shine in soft skills and excel in performance. Ethics is learnt early in life and other skills may not be a substitute for it and

36

are intertwined with lifelong learning (Clark, 1993). Discomfort arises out of discrepancy between what is known and the latest information. In this, soft skill attainment enables the students to monitor their thinking and process what they have learned and how they can be reflected upon for better interpersonal relations (Dettori and Paiva, 2009). Where teaching contains experiential learning techniques, the results have been very positive.

3.5.2 Experiential learning at the workplace

The objective of this section is to show that soft skill development can be achieved through learning from experience since it is a part of life cycle. However, soft skills have been considered to be equally or more difficult to learn than technical skills (Federico, 2008), which makes experiential learning as a specific tool of soft skill development.

> *Tell me and I will forget*
> *Show me and I may remember*
> *Involve me and I will understand*
> - Confucius (circa 450 BC)

In a study on 'The hard truth about soft skills' (Federico, 2008), it was shown that soft skills were equally or more important than technical skills and the ability to communicate was the most important of all skills. Organisations providing soft skills training reported a higher level of initiative success than those that do not provide soft skills training. Hence, soft skill development may be accomplished as pointed out by Kolb (1984) by experiential learning through concrete experience (relating learning to a personal experience), reflective observation (reflecting on experience), abstract conceptualization (hearing what specialists say, understanding theories and forming conclusions) and active experimentation (practising new behaviours with guidance and coaching).

Learning stems from experience leading to acquisition of skills and thereby development of human capital. The concept of experiential learning explores the cyclical pattern of learning from experience through reflection and conceptualising to action on to further experience (Kolb, 1984). Kolb's typology of individual learning styles is based on experiential learning, deriving from the manner in which an employee tends to grasp new information and the methods that he or she tends to use when processing new concepts. Trainers employ the typology during the process of developing instructional material, so that each of the learning style types will benefit from appropriately adapted instruction. Experience leads to observation and reflection, followed by concept formation, wherein new concepts may guide choices for new experiences (Kolb, 1984). Knowledge acquired either by concrete experience or abstract conceptualisation is processed through reflective observation or active experimentation as shown by figure 3.3.

Figure 3.3: Kolb's learning cycle

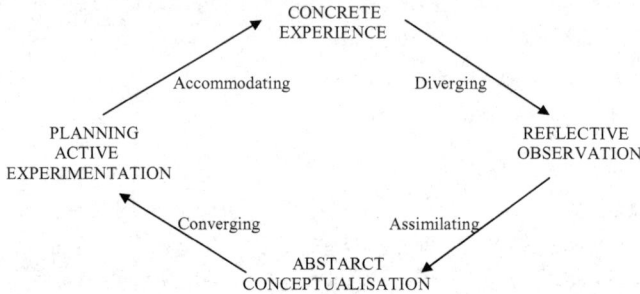

The employee has a concrete experience (something happens) and then makes reflective observations (what happened) about it, which forms the basis of abstract conceptualisation (so what). These concepts in turn are tested through active experimentation (now what). Concrete experience denotes feeling and actually doing the activity. The learner takes part in a training course, attempting to acquire soft skills. Reflective observation indicates observation and reflecting on performance in the activity, considering successes and failures. The trainee considers his soft skill performance and scoring attempts. Abstract conceptualisation is learning from experience and application of theory to the experience of doing the activity. The trainee talks to the trainer or mentor who provides insights into scoring. The planning and active experimentation stage involves consideration of theory and reflection to guide planning for subsequent experiences. The employee uses insights from training and experience from the previous course to plan for the next course to score high.

The tendency for knowledge to be acquired in concrete experiencing compared to abstract conceptualisation is described as a distinct dimension of learning style and the tendency for knowledge to be transformed in terms of reflective observation compared to active experimentation (Kolb, 1984). The learning style is derived from the relative emphasis the employee places on the different stages of the learning cycle. Different employees prefer different learning styles and various factors influence the preferred style. Kolb defines three stages of personal development, wherein the propensity to reconcile and successfully integrate the following stages (Kolb, 1984).

- Acquisition: development of basic abilities and cognitive structures
- Specialisation: schooling, early work and personal experiences of adulthood
- The development of a particular specialised learning style shaped by social, educational and organisational socialisation

Acquisition of soft skills is a lifelong process. Learning is an experience that occurs inside the learner and includes acquiring facts, skills and methods that can be retained and used (Hillmer,

38

2007). It is the discovery of the personal meaning and relevance of ideas and arises as a consequence of experience. It is a cooperative and collaborative process and problem solving becomes an essential ingredient of the process. Eraut (2007a) argues that to gain knowledge through learning at the workplace, one has to understand the relationship between time and the method of understanding of cognitive skills. 'Situated learning' is a method wherein understanding of knowledge takes place socially and individually by the context in which it is acquired and used. The process revolves around 'what is being learned?', 'how is it being learned?' and 'what factors affect the level and directions of learning effort?' (Eraut, 2004). In this way, knowledge can be represented by a process wherein remembrance, decision making and problem solving skills determine the learning style (Eraut, 2007b).

Through learning, it may be possible to develop soft skills since these involve comprehending the challenge and value of work through necessary feedback and support to achieve confidence and commitment (Eraut, 2007c). Workplace learning consists of exercising proper capability within the context of work and learning at both individual and team levels (Eraut and Hirsh, 2007). The typology of learning has been divided into task and role performance, awareness and understanding, personal development, acquisition of knowledge and skills, teamwork, decision making and problem solving (Eraut, 2007c). It can be discerned that soft skill development plays an important role in these different stages. Learning takes place through work processes and is motivated by challenges and by consulting or working alongside others. An effective way of learning is from shared experience, either by discussing past experiences or by developing new experiences through practical exercises. Participants learn from each other and the trainer often learns from the participants. Reflection from experience occurs when the worker takes the time to reflect back upon it, draws conclusions and derives principles for applying to similar experiences.

In the context of the current study, learning by the sample managers has been assessed by means of case studies and narratives in chapters 5-8. Proper allocation and structuring of work have been found to be crucial for this learning. For example, learning from seniors depends on good relationships and a learning culture in the workplace. Support from colleagues is crucial during the initial period and coaching may be important for skills requiring emotional support. Senior managers have a role in creating mutual trust and learning culture with opportunities for juniors to learn together on challenging tasks (Eraut, 2007c). Where the required motivation is not forthcoming, achievement of the set personal and organisation development goals becomes time-consuming and tardy as reported by Eraut (2007a). This motivation is facilitated by different kinds of tacit knowledge and modes of cognition which are combined in the workplace learning, distinguished by Eraut (2000) as 'implicit learning', 'reactive on-the-spot learning' or 'deliberative learning'. Implicit learning is the process through which the worker becomes sensitive to certain regularities in the environment in the absence of intention to learn about those regularities or awareness that he or she is learning or in such a way that the resulting knowledge is difficult to express. Since workplace learning involves both technical and general learning through the adoption of best practices like effective coaching or mentoring, assessment of such practices has to envelop holistic measures like 360-degree appraisal and personal development plans (ILO, 2006).

Practice of Kolbian learning styles depend on the nature of training or coaching and reflect how far personal development and team plans would be effective in achieving performance efficiency and confidence in the participants (Fidler, 2008). As mentioned in Figure 3.3, new learning styles result in the managers to assume roles of activists (action-oriented content of training), reflectors (evidence from the experience of others), theorists (connecting theory with practice) or planners (developing frameworks for discussion) to position their learning process in achieving the set goals. Through experiential learning, the following benefits accrue to the employees (Eraut and Hirsh, 2007).

- Development of skills and employment experience that help ease the transition to the workplace upon graduation
- Learning and enhancement of soft skills required in the workplace
- Becoming highly trained in specific tasks
- Exploring career goals to determine suitability for jobs
- Building self-confidence in professional abilities
- Enhancement of self-awareness of strengths/weaknesses, likes/dislikes and interests
- Establishing networks of professional contacts, mentors and references
- Awareness of skills that are transferable to the work force and graduate school
- Fostering opportunities to apply classroom knowledge to the workforce
- Chances for employment upon graduation and developing competencies to career goals

To achieve the above, the individual needs to acquire the required competencies such as positive motives, traits, skills, improved self-image or social role (Boyatzis, 1982). These qualities represent what are called employability skills. Competencies such as delegating work and providing feedback have been acknowledged as critical skills for better job performance (Rausch et al., 2002). It is illustrative to compare and contrast the competencies needed for effective job performance for two very different jobs of a surgeon and a computer technician (Boyatzis, 1982). In terms of task skills, each must have the skill to diagnose a problem of the system they are treating, possess fine psychomotor skills to operate with precise movements and take initiative to find additional information needed to solve problems (Tissot, 2000). However, a surgeon works in conjunction with other surgeons, nurses and an anaesthetist, while a computer technician may often work alone. The surgeon needs skills related to performing effectively in a team during an operation and needs to effectively build rapport with other members of the surgical team and build and maintain good relationships. A computer technician needs more intrapersonal and self-management skills in order to regulate impulsive tendencies and follow through commitments and tolerate stress (Boyatzis, 1982).

Skill becomes goal-oriented and well-organised behavior that is acquired through experience and performed with economy of effort (Proctor and Dutta, 1995). Skill develops over time, with practice and is goal-directed in response to some demand in the external environment. Further, it is acquired when behaviour is structured into coherent patterns and cognitive demands are reduced as skill develops. Learning outcomes involve subject-based knowledge and understanding, practice (applied knowledge and understanding), generic cognitive skills like evaluation and critical analysis, communication, numeracy and IT skills and autonomy, accountability and working with others (SCQF, 2003). Learning outcomes are packages of knowledge, skill and competence put together, where knowledge is declarative having meaning outside any specific context of application. Skill is defined as the goal-directed performance of a task and can be acquired by training. Competence relates to specialised competence of acquiring knowledge and skills, methodological competence requiring planning and problem solving procedures, social competence requiring individual social skills and interpersonal skills and participatory competence for effective decision making and leadership skills. The competence is directly related to the ability to solve problems and see the problem as a starting point to reach the set goal (NFQ, 2003). The workplace competencies include an ability to productively use resources, interpersonal skills, information systems and technology. Experiential learning is closely related to soft skill training at the workplace and hence it requires some space.

3.5.3 Soft skill training

Soft skill training programmes at the workplace assess the returns on the investment on human capital, as pointed out by Kirkpatrick (1994), who has devised four levels of evaluation to assess its effectiveness. Level one evaluation measures how participants in a training programme react to it and questions regarding their perceptions and relevance to their work. This type of evaluation is called a 'smilesheet' and every programme has to be evaluated at this level to improve the intervention. Further, the reactions of the participants have important consequences on the learning outcomes. At this level, evaluation is done before and after training to assess the amount of knowledge acquired. However, measurement at this level is more difficult and range from formal to informal testing toward self assessment. The latter stage evaluation measures the kind of transfer that has taken place in the behaviour of the learners due to intervention. Evaluation at this stage represents the true assessment of effectiveness in finding out how the newly acquired skills are being used. Since it is difficult to predict when the change in behaviour will happen, evaluation has to concentrate on the timing, frequency and its method. The final evaluation assesses the intervention in terms of business results like increased production, improved quality, reduced cost, reduced frequency of accidents, increased sales and higher return on investment. In the final analysis the results of the training programme have to be compared with the cost of undertaking the programme (Kirkpatrick, 1994).

The performance of the soft skill training programme can also be measured with reference to the objectives of the programme (Onisk, 2006), where key metrics for the effectiveness of the programme are developed. For example, if the objective is strategic relevance, the related metric will be whether the certification of the intervention is still relevant to the ultimate strategy. If the objective is one of focused outcome, the metric will measure the knowledge of the participants leaving the training to sit for the training certification examination. In case this outcome is measurable, the question would be: how many participants have obtained their certification in the relevant skills? Suppose if the objective is 90 percent of certification, the metric assesses the certification attainable within say, a particular time period of the training. On the other hand, if the objective is cost-centric, the metric will measure the cost per participant, both direct and indirect. If the objective is time-bound, the metric will explain how long after training the participants would obtain their certification. Once these metrics are established, controlling the programme to ensure its viability and support of management and workers becomes crucial. Maintenance of a periodic and systematic reporting process and periodic evaluation of the objectives are required in the case of certification.

As regards soft skill development in the study region, it may be mentioned that the unemployment rate in the gulf countries (including Oman) is high owing to lack of employable skills and lack of synchronisation between job requirements and curriculum. However, the higher education institutions have been focusing on development of core soft skills and intensification of this process at a wider scale will reduce the skill gap by improving employability of the local youth.

As will be discussed in the eighth chapter, the success of an organisation depends on the performance of its employees and the ability to grow continuously on learning and developing knowledge (O'Donoghue and Maguire, 2005). Soft skills have to be identified and developed so that they can be diffused into a larger segment of the workforce through practices like 'Communities of Practice', wherein groups of people share a concern and a set of problems in deepening their knowledge and understanding in their areas (Wenger et al., 2002). Since training has to result in knowledge, know-how skill and competence, this objective of human capital development has to be intertwined into the objectives of the organisations.

42

In the knowledge economy therefore, employability, if it wants to be effective, has to focus on the following issues (O'Donoghue and Maguire, 2005).

- Development of existing skills with positive motivation
- Short and long term needs of skill development
- Internal and external influences of skill enhancement and
- Integrating various sources of soft skill acquisition

The seventh chapter on reference group analysis captures these issues into the framework of soft skill acquisition and assessment.

3.6 A critique of soft skill enhancement techniques

The critical role played by soft skills in employment and lifelong learning prompts a fresh look at the sources of acquisition of the skills. In the context of increasing globalisation of economies, a different understanding of learning and training in the workplace is essential (Ford, 1990). Ford critiques that the overall impact of change is such that the standard concepts that have been used for thinking about workplaces, such as 'technology', 'work organisation', 'employment relations' have lost their currency. Following Ford, we may argue that soft skills training has assumed importance as is evidenced by orientation courses offered for new entrants in many organisations on basic .skills. Only through such interventions, organisations transform themselves to provide greater quality; improvement and innovation; adaptability and service. The required transformations by organisations centre on the need for a more multifunctional and multiskilled workforce. This is facilitated by the creation of a responsive workplace culture incorporating soft skill training. As Ford points out, there are diverse strategies for achieving this, but they generally integrate new kinds of work organisation, innovations in technology, innovative skill formation practices, innovations in employee commitment, participation and remuneration. Many of these, especially new kinds of work organisation and innovations in employee commitment are just the kinds of strategies that have caused successful workplace conditions. Soft skill formation has to be viewed to embrace and integrate formal education, induction, continuous on-the-job learning, recurrent off-the-job learning and personal development (Ford, 1990). Soft skills may be developed by continuous on-the-job learning in which skill formation indicates a wider notion of learning in the workplace. It may be argued that technical skills are essential for technological development, but it is soft skills which provide the necessary complementarity. However, when compared to hard skills, soft skill development which has to concentrate on individual needs becomes enigmatic.

Though soft outcomes are viewed as important very few have developed any systematic tool to measure them according to the ESF-funded projects (Dewson et al., 2000b). Further, the assessment model may be specific to the individual projects and can be subjective. The outcome from the intervention in respect of skills related to work, attitude, practice and personal may be for particular target groups and hence may not apply to others. According to the authors many ESF projects measure soft outcomes using paper-based techniques to assess the changes in attitudes and feelings over time. Quite a few have used ongoing reviews between trainers and beneficiaries to record the outcomes which draw on the evidence produced by the trainees. Such reviews are recorded on individual training plans, though not in systematic format. Some improvements are accorded even though there may not be any formal measure of distance travelled in these skills.

The reviews pinpoint the fact that soft outcomes and indicators do not take into account skills gained during work experience and voluntary work as an indicator of soft outcomes or distance travelled (Dewson et al., 2000b). It may be problematic to attribute all the positive soft outcomes and distance travelled towards greater employability solely to the training intervention. In the case of self-assessed questionnaires will have a high degree of subjectivity and facilitated assessment maybe biased depending upon the relationship between the employee and the facilitator. In certain cases the business language becomes inappropriate for certain groups, the multiple groups compelled to consider different baselines thus negating one particular model for all the projects. All these suggest that there is a need for projects on soft outcomes to go in for a more systematic measurement. The Institute for Employment Studies has recommended longitudinal case studies of evaluation and effective follow-up of all beneficiaries for improvement of the measure. Skill enhancement requires changes in teaching and training as extensive activities. Learning to teach or train may also be non-formal and practice-based and hence extensiveness and practice-based learning would lead to the enhancing of the quality of skill formation.

In emerging countries like Oman, higher education institutions have been developing hard skills of local youth but soft skill development is a new phenomenon. When compared to the high unemployment rate in certain occupations, the reason turns out to be either lack of interest in those activities like construction or absence of soft skills in activities requiring interactions with customers. Soft skills acquire importance in improving the existing knowledge base and not only the employers but also the colleges and universities have a role in facilitating such a process so that the local youth are trained in all those avocations requiring soft skill. This process indeed would not only empower the locals with high quality human capital but also reduce the unemployment rate and the dependence on expatriates. If the higher education institutions accord importance to soft skill teaching and training as is done at the workplace though experiential learning and other tools, skill development would be smooth leading to lifelong learning besides fulfilling the expectations of the employers.

3.7 Conclusion

The chapter started with an introduction to soft skills, after establishing their importance. Its conceptualisation has been in terms of personal, interpersonal and situational skills to match its different attributes complementing the hard skills. In the service-oriented economy, the importance of soft skills has increased tremendously and the employers evaluate the new recruits based on the soft skills. Soft skills also play an important role in promotions and positions requiring strategic decision making.

Soft skills may be assessed through what is called 'distance travelled' due to some intervention programmes intended to impart these skills. A skill wheel explains the totality of all the soft skills and how they undergo changes owing to the intervention process. Since soft skills are intangible, their measurement will be subjective, more so under self-assessment. With appropriate cross checking and facilitated assessment we can reduce the element of subjectiveness. We follow the Hackney method of evaluating the performance of the employees before and after an intervention like training take place to improve the soft skill base of the employees. Taking into account the three major groups of personal, interpersonal and situational skills, if the soft skills are evaluated before and after the intervention the change will explain the improvement in the performance of the employee through the distance travelled method. Since the evaluation bears subjectiveness, standardised and quantitative measure will pose a big problem and hence a self-assessed rating has been adopted. The different sources of soft skill acquisition and the role played by experiential learning at the workplace have also been discussed with a critique on the skill enhancement techniques.

The fourth chapter on methodology will attempt to explain how soft skills can be investigated, illustrating the sample cases of banking and oil and gas industries in Oman and provide a measure of distance travelled in respect of different skill occupations.

CHAPTER

4
Research Methodology

4.1 Introduction

Development of human capital is time consuming and as and when educational planning strategies and economic growth prospects change, the importance accorded to human capital also changes. The experience of the advanced countries has shown that higher the level of investment on education, higher has been the contribution of human capital and when compared with that of physical capital, the rate of return on human capital has been higher (Becker, 1993). The fact that human capital has assumed a better status than physical capital and that under an endogenous technological regime which instigates augmentation of both the factors, human capital assumes the role of the leading factor. Human capital is proxy by educational attainment; however, in the service oriented world, mere educational attainment is no guarantee for employability and hence interest on soft components of human capital has ushered in a new field for research.

The concept of soft skill and its measure developed in the third chapter is employed to generate a soft skill framework for empirical testing in Oman. Section 4.2 identifies the research areas of the study – the problem of soft skill measurement and its application. Section 4.3 presents the research questions that become relevant for the methodology. Based on the questions, the objectives and propositions are listed in section 4.4. Section 4.5 discusses the broad research approaches in social science research. Section 4.6 elaborates the research design wherein qualitative and quantitative methods are described along with quasi-experimental design. The theoretical framework is constructed through development of skill wheel, distance travelled, soft skill index, human capital quality and the focus group analysis. Section 4.7 explains the sample design wherein data collection procedures and practical issues encountered in sample selection are discussed. The institutional and individual sample structure is presented in the section. Section 4.8 explains data analysis which includes data triangulation, the regression method to showcase the relative contribution of hard and soft skills and the ethical issues in research. Section 4.9 concludes, pointing out the limitations of the study.

4.2 Research areas

In the past, the hard S's were identified with strategy, structure and systems necessary for success of the organisation (Nonaka and Johansson, 1985), whereas the soft S's- skills, staff, style and super-ordinate goals complemented them. When the degree of consistency between these two S's is high, it indicates a better managerial performance. While the level of educational attainment has been taken to indicate the quantum of human capital available in a particular organisation, supplementary skills called as soft or generic or people skills become essential for the effective performance in realising goals. There are many studies on the measurement of human capital relating to educational attainment which we treat as hard skills, whereas the focus on soft skills is a new area. Because soft skills are intangible, measurement and standardisation are difficult and those studies which attempt its measurement have been constrained by many limitations (Moss and Tilly, 1995; Onisk, 2006). Soft skills and personal values may be augmented by training, mentoring, coaching or learning-by-doing process (Simpson, 2006). Hence, the measurement has to consider lapse of time in assessing the change brought about by these interventions which is the focus of methodology. The level of soft skill may or may not be positively related with the level of hard skill and this factor delineates the significance of soft skills in the realm of employability. Comparing how an individual's performance before and after an intervention like training is affected in terms of changes in communication, teamwork or attitude will examine what is called distance travelled in skill development and the extent of employability.

Not much academic interest has been shown in the concept or measurement of soft skills owing to the subjectivity element in this measurement. Hence these measurements lack standardisation which prompts the measure to be firm-specific, time-specific or location-specific (Lloyd and OSullivan, 2003). An attempt is made to generate a methodology which captures the nuances of the measurement. In a way it could act as a facilitating tool amenable for standardisation and application. We are interested in assessing whether soft skills play an important role in the early stages of human capital augmentation process. The fact that a country can have accumulated human capital stock indicates the growth of knowledge development; the annual flow will indicate the rate of growth of that development. On the other hand, when we talk of soft skills stock or flow, as stated already they exhibit elements of specificity. If the hard skill of a person is indicated by the number of years of schooling attended, the type of communication or interpersonal skill one has can be measured in terms of impact rather than the inputs. There are studies on topics like labour market situation in Oman (Al Dhahab, 1997; Goodliffe, 2004), higher education and Omanisation (preference for employment of nationals) (Al-Lamki, 2000, 2002) or education development related to Oman (ESCWA, 2003; Rassekh, 2004; Murphy, 2005). But there are no studies dealing with soft skill application in Oman and how these skills are related with hard skills. In attempting to investigate this and other aspects, we have set forth the research questions in the following section.

4.3 Statement of the research questions

Since human capital plays a crucial role in the production process when compared to physical capital and is composed of both hard and soft skills and owing to the recent emphasis on soft skills by many organisations, this study focuses on the role and significance of soft skills. Hence the research question to be posed would be:

- What is meant by human capital and what are its components?

  Soft skill is personal and subjective and not only enables personal development but also leads to interaction with other people in given situations. The corresponding research question would be:

- What is meant by soft skill and how soft skill grouping may be accomplished?

  Soft skills endowment will be different in different skill categories or functions and would vary according to the emphasis shown either to personal, interpersonal or situational soft skills in different organisations as indicated by a skill wheel. The research question to discuss this would be:

- What type of treatment the higher education institutions in the region give to soft skill development?

  The individual soft skills may be rated by scores and based on the weightage of each soft skill, an overall index to denote the relative significance of the soft skills can be constructed. The research question in this context would be:

- How may soft skills be measured and an index constructed?

  Distance travelled indicates the attainment of hard outcomes (better employability through accomplishment of soft outcomes which can be measured in terms of enhancement of soft skill in the post-intervention period when compared to the before intervention period). It indicates the movement to better employability consequent on the acquisition of soft skills. The skill wheel is constructed accordingly. The relevant research question in this regard would be:

- How is distance travelled measured and assessed?

  Intervention programmes like training, coaching and mentoring influence soft skill acquisition and the different sources of acquisition may be from family, schooling, higher education and workplace. At the work place, training, experience, ideastorming, business reading and mentoring may enhance the intensity of soft skill acquisition. The impact can be assessed by comparing before and after intervention scenarios. Following are the research questions to discuss these issues.

- How soft skills are acquired and what are the different sources of their acquisition?
- What is the relative contribution of various soft skill enhancement sources across different categories?
- What is the impact of various intervention programmes to enhance soft skills?

The relative contribution of soft skill as contrast to hard skill may be assessed in terms of regression analysis where performance of an institution will be compared as before and after intervention. Experience and promotion are embedded in hard skill. The research question to examine this would be:

- What is the relationship between soft skill endowment and performance/productivity?

Since soft skill study is subjective, qualitative data have been collected in addition to quantitative data. The research design chosen has been quasi-experimental. Pre and post-intervention scenarios are compared with reference to the sample groups to assess the impact of intervention programmes. The analysis includes use of regression technique to bring out the significance of soft skills and narratives to illustrate the practice of several soft skills.

4.4 Objectives

Being one of the first studies on the measurement of soft skills for a region like Oman, the study has the following objectives:

1. To study the interaction between soft skills and hard skills components of human capital.
2. To study the importance of soft skills and to measure their contribution to the improvement of human capital quality and also to productivity.
3. To attempt measurement of soft skills and construction of a soft skill index in respect of high and low skill groups especially in banking and oil sectors.
4. To evaluate the contribution of training on the performance of the specific establishments.

The propositions with regard to the research questions to be considered would be:

1. Requirement of soft skill will vary according to the skill groups or functions.
2. The relative contribution of soft skill vis-à-vis hard skill improves after intervention.
3. Changes in situational soft skills are more prominent than in personal or interpersonal soft skills.
4. Hard outcomes depend on soft outcomes for distance travelled to be realised.
5. Leadership, communication and teamwork are the major training courses that impact all the three soft skill groups.

6. Training, mentoring and experience are major sources of soft skill acquisition in the workplace.

4.5 Broad research approaches in social science research

There are two major approaches to social science research - quantitative research, involving conversion of observations to numbers and analysing them statistically and qualitative research, which looks at participants' opinions, behaviours and experiences from their own points of view and in a more subjective way (Bryman, 2008). Quantitative research is useful if there is a clear idea of the overall situation and types of answers likely or if there is a clear need for numbers and data can be clearly quantified. Qualitative research is good for finding out things we do not expect and is good for understanding complex relationships. Besides, it is useful for finding out about meaning, motivations, ideas and beliefs and why people adopt certain strategies (Krathwohl, 1998). Quantitative research may be mixed with qualitative research to decide what groups, categories and questions are relevant and to better understand results. Quantitative methods include experiments and surveys. An experiment is a random treatment and a survey may be cross-sectional or longitudinal. Qualitative methods include ethnographies which are observations of groups; grounded theory using multi-stage data collection and phenomenal studies which study subjects over a period of time through developing relationships with them and report findings based on such experiences. Case studies are a unique system of qualitative method wherein various data are used to investigate the subject over time and by activity (Gubrium and Holstein, 1997).

Shank (2002) defines qualitative research as a form of systematic empirical inquiry into meaning where 'systematic' means planned, ordered and public, following rules agreed upon by members of the qualitative research community and 'empirical' means that this type of inquiry is grounded in the world of experience. Inquiry into meaning indicates that researchers try to understand how others make sense of their experience. Denzin and Lincoln (2000) claim that qualitative research involves an interpretive and naturalistic approach of studying things in their natural settings, attempting to make sense of or to interpret phenomena in terms of the meanings people bring to them. The advantages of doing qualitative research include (Bryman et al., 1988) flexibility to follow unexpected ideas during research and explore processes effectively; sensitivity to contextual factors; ability to study symbolic dimensions and social meaning; increased opportunities to develop empirically supported new ideas and theories for in-depth and longitudinal explorations of leadership phenomena and for more relevance and interest for practitioners.

By qualitative approach, we can explore a phenomenon that has not been studied before (and that may be subsequently developed quantitatively) and add detail and nuance that illustrates or documents existing knowledge of a phenomenon generated quantitatively. A topic may be better understood by studying it simultaneously (triangulation) or concurrently with both methods (mixing quantitative and qualitative methods) at the same time or in cycles, depending on the problem. It may be possible to advance a novel perspective of a phenomenon well studied quantitatively but not well understood because of the narrow perspectives used before and try to understand any social phenomenon from the perspective of the participants involved, rather than explaining it from outside. It also enable us to understand complex phenomena that are difficult or impossible to approach or to capture quantitatively and to understand any phenomenon in its complexity or one that has been dismissed by mainstream research because of the difficulties to study it or that has been discarded as irrelevant, or that has been studied as if only one point of view about it was real (Ospina et al., 2004).

Combining quantitative and qualitative methods in a single study is common in social research, although there may be difference between qualitative and quantitative research methods with each belonging to distinctively different paradigms. The advantages of mixed modes of data collection are purpose, process and analysis and interpretation. In terms of purpose, qualitative research identifies the relevant variables for study and develops an instrument for quantitative research to examine different questions such as acceptability of the intervention, rather than its outcome and to examine the same question with different methods like using participant observation or in-depth interviews. Process includes the priority accorded to each method and ordering of both methods which may be concurrent, sequential or iterative (Bryman et al., 1988). According to them, researchers rely on a method associated with either quantitative or qualitative methods and then conclude their findings with a method associated with the other tradition. Both datasets may be brought together at the analysis and interpretation stage. Brannen (2005) suggests that most researchers have taken this to mean more than one type of data, but she stresses that Denzin's original conceptualisation involved methods, data, investigators or theories. Bringing different methods together almost inevitably raises discrepancies in findings and their interpretation.

Mixed mode of data collection provides a comprehensive assessment of the soft skill scenario and accomplishes the integration of quantitative analysis with the case studies (Bryman, 2008). In a study concentrating on attitudes and personal behaviour, integration of quantitative and qualitative data would provide insights into the best practices followed at the workplace. Further, as Bryman (2008) points out, such integration identifies areas where both data can be accommodated to bring out the totality of the given situation. Since soft skills development is subjective, mere quantitative measurement would be problematic. However, once the skill index is computed, comparisons may be made between different groups or institutions as the case may be, based on the scores obtained before and after the intervention programmes. Further, assessment of soft skills has to take into consideration the rate of enhancement in the soft skill index in the treatment group as compared to

51

the pre-training situation which also would yield ordinal values owing to the personal and self-assessment nature of the subjects. Since the study assesses the contribution of soft skills as vis-à-vis hard skills, longitudinal data pertaining to pre and post-intervention scenarios in respect of different groups have been tested for their significance by using the regression technique which also provides a quantified measurement of soft skills. Hence, this study adopts a mixed mode approach wherein both qualitative and quantitative aspects of research are considered and modes of data collection are more than one. For example, besides the questionnaire and interviews, telephone calls, emails, personal observations and focus group studies have been used to elicit the necessary information from the participants.

4.6 Research design

4.6.1 Quasi-experimental research design

There are different types of research designs- experimental, quasi-experimental, descriptive, surveys, observational, relational and causal (Berg, 2003). In experiments, we have control over the variables and can establish the causality. But these are expensive and time consuming and hard to generalise with small sample size. Quasi-experiments are very similar to true experiments but use naturally formed or pre-existing groups. A treatment group is compared with the pre-training situation to assess its performance over the years. For example, if we wanted to compare senior and junior managers or the reference group with the general group regarding training impact, it is impossible to randomly assign subjects to either senior or junior (naturally formed groups). Therefore, this cannot be a true experiment. When one has naturally formed groups, the variable under study is a subject variable (in this case - position) as opposed to an independent variable. As such, it also limits the conclusions we can draw from such studies (Berg, 2003). If we were to conduct the quasi-experiment, we would find that seniors had more training as compared to the juniors. We might conclude that being senior or reference group member thus results in having a higher quantum of training. But other variables might also account for this result. It might be that repeated exposure to day-to-day organisational problems has caused the difference in training impact. Perhaps more of the seniors had training in their early years as compared to the younger group due to increased awareness of the organisational issues. The point is that there are many differences between the groups that we cannot control that could account for differences in our dependent measures. Thus, we must be careful concerning making statement of causality with quasi-experimental designs.

If an institution wants to test the effectiveness of a new training programme, it might decide to implement the programme on one group of employees and use a comparable group (no training programme) as a control. As the employees are not shuffled and randomly assigned to work different positions, the study has pre-existing groups. After a few months of study, we could then see if the training had better performance in the treatment group when compared to the pre-training situation. The results are again restricted due to the quasi-correlational nature of the study. As the study has pre-existing groups, there may be other differences between those groups than just the presence or absence of a training programme. For example, the training programme may be in a significantly newer, more attractive atmosphere or the manager from hell may work in respect of non-training situation. Either way, if a difference is found between the two situations it may or may not be due to the presence or absence of the training programme. With the exception of no random assignment, the study looks similar in form to a true experiment. As no random assignment exists in a quasi-experiment, no causal statements can be made based on the results of the study.

In observational research, involvement of the researcher with the group of study results in detailed analysis of its behaviour, but the problem of subjectivity and ethical issues may occur. In the case of surveys, questionnaires or interviews may be used depending on the nature of sample and quantification of the results. Since the research questions relate to assess the soft skills before and after the intervention programmes, quasi-experimental and qualitative methods have been used to assemble and analyse the data in this study. The use of quasi-experimental methods in the examination of this experience allows us to get a better understanding of the perspective of the study participants grouping them into treatment and control groups. One of the benefits of qualitative research is that it describes and analyses individual and collective social actions, beliefs, thoughts and perceptions (McMillan & Schumacher, 2001). The goal of this research study was acquisition of information related to thoughts, perceptions and beliefs of individuals that participated in the training programmes. Qualitative studies are important for theory generation, policy development, training practice improvement and action stimulus (McMillan and Schumacher, 2001). Many goals can be accomplished using a qualitative research method; however, it was the goal of improvements in training practice that served as the impetus for selecting a qualitative research design for this study.

Case studies are characterised as being descriptive, focusing on the case and accommodating a variety of disciplinary perspectives (Merriam, 2001). Case studies are differentiated from other types of qualitative research in that they are intensive descriptions and analysis of a single unit or bounded system. The study involves determining the number of people involved and the amount of time for observations wherein the case is a single entity, a unit around which there are boundaries (Merriam, 2001). Case studies help us to understand the processes of events and programmes in discovering context characteristics that will shed light on an issue or object (Sanders, 1981). Merriam (2001) states that insights gleaned from case studies can directly influence policy, practice

53

and future research. By analysing the data for emerging themes and patterns, the data collection process was examined repeatedly to ensure the data was providing the most accurate picture from the perspective of the participants. Once the research method was selected it was necessary to select the data collection instruments. In qualitative case studies, interviewing, observing and analysing documents are commonly used to collect data (Merriam, 2001). Individual interviews were used as the primary data collection instruments for this study. Thus, we have used a mix of quasi-experimental (pre and post training) and qualitative survey method (questionnaires for the general group of 120 and interviews for the reference group of 40).

In the quasi-experimental and qualitative method, we consider the demand and supply sides of soft skills which have to match each other for market perfection and optimal employment at the organisation level. The demand for soft skills will depend upon the functional requirements and expectations of the employers, technological domain contributing its own demand. The government and private policy may revise the skill requirements of particular jobs over the years. Further, labour market characterisation and human capital development may also exercise their markings on the soft skills market (Anderson et al., 1979; Gribbons and Herman, 1997). The personal abilities, training, learning-by-doing, role analysis, following benchmarks and the necessity for interaction with others will determine the supply side of the balance sheet. Given these factors, we have then analysed the pre and post training scenarios so as to assess the development of soft skills and how the organisations are able to bridge the skill gap toward achieving increased productivity and competitive advantage.

The pre and post-intervention scenarios require longitudinal data from the same respondent at two periods of time and analysing these data through regression analysis is intended to focus on the changes in the contribution of hard and soft skills over a period of time due to the intervention programmes. While assessment of qualitative data shows the status of soft skills in different institutions, comparing the performance of both hard and soft skills through the regression analysis pinpoints the relative contribution of soft skills in the performance of an individual which otherwise would have been problematic only with qualitative data. Hence, the research design employs this technique so as to quantitatively test the significance of soft skills and their impact on own and company's development. The quasi-experimental-type narratives and the regression results complement each other in bringing out the essence of soft skill measurement on the one hand and how it has been nurtured and developed on the other hand.

4.6.2 Theoretical construct

This section extends the concept of soft skill as explained in chapters two and three by conceptualising it into three categories of personal, interpersonal and situational and constructing a skill wheel and the distance travelled methodology. The soft skill wheel as explained in figure 4.1 may have different ramifications for different categories of workers in different work cultures. The skill wheel has been developed based on the literature review of studies like European Social Fund projects (Balgobin et al., 2004) but also from empirically validating with the management of sample institutions as to the relevance and significance of such task wheels in performance appraisal of the employees. Not only the soft skill requirements will be different for different skill groups but also in different functional attributes. Because of this, the significance of soft skills will depend upon the specificities related to the individual, institution or location. Hence, this study constructs a soft skill index based on the incidence of the different skills in different skill groups. The intensity of the soft skill index indicates the nature of employability and competence of the workers in achieving the goals of the organisation. The transformation from basic to core and from core to advanced skills is indicated as 'distance travelled' as developed in the third chapter.

Figure 4.1: Soft skill wheel

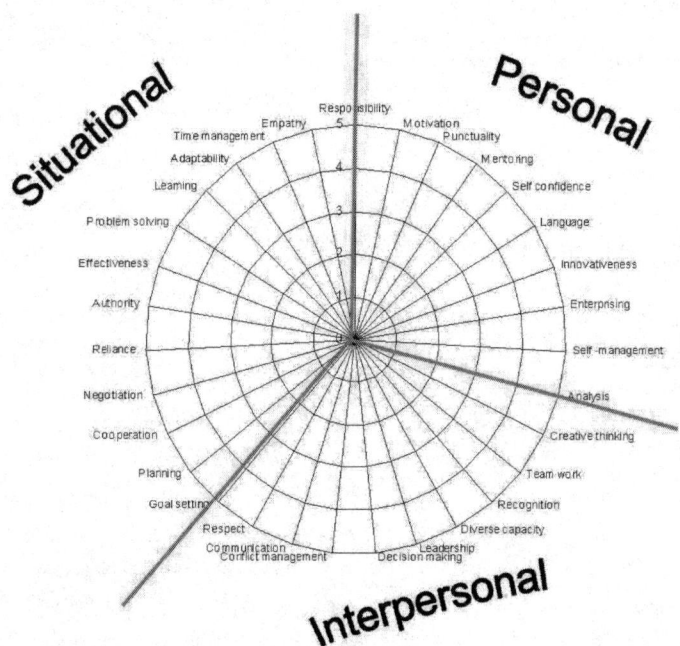

Soft skill index, constructed by the combined effect of the three skills indicates value addition to the particular individual in skill endowment. Since the index is made up of three skills which are crucial for overall job requirement (some of them may not be that much required for particular jobs), the scores in each skill is aggregated to obtain the index. If many skills are the most sought after, the index considers all those skills.

Since the focus is on the above three skills the differences in group weightage may be due to difference in employee categories (such as senior or junior managers), work culture or location. In case if they are of equal weightage to the groups the above illustration shows how the soft skill index can be computed. The index constructed before and after the intervention expresses distance travelled (as in figure 4.1) as rate of growth in the index. For instance, if the combined soft skill score increases to 2.85 as a result of training when compared to 2.65 in the case of non-training cases, the index increases to 57 (2.85 divided by five into 100 since the maximum score is five) after intervention when compared to 53 (2.65 divided by five and multiplied by 100) before, the rate of growth in the index is about eight percent (57 minus 53 = 4 divided by 53).

Table 4.1: Hypothetical soft skill index

Skill group A	Weightage B	Maximum score C	Actual score* D	Index (%) E (D/C)
Personal	33.3	5	3.5	70
Interpersonal	33.3	5	2.9	58
Situational	33.3	5	3.0	60
Overall	100	5	3.1	62

Note: * Hypothetical score where weights are equal

For different categories and intervention modules, the varying growth in the soft skills indicates the relative importance of particular soft skills and also training programmes in particular timeframes. Apart from skill wheel and the consequent distance travelled mode, soft skill development may also take place as a result of following the examples of the reference groups and narratives besides institutional analysis which exhibit the characteristics of model skill development. Though a score of five may indicate a 100 percent accomplishment theoretically, it may not be possible in real world, given the dynamic nature of competition and ever-increasing demand for high soft skill score. Hence it is assumed that the maximum score is subject to dynamic changes as and when intervention programmes take place, targeted at increasing the maximum limit. Also subjective judgements of individuals and these may vary over time and between groups.

Once the distance travelled is assessed, contribution of soft and hard skills before and after the intervention programmes would establish their relative strength in the individual's profile. Further, when soft outcomes emanate as a result of intervention programmes, the quality of human capital stock available with the institutions would also be improved. Taking the higher secondary schooler as the base, changes in quality of human capital may be assessed for higher educational levels combining both soft and hard skills.

4.6.3 Soft Skills and their analysis

The literature review revealed that soft skill have been classified as personal, interpersonal, leadership, problem solving, presentation, communication and so on.

It was decided to narrow down the soft skill groupings to three- personal, interpersonal and situational, since any soft skills at the workplace can be narrowed down to a combination of intra, inter and situational skills. We were interested to know how an individual performs with respect to one's own stand and that of others in a given environment and hence the three-way grouping of soft skills.

Soft skills have been grouped under five broad categories by Motah (2007) and Simpson (2006) - personal, interpersonal, communication, teamwork and problem-solving. Considering the importance of personal abilities in critical assessment of own development, personal soft skills have been placed at the top. The behavioural patterns are captured by the way the person communicates with others and hence interpersonal skills assume importance. The objective of acquiring soft skills is to develop personal attributes and how an individual interacts with others and how one performs in a given situation provides the basis for situational skill being a separate entity. Hence, the three-way grouping to indicate intra, inter and situational traits. Personal soft skills are intrapersonal skills that lead to personal development and include nine sub-skills- responsibility, motivation, punctuality, mentoring, self-confidence, language, innovativeness, enterprising and self-management.

Interpersonal skills are required for smooth interaction between co-workers on the one hand and with customers on the other hand and include 10 sub-skills- analysis, creative thinking, team work, recognition, diverse capacity, leadership, decision making, conflict management, communication and respect to others. Situational skills are those skills that have relevance in given situation and may be firm or individual specific. These may be a combination of various personal and interpersonal skills applied to specific situations and hence exhibit characteristics of situational analysis. There are 12 sub-skills under this category- goal setting, planning, cooperation, negotiation, reliance, authority, effectiveness, problem solving, learning, adaptability, time management and empathy. The skills have been grouped considering the appropriate personal, interpersonal and situational affiliation of the particular sub-skills. The sub-skills were identified and grouped on the basis of their affiliation to one of the three skill groups and in keeping with the existing skill methodology and improving it.

4.7 Sample design

4.7.1 Data collection

While an empirical research style has been adopted for the study, the different data collection methods pertain to a combination of questionnaires, personal interviews, focus group approach and personal observation. Primary data collection uses surveys, experiments or direct observations, while secondary data collection is conducted by collecting information from a diverse source of documents or electronically stored information. We have used a mixed type of data collection to accommodate the subjective nature of soft skills. A questionnaire is a data-gathering device that obtains answers or reactions from a respondent to pre-arranged questions presented in a specific order (Malhotra, 2004). A questionnaire is the main means of collecting quantitative primary data. A questionnaire enables quantitative data to be collected in a standardised way so that the data are internally consistent and coherent. Questionnaires are flexible and adaptable to a variety of research designs, populations and purposes. Questionnaire surveys depend on the frankness of the subjects' responses and need to be designed and carried out carefully so that they provide a genuine reflection of the attitudes and beliefs of the respondents. We have used both open and closed type questions providing balance between depth and authenticity. For exploring feelings, attitudes and behaviour types, open-ended questions are more appropriate and where time, subject or topic is sensitive and objectivity is required, closed-type questions are appropriate.

The questions have to be easy to read and relevant to the subject under investigation. As a first step in questionnaire design, we had specified the information needed from the target respondents in mind, taking into account their educational level, position and experience. The language used and the context of the questions has been familiar to the respondents. Questions that are appropriate for postgraduate workers may not be appropriate for those with only a high school education. Further, questionnaires that fail to keep in mind the characteristics of the respondents, particularly their educational level and experience, lead to a high incidence of uncertain or no opinion responses. It has to be decided whether a question is necessary and whether more than one question is needed to obtain the information in an unambiguous way.

Respondents may not always be able to answer the questions posed to them. They have been helped to overcome this limitation by keeping in mind the reasons people typically cannot answer a question. Questions have been designed to aid recall depending on the research objectives. A question that employs aided recall attempts to stimulate the respondent's memory by providing cues related to the event of interest. While most individuals are willing to participate in a survey, this sense of cooperation may vanish if the questions require too much effort to answer. Sensitive information was obtained in the form of response categories rather than asking for specific figures.

Unstructured questions are open-ended questions that respondents answer in their own words and we have used them where the respondents were willing. They are also referred to as free-response or free-answer questions. Open-ended questions are good as first questions on a topic (Malhotra, 2004). They enable the respondents to express general attitudes and opinions that can help us to interpret their responses to structured questions. Open-ended questions allow the respondents to express their attitudes or opinions without the bias associated with restricting responses to predefined alternatives. They have been useful in identifying underlying motivations, beliefs and attitudes. The disadvantages of unstructured questions relate to recording error, data coding and the added complexity of analysis. In personal or telephone interviews, successfully recording verbatim comments depends entirely on the recording skills of the interviewer. Interviewer bias is introduced as decisions are made regarding whether to record answers verbatim or write down only the main points. Tape recorders have been used if verbatim reporting was found important. In general, open-ended questions are useful in exploratory research and as opening questions. Structured questions specify the set of responses as well as their format. A structured question may offer multiple-choices or a scale (Likert scale, for example). In multiple-choice questions which we have posed, the author has provided a choice of answers and respondents were asked to select one or more of the alternatives given. They were easier for respondents to answer and easier to analyse and tabulate than open-ended questions. Interviewer bias is also reduced, given that these types of questions work very well in self-administered conditions. Respondent cooperation was improved since the majority of the questions were structured. An itemised rating scale (5-point) has a number or a brief description associated with each response category. The categories are typically arranged in some logical order and the respondents are required to select the categories that best describe their reactions to whatever is being rated. The respondents are asked to indicate their degree of agreement by checking one of response categories or ratings. To validate the nature of responses, the questionnaire was pre-tested in a pilot survey to improve its authenticity. All aspects of the questionnaire, including question content, wording, sequence, form and layout, question difficulty and instructions have been tested (Martin and Polivka, 1995).

We have also made use of interview method of data collection especially in the case of in-depth analysis of reference groups. Interviewing is one of the most common methods for collecting data in qualitative research. Interviews allow the respondents to provide rich, contextual descriptions of events. But the process of interviewing is time-consuming and the quality of data often is dependent on the aptitude of the interviewer. Face-to-face interviews have a distinct advantage of enabling the researcher to establish rapport with potential participants and therefore gain their cooperation. These interviews yield highest response rates in survey research. They allowed the author to clarify ambiguous answers and when appropriate, seek follow-up information (Leedy and Ormrod, 2001).

Telephone interviews are less time consuming and less expensive and the researcher has ready access to anyone who has a telephone or mobile. Disadvantages are that the response rate is not as high as face-to-face interview, but considerably higher than the mailed questionnaire. Computer-assisted personal interviewing is a form of personal interviewing, but instead of completing a questionnaire, the interviewer brings along a laptop or hand-held computer to enter the information directly into the database. This method saves time involved in processing the data and saves the interviewer from carrying around hundreds of questionnaires. However, this type of data collection method can be expensive to set up and requires that interviewers have computer and typing skills. We have used telephonic interviews wherever found necessary.

The focus group approach which we have adopted to elicit information from the reference groups is a special type of group in terms of purpose, size, composition, and procedures (Krueger, 1994). A focus group is typically composed of five to twelve participants (our group has five) who may be unfamiliar with each other and conducted by the author. These participants have been selected because they have certain characteristics in common that relate to the topic of the focus group. The author created a permissive environment in the reference groups that nurtured different perceptions and points of view without pressuring participants to vote, plan or reach consensus. The group discussion was conducted several times with similar types of participants to identify trends and patterns in perceptions. Careful and systematic analysis of the discussions provided clues and insights as to how soft skill and its development is perceived. The discussion was relaxed, comfortable and often enjoyable for participants as they shared their ideas and perceptions. Group members influenced each other by responding to ideas and comments in the discussion.

Questionnaires, interview and focus group analyses have been used to improve the quality of survey-based quantitative evaluations by helping generate evaluation hypothesis and strengthening the design of survey questionnaires and expanding or clarifying quantitative evaluation findings. These methods tend to be open-ended and have less structured protocols (data collection strategy has been changed by adding, refining, or dropping techniques or informants). They also rely more heavily on interactive interviews as respondents may be interviewed several times to follow up on a particular issue, clarify concepts or check the reliability of data. They use triangulation to increase the credibility of their findings where multiple data collection methods to check the authenticity of their results have been used. Lastly, their findings are not generalisable to any specific situation or population; rather each case study produces a single piece of evidence that can be used to seek general patterns among different studies of the same issue.

4.7.2 Practical decisions

This section intends to explain the process of sample selection and the problems encountered in the selection and survey. The author has compared establishments which have high soft skill component of human capital with those having a lower level to bring in the importance and measure of soft skills in different skill groups. In Oman, of the six major sectors – retail, automobile, telecommunications, tourism, banking and oil, soft skill requirement seems to be high in sales, banking and tourism sectors. Soft skill requirement was not found to be high in oil companies; automobiles and telecommunications present a similar picture but as contrast to oil, the gap between requirement and endowment seems to be lower. After sifting through available information, it was decided to select the banking sector to represent high soft skill requirement and endowment and oil companies to indicate relatively low levels. To assess whether there would be differences to soft skill orientation between the banks or the oil companies, sample institutions representing highly-oriented and another lowly-oriented have been selected. Further, as among the banks and the oil companies, soft skill requirement and endowment will be different for different skill groups like senior and junior managers, it was decided to do sampling within these institutions. Hence, this study concentrates on these two skill categories in banking and oil companies and the total sample size is 120 as follows:

a) Relatively high soft skill (senior managers) in banking sector   30
b) Relatively high soft skill (senior technicians) in oil sector   30
c) Relatively low soft skill (junior managers) in banking sector   30
d) Relatively low soft skill (junior technicians) in oil sector   30

A pilot survey was conducted so as to verify the existence or awareness of soft skills in the Omani economy and to refine the questionnaire so as to include the essentials of soft skill development. The pilot survey had the objective of narrowing down the sectors to banking and oil and covers 10 samples each in the two sectors. To identify the above four levels amongst the skill groups; random sampling was adopted wherein 30 respondents in each of the four samples was selected for the Part A questionnaire, which is described below.

Based on the final survey of 120 samples in the two sectors, 10 respondents each in the two banks and two oil companies was identified as references, giving the in-depth sample size as 40 to give representation to both high and low soft skill groups. A detailed in-depth interview was conducted to elicit information on soft skill development because of intervention from the 40 respondents. Among these respondents five each in the two sectors was considered as reference groups for obtaining qualitative data. The selection of reference group members from the intervention group is based on their better scores when compared to others and their willingness to participate in the in-depth investigation.

In-depth (reference group) sample size

I. *Banking (two banks)*
a. Junior managers   2x5 = 10
b. Senior managers   2x5 = 10

II. *Oil (two companies)*   Total = 40
a. Junior managers/technicians   2x5 = 10
b. Senior managers/technicians   2x5 = 10

Through interviews, personal rapport was established since the group was small while understanding of the respondents' behaviour relating to training and related issues was made possible. The narratives involved case study approach wherein personal views of select participants were obtained to illustrate their opinion about soft skill development. However, the narratives paraphrased subjectivity and may not be generalised. The questionnaires were mostly psychometric in scaling relation with productivity and performance. Face-to-face personal interviews was accomplished in view of large number of questions asked and also taking into consideration the longer time required to fill in the questionnaires. The questionnaire has several sections dealing with personal, organisational and soft skill development aspects. Aspects included in the questionnaire were on different educational levels, training and experience differentiation and the broad categories of hard and soft skills. Each soft skill group (personal, interpersonal and situational) was divided into many sub-skills and the respondents were asked to rate their score in each of the sub-skill. Care has been taken to distinguish between the judgement about the development of the individual and a judgement about contribution toward work performance. In this, personal development is of utmost importance to the individual, though company's development is also captured when 'performance' of individual is assessed as in the regression analysis. While development of the individual was assessed by ratings of the appropriate soft skills in the skill wheel, the employees were asked to indicate the nature of their contribution to company's development in terms of productivity, the earnings capacity of the individual taken as proxy for it. The regression analysis assessed both these developments in order to bring out the relative importance of soft as against hard skill component of human capital. Personal and company's development are inseparable in so far as performance is concerned. The scores in the 5-point scale were rated as before and after the intervention programmes wherever it was required so. Through interviews and case studies, specific narratives have been obtained from the respondents. Through cross-checking with the peers, the narratives have been moderated by the author as regards controversial opinions, language and content.

Data from the use of questionnaires information in respect of 120 general sample respondents spread over the following eight categories (24 trained and 36 non-trained senior mangers and 34 trained and 26 non-trained junior mangers) have been collected.

Figure 4.2 Sample distribution

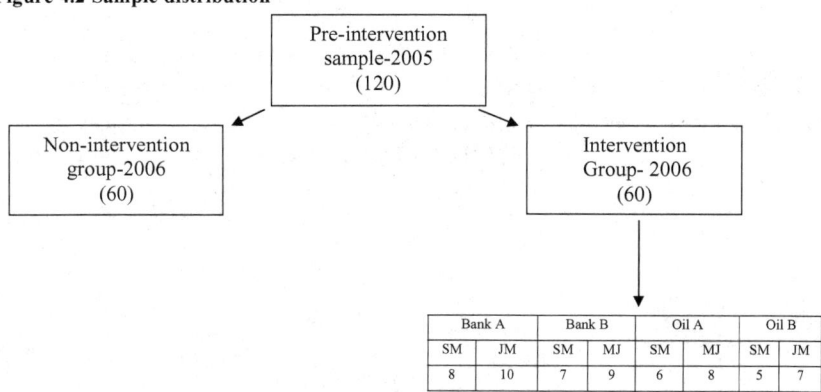

Bank A		Bank B		Oil A		Oil B	
SM	JM	SM	MJ	SM	MJ	SM	JM
8	10	7	9	6	8	5	7

Through questionnaires, personal and telephonic interviews, electronic mail and focus group approach information has been collected and also case studies and narratives from the 40 reference (five each in the above eight categories) group members. Personal observation has also been resorted to in eliciting information in respect of narratives from the participants. The reference year has been 2006, the baseline being 2005.

After the general sample was contacted, they were given the questionnaires and later through personal interviews and contact, the questionnaires were filled in between May to July, 2007. Options were given to them either to write down their ratings or the interviewer would note down the ratings based on the assessment of the respondents. The data collection techniques chosen were appropriate and linked to key research questions and predictions. The respondents were aided to recall information as to the nature of intervention programmes undergone during 2006 and their perception regarding soft skill augmentation owing to training, mentoring and coaching. The narratives from select participants were also obtained. From the general list, the willing-reference group members' information was collected at a later date (between August and November 2007) convenient to them through personal interviews and focus group approach. Since in the case of the 40 reference group participants, second and repeat visits were made to collect the information for the in-depth study, same scoring method has been adopted to the before and after intervention scenarios. Narratives and case studies for the reference group were obtained, in certain cases from the same respondents who provided the general sample narratives. Information on training policies by the four institutions was collected by visiting frequently and meeting the appropriate decision makers. The human resource, training and personnel managers were of much help and provided the particulars. Besides, some of the general managers and directors were also contacted to elicit policy decisions concerning their institutions.

As regards the selection of higher education institutions to assess their involvement in soft skill development, of the many universities and colleges which have been started recently in Oman, field survey was conducted during July-August of 2008. We have selected the state-run university (HEI 1 to represent university education), a private engineering college (HEI 2 to represent technical education), a private arts college (HEI 3 to represent general education) and a business college (HEI 4 to represent business education) in empirically finding out the nature of treatment meted out by these institutions on soft skill development. Apart from collecting information about the HEIs, the deans (and a few faculty members) of the institutions were contacted as to evaluate their treatment of soft skills in higher education in Oman.

4.7.3 Sampling and data collection

Sample formation involved five stages. First, based on the informal discussions the author had with some industrialists and university faculty in a conference on higher education in 2005 in Muscat prompted him to focus on the treatment given to soft skills by the institutions. Establishing contacts with the captains of industry in several sectors, it was found out that banking was an important sector in which awareness of soft skills was widely prevalent and soft skill training was incorporated in its human resource development policy. Hence it was decided to focus on the banking sector.

In order to contrast the importance given by the banks to soft skill training, a sector where the awareness was not so emphatic was to be selected for comparison. Here again, contacts with a number of industrialists resulted in deciphering the oil and gas sector to represent lower intensity of soft skill awareness. Therefore, this sector was selected so as to contrast with that of the banking sector.

Since within the banks or the oil companies, intensity of soft skill awareness could be different, it was decided to select two banks and two oil companies that had high or low soft skill intensity. By looking at the annual reports of the major banks and oil companies in Oman and by identifying with parameters like size, recent performance, employee profiles and HR policy, Bank A was selected as high soft skill intensity institution and Bank B was selected to represent low intensity. Likewise, Oil A and Oil B were selected to represent higher and lower intensities within the overall low soft skill awareness in the sector.

The second stage involved the selection of the general sample of 120 respondents. Narrowing down to four institutions to represent high and low soft skill intensity within high and low soft skill awareness regimes, it was decided to survey the institutional profile and also the employee profile in soft skill endowment. The institutional particulars were gathered from the general, HR and personal managers of the respective institutions. The assistance of these officials was sought to select the sample employees. In the selection of sample, both random and purposive sampling methods have been employed. The selection of general sample was randomly done, while the sample for reference group analysis was purposive.

From the list of employees provided by the institutions and discussions held with the HR managers, it was observed that between senior and junior staff, soft skill endowment was varied and hence it was decided to include both senior and junior staff of different educational levels as respondents. Recently recruited, having not been promoted more than once and managers who are classified as junior management cadre and those who are mentored by experienced managers have been identified as junior managers. Those who are experienced and are in the senior management cadre and who are mentoring other managers have been identified as senior managers.

The total number of senior managers in Bank A amounted to 81, whereas in Bank B, the number was 53, in Oil A 49 and in Oil B 27. The listed junior managers numbered 190, 110, 96 and 65 respectively in the four institutions. Since the number of senior and junior managers who were willing to participate in the soft skill survey was not forthcoming large, it was decided to restrict the sample only to those who were willing to participate. The volunteered sample included 30 senior managers in Bank A and 25 in Bank B and 35 senior managers and engineers in Oil A and 23 in Oil B, while in the case of junior mangers, the list included 37 and 30 in Bank A and Bank B and 36 and 34 in Oil A and Oil B respectively. From the random list, names of employees who had not undergone soft skill training in the past two years were deleted. The assistance of HR managers of the respective institutions was quite helpful in this matter.

Final selection rested with 30 and 25 senior managers in Bank A and Bank B and 35 and 23 senior managers and engineers in Oil A and Oil B, while in the case of junior mangers, the list included 37 and 30 in Bank A and Bank B and 36 and 34 in Oil A and Oil B respectively. It was decided to give equal representation to all the institutions and senior and junior managers and hence the sample size of both the categories was balanced to represent the same numbers. The possible number of members in each group amounted to 113 senior and 147 junior managers. Purposive sampling has been used to restrict the sample size to the present number owing to the intervention effect.

Selecting an equal number of sample respondents from each institution has the advantage of not only systematic comparison, but also the intensity of training impact can be assessed by the number of training programmes conducted by the institutions and the number of managers who had undergone training. It was also decided to give equal representation to those who were trained during 2006 and those who were not trained during that year. The final sample formed represented 55 (30) and 52 percent (30) for seniors and 45 (30) and 43 percent (30) for the juniors contacted in the banks and oil companies respectively, making the total sample size as 120 (both pre-training and post-training).

The sample was distributed equally between the seniors and juniors and also between the banks and oil companies to facilitate minimum number of samples (especially for regression analysis) and purposive comparison. In the third stage, reference group analysis was involved and hence, from the general sample of 120, a smaller sample of those who were willing to be in-depth interviewed was selected and even here equal representation principle was safeguarded.

Data collection was an elaborate process which involved the author in collecting information from secondary sources, sample institutions and sample respondents. The author hired four students (undergraduate accounting awards level 2), oriented them with the topic and questionnaires and they have been very helpful in filling up the questionnaires, given and explained by the author with the respondents. The scoring of the soft skills was self-assessed and the author with the help of the HR and training managers of the concerned institutions triangulated the scores into the present form.

Scoring on own and to company's development was self-assessed as in the questionnaire and each triangulated with the help of cross-checking with management and peers. For example, in three cases of Oil A JM, one case of Oil B SM and three cases of Oil B JM, there were some differences between the scores, ranging from 15 to 25 percent. These differences were toned down by re-cross-checking with the help of the Personal Managers, Training managers and the top management of the institution and then agreed upon. The total number of managers contacted was 250 at the first stage, wherein 120 were purposefully identified. The pre-training sample (120 as on end of 2005) was contacted once and the intervention sample (60) was contacted twice. There were no drop-outs since all the selected sample was asked of their performance as at the end of 2006 when compared to end of 2005. The reference group sample of 40 was contacted for the third time and those who provided the case histories and narratives for the fourth time to complete the narration process. Apart from the questionnaire, personal interviews and observation have been used to elicit information on the case studies. Thus the pre-training group who did not participate in training during 2006 provided data once. The intervention group provided data twice (for 2005 and 2006). The reference group provided the data thrice- general, intervention and in-depth. The managers who provided the narratives were contacted four times.

The post-training sample was selected such that the treatment group and the control groups would have equal numbers. The HR and training managers of the sample institutions helped the author to narrow down to this number based on the training profiles of managers well-versed with soft skills. Though the two groups had equal number, among the institutions and skill categories there were slight differences in the composition of the two groups, but overall, the post-intervention sample was formed such that numbers in both the groups would be the same for purposive comparison. .

As there was a general group and an intervention group, there was only one reference group, but distributed equally among the institutions. Hence, nominally, each institution had one reference group. From the general sample of 15 in each institution and from the willing respondents, five of them were identified for in-depth interview with the assistance of the HR and training managers. The focus group approach and interview method were followed in the case of the reference group to obtain the information. The author and the four students hired by him contacted the reference group members and through the questionnaires, interviews and personal observations, data were collected from the reference respondents.

4.8 Data analysis

Apart from secondary data collected from the government agencies and the institutions, primary data were collected in respect of various training and other intervention programmes, besides data on employment, educational qualification, experience and promotional avenues. These were collected from annual reports, brochures and account reports of the respective institutions. The narratives of managers and participants of training programmes were sourced from the respective sample respondents through an in-depth survey. Particulars on skill development in the workplace and impact of different training programmes were obtained from the participants after due cross-checking with the concerned management and co-workers. In all these, the author canvassed the questionnaire to the respondents and the information was directly filled in by the respondents wherever it was feasible, otherwise written down by the author. In a few cases, some of the reference group members acted as the informants to collect information from other employees of the sample institutions.

4.8.1 Data triangulation

Triangulation enabled to decrease, negate or counterbalance the deficiency of a single strategy, thereby increased the ability to interpret the findings (Denzin, 1989). Cohen and Manion (1994) define triangulation as an attempt to map out and explain the richness and complexity of human behaviour by studying it from more than one standpoint. Triangulation provides a more detailed and balanced picture of the situation since it is a method of cross-checking data from multiple sources to search for regularities in the data. Triangulation is simply using different methods to research the same issue with the same unit of analysis, thus cross-checking one result against another and increasing the reliability of the result. Contradictory results often bring up important problems with question design, as well as fundamental issues surrounding researcher understanding of a topic. According to Denzin (1989), triangulation involves elements of time, space and person. With regard to time, data was collected on the same phenomenon at different points of time (not longitudinal) to validate the congruence of that phenomenon across pre and post training points of time. In space triangulation, data collection for the same phenomenon at different locations was undertaken so that multi-location consistency takes place. Collection of data of at least two of three persons and testing for consistency among them in the workplace involves person triangulation. As a matter of fact, the regression analysis to assess the contribution of soft and hard skills at the workplace of different managers has triangulation as the objective. Productivity, as achieving the desired level of own and company development and soft skills, in terms of scores have been triangulated after cross-checking with peers for any discrepancies and in keeping with the general norms.

4.8.2 Regression analysis

Ordinary least square linear regression analysis was employed by using longitudinal data to bring out the relative influence of hard and soft skills on performance, where performance is the job achievement according to the particular employee in improving the image of the institution and one's own standing. Improvement in human capital quality due to any intervention will improve performance. As mentioned in section 3.2, a low level of job achievement had a score of less than one, a low medium level achievement a score of one to two, a medium level achievement a score of two to three, a high level of achievement a score of three to four and a very high level of achievement a score of four to five in the scale 1-5. Distance travelled (section 3.4.2) was measured based on both soft and hard outcomes as a result of acquisition of soft skills due to various intervention programmes. The soft skill index indicated changes in relative skill endowment in the changing scenario. Further, evaluation of the effectiveness of training programmes conducted by the particular organisations and soft skill endowment (hard skill notwithstanding) of the employees was accomplished through the analysis of a regression model. The reference period will be 2006, with 2005 being used for comparison. In order to assess the contribution of soft skill along with hard skill, a multiple linear regression equation was fitted

Performance = function of (hard skill + soft skill)

This can be expressed in a regression equation

$$Y = \beta_0 + \beta_1 X_1 + \beta_2 X_2 + \varepsilon$$

where

Y = performance, the dependent variable, indicating contribution to one's own and company's development, realised through the interplay of hard and soft skills and measured as an actual score in the scale 1 to 5.

β_0 = constant (intercept)

β_1 and β_2 = regression coefficients of explanatory variables X_1 and X_2

X_1 = assessed individual score in soft skills (aggregation of personal, interpersonal and situation skills) in the scale 1 to 5

X_2 = assessed individual score in hard skill endowment in the scale 1 to 5

ε = error term

The share of each worker to the total in respect of dependent and independent variables was considered for easy comparison and generalisation. The model has the usual assumptions: the disturbance term (ε) having zero value and are homoscedastic and not autocorrelated and independent variables being non-random and linearly independent. It has two regression equations, one for the pre-training and another for the post-training stages to assess the relative contribution of skills before and after the intervention programmes. The specific assumptions are that the hard and soft skill endowments of the employees in a particular category are aggregated and each employee's share in the total gives the percentage share in the respective skill in the total sample. The percentage share of each employee in total sample performance was regressed on the percentage share in respective skills to assess their contribution. Performance indicates the extent to which an employee realises one's own development and also contributes to organisational development. Improvement in performance through the combined effect of soft and hard skills indicates increase in an employee's earning capacity and also improved contribution to organisational productivity through the human capital theory. The soft skill index of an employee indicates the extent to which it has been possible to achieve this improvement in performance, so captured in the regression analysis.

As the purpose of the regression analysis is not to compare the relative contribution of hard versus soft skills, rather to indicate the changes in their composition as a result of intervention, a separate regression was also run regressing performance separately on hard and soft skills. In either cases, the relative changes in the skills before and after intervention would indicate the rate of skill augmentation- in which skill group the rate is higher and in which component of human capital.

The performance index was taken to indicate the rate of growth in productivity or earnings capacity. Productivity is indicated by the earning capacity of the employee, which can be proxied in terms of achievement of own and company's development. How the increase in the earning capacity or incentives and awards after the intervention (training) when compared to before-intervention will be determined by the different skill indices. The educational attainment (hard skill) index was constructed taking the baseline value of 100 in the case of higher secondary worker, the wage index increasing over the subsequent higher education levels. The index value may differ depending on the productivity levels of different education levels in given situations and for our analysis, the following values seem to be appropriate, wherein a postgraduate with training and mentoring capabilities is 40 percent more productive when compared to a higher secondary worker. This is similar to the approach of ILO (section 3.2) wherein if no-schooling is treated as the baseline, the quality of human capital improves over subsequent years of education which assumes a linear rate of growth over subsequent education levels as noted below.

The following assumptions of human capital index is made to assess the changes in human capital stock as a result of intermix of both hard and soft skills.

Higher secondary (HS)	= 100 (baseline index)
HS + Training	= 105
HS + Training + Mentoring	= 110
Graduate	= 115
Graduate + Training	= 120
Graduate+ Training + Mentoring	= 125
Post graduate	= 130
Postgraduate + Training	= 135
Postgraduate + Training + Mentoring	= 140

Source; adapted from ILO, 1972

The soft skill index was constructed juxtaposed to the corresponding hard skill for the different groups. This indicated the changes in the human capital stock in respect of the given institutions. The rating of the scores involved subjective judgement and the assessments were related to the age and category of employees on the same scale. Necessary steps were taken to ensure that different institutions make comparable judgements. This is a tricky issue and yet underlies the quantitative assessments. There are difficulties in this type of qualitative assessment and hence we strike a compromise between admitting the difficulties and not being seen to have collected shaky data.

4.8.3 Ethical issues

In any social science research involving human participants, including questionnaires, surveys, focus groups and other interview techniques and research involving human data or records, ethical concerns are strongest where these data are gathered directly from the subjects and ethical approval is usually required (Diener and Crandall, 1978). Ethical issues invariably revolve around right to privacy or non participation, right to anonymity, right to confidentiality and right to expect experimenter responsibility (Beauchamp et al., 1982). We are to be honest if possible, but if we have to mislead people we have to debrief them immediately after their participation.

70

The principle of voluntary participation requires that people are not to be coerced into participating in research. This is especially relevant where researchers had previously relied on captive audiences for their subjects. Closely related to the notion of voluntary participation is the requirement of informed consent, which means that prospective participants must be fully informed about the procedures and risks involved in research and must give their consent to participate (Beauchamp et al., 1982). Ethical standards also require that researchers not put participants in a situation where they might be at risk of harm (physical or psychological) as a result of their participation. As regards privacy of research participants, research guarantees the participants confidentiality and they are assured that identifying information will not be made available to anyone who is not directly involved in the study. The stricter standard is the principle of anonymity which means that the participants will remain anonymous throughout the study and even to the researchers themselves. The anonymity standard is a stronger guarantee of privacy, but it is sometimes difficult to accomplish, especially in situations where participants have to be measured at multiple time points (pre-post study). When training programmes may have beneficial effects on the intervention group, persons assigned to the no-treatment control may feel their rights to equal access to services are being curtailed and hence this aspect has been considered.

Where records are in the public domain or where the subjects are no more, ethical considerations still are relevant but such research does not normally require ethical approval. Research using personal information or samples stored from previous research (either initially or when a proposal is revised) and the use of biological samples that are anonymised or that consisting of surplus tissue from routine operations need ethical approval. We are aware that any research which constitutes or could be interpreted as constituting, an encroachment on personal privacy requires careful ethical consideration. Care has been taken to maintain the names of the respondent institutions and individuals anonymous and not to encroach into their personal privacy in keeping with the international norms of research ethics. The narratives of the select respondents have been in their words and since all of them were either junior or senior managers or technicians, their narratives have been in English. The author has edited them for grammar and language.

The researcher is responsible for ensuring that the data collected and cases developed are accurate representations of each participant. Doheny-Farina (1993) emphasised that the results of a study are based on what the researcher brings to the research. The author is aware of the influence he has on the respondents and the context of the study. This study was designed to ensure that the impact on the informants and the research environment is non-detrimental and as minimal as possible. The identity of informants, the institutions and the training systems for each participant is protected and there will be no damage to any of the institutions, participants or trainers as a result of this study. The training community, professional development community and the communities of

71

origin for the informants will benefit from gaining greater insights into how to create successful training courses to meet the needs of trainees. All informants were assured that their identities would remain confidential and that the information they provided during this study would have no bearing or influence on their performance appraisal. A member check system was established to ensure that the researcher accurately portrayed the views of the informants. The informants were informed that they could access the transcribed interview prior to the final analysis of the data. Any questions about any portion of the interviews were addressed with each of the study participants and clarifications in relation to the data were noted in the transcriptions. All of the participants felt they were accurately portrayed in the interviews and no corrections to transcripts were requested. Several steps were taken to ensure the informants had a sense of comfort and legitimacy related to this research study.

Beyond personal interests, the research benefits by way of providing the necessary information the participants required for a clear understanding of soft skills and in not wasting their time and effort in unnecessary endeavours. Since the author is responsible for all the information provided in the thesis, care has been taken to ground the questions and narratives in theory and not to divulge any information that may hurt the feelings of the participants or the institutions. Further, care has been taken to see that no psychological discomfort results in the participants and not to deceive the participants about the aspects of the research that might influence the willingness to participate in the survey and no discomfiture resulted in them.

4.9 Conclusion

The research questions relate to the nature, measurement and augmentation of soft skills and their impact in the workplace. Depending on the soft and hard outcomes, distance travelled is assessed, besides computation of overall skill index as an arithmetic mean of all skills. The research design uses a mixed mode of data collection and a quasi-experimental analysis. Performance, measured as contribution to own and company's development, is regressed on hard and soft skill before and after intervention so as to bring in the significance of the theory of human capital. In addition, the methodology involves qualitative case study analysis to justify the mixed mode. The data collection procedures, practical issues encountered in institutional and individual sample selection and the need for data triangulation and ethics are also discussed. The next chapter will describe the sample profiles of both institutions and individuals. The different strategies adopted related to soft skills training in the selected institutions is explained with the impact of the same on work ethics in particular institutions.

CHAPTER

5

**Soft skill orientation of the
sample institutions**

5.1 Introduction

Since soft skills are purely personal, any quantification will have its own subjective limitation and hence narratives by the participants will to a large extent compensate for this limitation besides providing a diverse view of skill assessment. The narratives by training managers, human resource managers, engineers and other staff and participants of the various intervention programmes explicitly caricature the importance of soft skills and how they are practised. Since soft skills are utilised by the employers for both internal and external purposes depending on the nature of interaction within or outside the organisation, the narratives consider not only the personal development aspects of soft skill intervention, but also the impact of these skills on the relationship of the organisation on the outside world as it relates to clients and customers. This chapter analyses the characteristics of the sample institutions and their orientation toward soft skill training and development. The analysis is accomplished both quantitatively through comparison of data and qualitatively through illustration of several cases involving the key participants in the training and development system.

Organisations implement soft skill development through formal training and development, coaching or mentoring programmes in order to provide the employees with an understanding of human performance improvement and an opportunity to apply this knowledge by developing appropriate communication materials through appropriate assessment and design. These training materials demonstrate the ability of the employees to make practical application of various soft skills. Through positive motivation and attitude the employees may be provided with necessary training for better organisational development (Goldstein and Ford, 2002). The purpose of training is to inculcate new and improved skills in the employees on specific tasks (as illustrated in Cases 3, 6a and 6b). The training sessions follow a defined purpose and logical progression starting with a general overview and ending with troubleshooting (Case 1). All these three methods of skill development (training, coaching and mentoring) may be practiced differently in different institutions depending on the quality of human resource endowment and financial resources. Highly networked institutions like banks will have to be up-to-date in information and communication technology so as to have competitive advantage over other sectors, while localised institutions like petroleum refining require advanced production and marketing technologies. Skill development of bank employees will require a different magnitude from those of oil company employees. This chapter probes into the effectiveness of the different skill development programmes in the sample institutions in order to assess not only their soft skill orientation but also the degree of importance given to the respective soft skill development programmes, providing answers to questions like: do institutions accord crucial role to soft skills and how the differences in soft skill development can be explained across different skills. The purpose is to distinguish the institutions and compare them as to their focus on soft skills and effectiveness of the different intervention programmes in achieving the outcome.

Section 5.2 provides an introduction to the skill development scenario in Oman, while section 5.3 distinguishes the characteristics of the four sample institutions (two banks and two oil companies) in terms of their different organisational characteristics and establishes the case for soft skills in the institutions. Section 5.4 assesses the performance of the institutions in terms of their size, productivity and profitability by suitable comparisons. Section 5.5 analyses the soft skill orientation of the institutions from the job requirement stage onwards by illustrating with many cases justifying the importance of soft skills. The next section discusses the various training programmes and coaching sessions implemented by the institutions by indicating the relative importance of each course by adopting a weighting system wherein number of courses and the duration in days are multiplied to get the weightage. Many cases on the role and status of soft skills in the opinion of trainers and trainees are illustrated. Section 5.7 summarises some of the critical issues in the intervention programmes while section 5.8 concludes.

5.2 Skill development in Oman

The Sultanate of Oman, a small oil producing country in the Arabian Peninsula with a population of three million, is geographically diverse consisting of mountainous uplands, deserts and expansive coastlines. The nationals enjoy free medical care and education through post-secondary school, vocational or higher education. Its culture is rich in heritage and traditions influenced by years of marine and desert ways of life and a diverse mix of ethnic groups. It joined the International Labour Organisation in 1994 and has initiated reforms in the labour market aimed at addressing some of the barriers that have precluded employment of nationals in the private sector. The broader economic reforms (Seventh Five Year Plan 2006-10) seek to diversify and privatise the economy and provide for a more efficient public sector. The employers are given incentives to hire nationals through quotas and efforts are underway to make private sector employment more attractive to nationals by equalising public and private-sector employment conditions. A scheme is also in the offing which entails inducing institutions to facilitate the transition of nationals to private sector work through training and financial support or through job matching (MONE, 2008b).

Raising the skills of the current and future workforce requires a focus not just on primary, secondary, and post-secondary education but also on training and development. The skill mismatch stems from the perception that the existing education and training systems do not effectively prepare students for the needs of the global economy. Hence, Oman has successfully expanded the primary-level education opportunities to all its citizens and literacy rates have risen rapidly. However, secondary school graduates are considered unprepared to directly enter the labour market with relevant skills or to enter competitive university programmes.

The higher education and training reforms are a mix of strategies designed to focus on quality through curriculum changes, international accreditation and other reforms and to expand access by introducing new higher education institutions and to strengthen links to the labour market through job placement programmes. Training issues are one focus of the coordinating education councils, which also focus on primary, secondary and higher education reforms. Efforts have been made to expand the number of technical and vocational colleges and to forge public-private partnerships to increase opportunities for training, especially in skills required for the labour market (MONE, 2008b).

Private sector organisations with the cooperation of the government have started to implement many training and Omanisation (preference to nationals in jobs) plans. The plan has now reached more specialised sectors and professions, especially in education and financial intermediation. The self-employment programme called SANAD (self-employment and national autonomous development) has been successful in training and employing the national workforce in many disciplines. Many organisations have full-fledged in-house training departments managed by qualified trainers. Regular training on technical as well as soft skills is conducted and an annual training calendar is formulated and circulated to all divisions of the company. Apart from need-based training identified by the division heads, employees are also encouraged to express their own training needs. Depending upon the number of participants and recommendations of the division heads, employees are nominated for the training programme. The human resource departments implement training and development programmes in various spheres of knowledge development inculcating into the employees competency in soft skills like leadership, communication skills, analytical skills and technical skills, besides imparting positive motivation and attitude. There are many national training institutes, which have undergone a change in image and outlook through

75

strategic re-branding. Some are ISO 9001:2001 certified and have expanded and upgraded their facilities. The next section introduces a description of the sample institutions to showcase the soft skill scenario in Oman in the emerging banking and oil sectors.

5.3 Description of the sample institutions

Any company has to have training programmes to involve its employees in improving their basic work skills and competency such as personal skill development, communication, project management, conflict management and leadership. The training sessions may last from a few days to months, especially in respect of orientation and strategy coaching. The training programmes can be as specific as that of self management, presentation, personal skill development or team training and so on. While the senior managers assume the role of coaches or mentors to the junior managers and new entrants, they can also participate as training faculty along with qualified trainers from outside the company either outsourced or hired. Promotions are determined according to not only the years of experience in the particular position and company, but also based on the assessment of soft skills. Depending on the growth prospects of the company and performance appraisal of the employees, promotions are made. Promotions include not only more pay, but also better facilities and benefits, more responsibility in managing people and more say about anything done besides possibilities for further studies or training.

The following profile of the sample institutions strives to focus on the organisational structure as it impacts on the development of the skill endowment of the employees through various intervention programmes as mentioned in the methodology chapter.

5.3.1 Bank A

Bank A is one of the largest banks in the region with a strong presence in corporate banking, consumer banking, investment banking, treasury, private banking, and project finance and asset management. The Bank has a network of many branches and ATMs in the region and has recently opened its operations in the neighbouring countries.

Bank A is the leading provider of corporate banking services, catering to domestic and overseas needs of the small businesses and medium and large companies by offering them traditional working capital finance, project finance and others. The Bank's clients include domestic and multinational companies engaged in activities across all sectors of the economy such as contracting, telecommunications and oil and gas. The bank offers a range of value-added personal banking products and services to customers like a comprehensive suite of e-banking channels that are of international standard.

The investment banking division provides a comprehensive suite of financial services: corporate finance, product structuring, brokerage and research and a host of treasury products. The Bank has a record of being the first to launch a debt product, an index tracker, a guaranteed product, a private equity fund, a subordinated loan, a convertible bond and an international product listed on the local stock market.

The asset management division manages investment portfolios for several premier institutional clients in Oman. In the mutual fund industry Bank A occupies a dominant position with an 87 percent share of the assets under management. The division offers portfolio management services, custodial and accounting services and is also involved in structuring, marketing and managing new funds in various asset classes for different sets of investors. Bank A's private banking division has a distinguished track record in banking and wealth management.

Staff members in the corporate division have to liaise with small and large enterprises while those in the investment division have to interact with domestic and international investment houses. Private banking requires an altogether different interaction of the staff with the customers. The skills required for each division may consist of core banking skills and specialised skills in the particular domain. As new entrants are not expected to have specialised skills, the same are being imparted after they join the bank. Where the new entrants have previous banking experience, they will have to be reoriented to the organisational structure of the bank and its unique way of functioning. Further, while on job the employees have to learn many skills like leadership, problem solving, interpersonal and situational analysis so that they acquire competitive advantage vis-à-vis other institutions.

Bank A emphasises development of human capital as evidenced by its various annual reports. A major mission of the bank is to develop and motivate its employees who are considered to be the source of its strength. The bank has introduced a service-oriented business structure and internet banking besides mobile banking services and intranet portal. To be up-to-date in these technologies, the human resources have to be developed accordingly. Mention may be made about Omanisation wherein the locals are being trained to cope with the emerging trends in banking technology. The bank's new human resource development initiative (called 'HRDirect') enables the employees to interact with the HR database, facilitating decentralisation of human resources in decision making on HR issues (Anon, 2007). The bank links its competency framework to various HR processes in developing business leaders and new managerial capabilities, new goal setting and problem solving areas. The bank stipulates that the employees acquire behaviour so that they can achieve high performance levels. Competency maps and indicators of behaviour that are rewarded are listed and HRDirect links the outcome of individual effort to identify leaders who can be interested in new assignments. Further, depending on the behavioural and technical aspects of competency, the identified leaders are given training in team building, problem solving and people management, so that the competency level further improves and is directly linked to soft skill endowment as revealed in case 1.

The training unit of the bank has created a mock branch and an e-learning suite to train the new recruits before posting them on the job. It conducts about 400 to 500 training courses every year (including those on soft skills) which are developed in-house and also conducts diploma programmes and certification in various business areas. The training manager of the bank opined that the bank is one of the foremost in the region in creating a band of skilled workers which enables the bank to have competitive advantage over its rivals. The following cases explain how soft skill training is used to improve the internal efficiency of the organisation and also how personal development leads to better mentoring capability. The respondents were asked to narrate their perception about the training and the same was edited by the author as to language and content.

Case 5.1: Training demands as narrated by a training manager, Bank A:

My experience as training manager in this bank can be summarised in one word: challenge! It is a challenge arising out of the pressures on the bank in maintaining a band of competent people who could deliver the stuff modern banking system demands. The training sessions help the participants to achieve "self-determination". A course on presentation skills introduces the essentials of good personal presentation to be followed by verbal and written presentations. The second session deliberates on the importance of good presentation skills that are considered as best practice in the bank. The third session allows the participants to go through a test to assess their skill endowment. In the last session, any deficiency in skills if noticed is tried to be bridged through special mentoring.

Case 5.2: Bank A senior manager on his experience of undergoing training:

I had already had four years experience in corporate banking before I joined this bank in 1996. I was dealing in refinancing payments and making advances against receivables till 2001 when my major focus shifted to real estate mortgage loans. The boom in housing construction, fuelled by high oil prices necessitated my bank to expand its housing loan facilities and my task became more intensive owing to large number of applications in that sector. I was sponsored by the bank to undergo a 21 days training programme in a neighbouring country on the real estate and mortgage business and the course enabled me to have a new direction looking at the issue. As a result, I was in a position to process the applications and fulfil the demands of the customers more quickly and effectively than before.

The narratives summarise the number of sessions a training course contains and the nature of deliberations of particular courses like presentation and about the adoption of good practices and mentoring in effecting development through training.

5.3.2 Bank B

Bank B, smaller in size when compared to Bank A is much older and has its own staff training centre to fulfil individual, departmental and organisational training requirements. The bank provides overseas training opportunities to its managers including corporate MBA programmes. Performance appraisals are made every year to calculate the year-end bonus for each employee based on rankings given by their managers for each of their goals.

In tune with specific skills of the managers, they are posted in various divisions where they could improve their competency. This particular tendency has been witnessed in all the sample institutions. This structure has enabled its corporate banking division to deliver a wide range of services such as term loans, working capital facilities, import and export financing, asset and project financing plus comprehensive cash management services. The investment division activities include discretionary portfolio management services, brokerage operations, asset management, distribution of mutual funds, lead management of public equity and bond issues plus domestic and international investment advisory services. The Bank also offers treasury solutions to meet the growing business demands of institutional, corporate and private banking clients. The following case focuses on the importance of internal soft skills like demonstration of personal attributes in the recruitment process

Case 5.3: Bank B HR manager's views about skill acquisition by old workers and
new recruits:

Though references, word-of-mouth and previous experience play important role in the recruitment process, demonstration of attributes and characteristics with work-related examples by the candidates as the most determining factor. We know about psychometric tests being used in Europe to measure and assess a candidate's level of verbal and numerical reasoning and feel that adoption of such a methodology here would enable to identify enterprising youth for our company.
The employers may be willing to disregard qualifications if the would–be recruits display positive attributes like adaptability to demands of the job, good customer service skills, communication skills, enthusiasm, positive attitudes and basic work discipline.
Experience can be a substitute for training and as the worker ages in his job, he acquires such of those abilities which cannot be imparted formally. A worker having lower level of formal educational qualification but with positive attitude is a better asset than say a worker with better qualifications but without positive attributes.

The narrative exemplifies the advantages of ideastorming (brainstorming), coaching and mentoring sessions and how the new recruits in Bank B have been able to learn productively from these intervention programmes. To a large extent, experience can become a substitute for formal training in not only internal but also external soft skills.

5.3.3 Oil A

Unlike the banks, the requirement of soft skills in the oil companies will be of lower order owing to the technical functionality. However, in oil marketing soft skills recently have become crucial in improving their profitability and customer servicing.

Oil A's retail operation started at a time when there was minimum infrastructure in the country and cars were few. The market for petroleum products was very small with the only major consumers being the armed forces and an oil prospecting company. In 1970, a marketing franchise was granted to Oil A for its retail business. The development, manufacture and marketing of fuels and lubricants are a highly specialised business, in which Oil A is a world leader. In Oman, the businesses have developed in all sectors of the fuel marketing business; retail fuel sales to the public via dealer-owned filling stations, direct fuel sales to government and commercial entities and users of aviation fuel and non-fuel sales of lubricants and greases.

The company has initiated programmes to train young Omanis in the development and diversification of the country's economy. Training is conducted in both Arabic and English in qualified institutes and the trainees learn how to prepare a full business plan and part of this plan is a feasibility study of their own business idea, based on practical market research. In line with this project, the government has recently initiated a support programme aimed at providing soft loans to young entrepreneurs to help them start their own businesses.

Oil A service stations have continually evolved 24-hour convenience stores, besides introducing oil cards as an electronic fuel payment system for commercial customers and a trial launch of an innovative way of changing motor oil that is clean, convenient and environmentally friendly.

Health, safety and the environment are among the company's primary concerns and the focus of attention in all areas of the company's operations. The management of the environment, together with the generation of profit and the support of social initiatives form its developmental framework. According to a senior executive, the company follows strict international standards to ensure that the company applies the latest techniques in environmental management. This is achieved by adopting both administrative and technical tools to assist in avoiding any harmful consequences to our environment. The company puts direct responsibility onto senior managers to achieve specific environmental targets and does not assess its performance on profit alone but also takes into account whether environmental conservation targets have been successfully met.

The Company participated in a number of initiatives to explore ways of introducing e-enabled services to its customers. In October 2000, its website was launched and the site is intended to give customers a forum where they can communicate directly and easily with the company. They can order fuel cards and see their balance on-line. The company has initiated a strategy of sustainable development in the region to save the natural resources as evidenced by the narrative of an executive.

Case 5.4: Oil A's resource management plan

The company has launched a strategy of sustainable development with the objectives of protecting the environment and managing the resources such that it benefits the communities and delivers values to customers. A major component of this strategy is to encourage local employment and to improve operational standards and develop the human resources such that a challenging work environment is created by various training programmes and performance management systems. It provides career guidance and business advice to Omani graduates in select colleges (Senior Engineer, Oil A).

5.3.4 Oil B

Oil B, a fully owned government company is focused on developing partnerships with private sector companies to pursue the development of gas-based industrial projects and other downstream energy and energy related projects. Through various projects, Oil B plans on pursuing the future which creates more jobs and private sector investment opportunities directly from the projects themselves as well as from the many ancillary projects that will be needed to support these developments. Its significant experience in developing energy related projects and its position as a government owned commercial company makes it an ideal partner for companies looking to invest in the energy sector in Oman. The company has four main areas of operations covering the retail, commercial, aviation and the lubricants markets. The B2B business supplies all sectors of the economy and is particularly strong in the civil engineering and construction industry. The aviation business has the largest market share and caters for the proposed expansion over the next few years.

Oil B, smaller in size when compared to Oil A, is a local company and does not purport to endorse the sustainable development strategy of Oil A. On the contrary, it strives to achieve regional development through a competent marketing strategy involving local youth in delivering the products and services as required by the customers. Unlike Oil A, this company places more importance to group motivation through coaching training, which raises the issue of training the mentors also.

Case 5.5: On mentoring in Oil B

As far as training programmes are concerned, they are routine programmes and we have to conduct them because all other companies are doing so. I would rather prefer individual-to-individual mentoring with a tinge of traditional wisdom which can be far more effective than participating in formal courses. Not only it is on the type of on-the-job-training, it also contains the elements of life-long learning. For this, the chemistry between the mentor and the mentee has to be very good (Technical Manager, Oil B).

5.3.5 The case for soft skills

As the training manager of Bank A pointed out, soft skills are most required to enhance the performance of the managers once they are employed. He cited the example of call centres to which his bank turned outsourcing for many services. The call centre employee has to be polite, understanding, not getting infuriated by the customer's outbursts, clearly communicating and having a pleasing voice as the appropriate means to attract customers and satisfy them. Similar skills are required for the bank managers especially when dealing with customers in the personal, corporate or private banking divisions. In the oil companies, though soft skills play a less dominant role owing to more technicalities, nonetheless, they also have to improve their brand image through development of appropriate soft skills, say in marketing and public relations. Of course, different institutions will have different approaches to develop soft skills but the core utility of soft skills will remain different for different organisations. It is not that a bank or oil company will attempt to impart all the soft skills as mentioned in section 3.1; it depends on the purpose and goals of the particular division or at times according to the demands of the top management.

The question then becomes to identify those soft skills that are most preferred by a specific institution and how they are promoted through different intervention programmes. In any case, it is people working together and interpersonal skills that are needed most by any organisations. The following sections will examine the performance of the sample institutions and how they are oriented to particular soft skills besides assessing their different approaches implementing the various intervention programmes like training, coaching and mentoring.

5.4 Performance of the sample institutions

Soft skill requirement may be a function of the organisational structure of any institution depending on the demands of the top management, the quality of the employees and its competitive advantage (Kelly et al., 2005). Size, productivity and profitability are some of the indicators of performance which may determine the nature and extent of soft skill requirement. Mention may be made that apart from soft skills, there are other influences like overall organisational performance which determine the level of profitability. What we intend to do in this exercise is just to see if soft skill endowment and profitability level besides size and performance have some association or not.

Table 5.1 presents an overview of the sample institutions during 2006 in respect of size, income and productivity.

Table 5.1: Structure of the sample companies (2006)

Indicators	Bank A	Bank B	Oil A	Oil B
Revenue (mil RO)	190	77	227	122
Profit (mil RO)	60	30	9	4
Assets (mil RO)	2927	1068	54	32
Share of profit to assets %	2.1	2.8	16.7	12.3
Number of employees	1945	1065	1550	925
Revenue per employee ('000 RO)	97.7	72.3	137.6	131.9
Asset per employee ('000 RO)	1504.9	1002.8	34.8	35
Revenue growth %	36.7	32.7	24.1	35.5
No of junior managers	190	110	96	65
No of senior managers	81	53	49	27

Source: Bank A/Bank B/Oil A/Oil B, Annual Reports and various issues.

The banks have a higher asset size when compared to the oil companies. The capital structure of Bank A has witnessed a three-fold increase while Bank B experienced a two-fold increase. The increase in capital was only eight percent in the case of Oil A while it was 75 in Oil B. Revenue is an indicator of current performance and Oil A has the highest revenue. It is evident that between

Bank A and Bank B, there are differences in size and performance, besides the rate of increase in these indicators. While Bank A has a sustained performance over the period, Bank B was able to register a satisfactory growth only in 2006. When compared to Oil B, the performance of Oil A is at a higher level. Given the recent increase in world oil prices, it is but natural to expect that the revenues of the oil companies would be increasing quite substantially.

If profit is taken as an indicator of the efficiency of performance, the banks had a higher profit to revenue ratio. Oil companies have a higher profit-to-asset ratio. Given the increase in oil prices, the profit ratio of the oil companies is bound to increase whereas in the case of banks, new international capital norms and risk measures would be constraints (Anon, 2008). Along with size and profitability, employee productivity can be considered so as to distinguish the institutions as to their performance-related skill requirement.

In Bank B there has been a decline in employment as contrasted to other institutions. Poor performance during 2003 and 2005 could have been responsible for this decline. The proportion of junior managers and senior managers in Bank A has remained more or less constant. In Bank B there is an increase in the proportion of both senior and junior managers. In Oil A, the proportion of junior managers and technicians has remained constant while there is a slight increase in the proportion of senior managers. In Oil B the proportion of junior staff slightly declines while that of senior staff shows an increase.

As regards employee productivity, revenue, profit and asset per employee have been considered as various indicators. The revenue per employee is highest in Oil A showing an increase of about seven percent in 2006 over 2002. In Oil B the increase is 50 percent. In Bank A revenue per employee increases by 31 percent, while in Bank B, there has been a decline till 2005 and only in 2006 it was able to show a better performance.

Profit per employee is higher in the banks. In terms of asset per employee the growth was 70 percent in Bank A, 67 percent in Bank B, six percent in Oil A and 34 percent in Oil B. The revenue growth has been zero in Bank A and negative in Bank B, Oil A and Oil B in 2003. If the relative performance of the institutions as a precursor to the assessment of different types of soft skills is assessed, Bank A's annual reports show sustained progress of the bank, Bank B had a loss making business during 2002-03 which was turned into a profit position only after their new CEO was appointed. Oil A and Oil B have shown a flourishing business owing to the increase in world oil prices since 2001. Apart from the annual reports, the executives of the sample institutions cautioned about the challenging days before the banks owing to stiff global competition and small market or as in the case of oil companies, the danger of resource exhaustion and its negative impact on the economy. To sum up, the oil companies have a lower profit share which has not been increasing over the years. In the banks too, the growth rate of profit has shown a decline especially in the well-performing Bank A indicating the stiffness of competition and how this can be contained by improving the skill and productivity of the employees.

Comparing the four institutions as regards changes in size, productivity and profitability over the five year period would provide a platform for assessing the importance given to training and development, coaching and mentoring among other things. When compared to 2002, the overall structure of the sample institutions in 2006 shows that size as shown by revenue growth increase has been faster in Bank A and Oil B, moderate in Oil A and low in Bank B. As regards productivity per employee, the growth is higher in Oil B and Bank A and moderate in Bank B and low in Oil A. Profit growth has been higher in Bank A, followed by Oil B, Bank B and Oil A. At the outset, the composite indicator consisting of only size, productivity and profitability shows that Bank A has a higher level of performance, followed by Oil B, Bank B and Oil A. If soft skill development was correlated with this composite indicator it would show a higher level of endowment in Bank A followed by Oil B, Bank B and Oil A.

5.5 Soft skill orientation

5.5.1 Emphasis on soft skills in banks

The changing focus on poverty alleviation, sustainable environment and good governance and norms on risk management have made the functions of the banks more dynamic wherein soft skill requirement to deal with various issues becomes essential. The banks have to follow various guidelines to measure the various types of credit, market and operational risks and the capital required to cover these risks. The banks may face the risk that some of its borrowers may not make timely repayments of loan, interest on loan or meet the other terms of contract. The banks can also suffer losses in excess of expected losses during economic downturns. These losses are called unexpected losses. Ideally, the banks can recover expected loss on a loan from its customer through loan pricing. The capital base is required to absorb the unexpected losses, as and when they arise. Bank managers when they will have to be fully equipped to tackle problems coming from these issues, also have to equip themselves with appropriate personal skills so that they do not go panic. Various training programmes are intended to attend to this issue.

When the banks are required to invest in liquid assets such as cash, gold, government and other approved securities, such investments are risky because of the change in their prices. This volatility in the value of a bank's investment portfolio is known as the market risk, as it is driven by the market. The change in the value of the portfolio can be due to changes in the interest rates, foreign exchange rates or the changes in the values of equity or commodities. Several events that are neither due to default by third party nor because of the vagaries of the market are called operational risks and can be attributed to internal systems, processes, people and external factors. It is here that the soft skill of the decision-makers is put to test with regard to risk management which is so crucial to a bank's development apart from team management and problem solving so that the three types of risks are minimised and thereby efficiency is increased. Banks' senior management will determine corporate strategy, as well as the country in which to base a particular type of new business.

Looking at the advertisements for the position of managers in the banks, it seems that soft skills are an important ingredient in the selection process. The following advertisements by the local banks illustrate this.

Case 5.6a: Job requirements for a senior manager in a bank

In the case of senior managerial position (The Head, Corporate Finance), a prospective candidate will
a) Lead the Bank's Corporate Finance team that is involved in corporate advisory, capital market offerings, private placements, M&A, etc: *here leadership skill is required*
b) Be in charge of marketing of corporate finance services and developing client relationships: *here customer relationship skills are emphasized.*
c) Business development: *this requires proficiency business and situational skills*
d) Preparation of strategy report on the basis of client's objectives: *this requires good presentation skills*
e) Lead on drafting issue documentation: *this involves good communication skills*
f) Interaction with regulatory agencies: *this requires good interpersonal skills*
g) Lead on marketing the transaction including preparation of presentations, marketing material, etc: *this requires presentation skills.*
h) Lead on financial modelling: *this requires numeracy skills*
i) Lead on Negotiations: *this requires negotiation skills.*
j) Organise and lead the team on transactions: *this requires teamwork skills.*

The above position requires a minimum of graduate degree in finance related subject and 10 years of experience in a bank. (Advt., Bank A, italics author's)

Case 5.6b: Job requirements for junior managers (Assistant Fund Manager)

A. Technical skills in investment scenario
B. Liaison with investment and regulatory institutions: *this involves interpersonal and situational skills*
C. Monitoring position of company client portfolios: *this requires situational and problem solving skills.*
D. Assist in the preparation for periodic reports prepared for senior management: *this requires teamwork, communication and presentation skills.*

The position requires Bachelors in Finance related subject and the skills required are strong knowledge base and technical skills in international funds and portfolio management besides excellent English communication and interpersonal skills (Advt., Bank B, italics author's).

The above illustrations show how in recruiting for senior and junior managerial positions in the banks, soft skill requirement is important from the viewpoint of the employers wherein we find that interpersonal, situational and problem solving skills seem to be more sought after. The emphasis on soft skills by the sample institutions may be documented by the opinions of top managers responsible for recruiting and training the employees.

The following are some of the views expressed by the trainers and senior managers as well as the participants as to the relevance, contents and importance of training courses in banks.

Case 5.7: Bank A participant on the importance of team and communication skills:

I cannot forget one of the training courses I attended on the development of communication and presentation skills, which was so much educative. The course consisted of five segments. 1) A series of attitude and aptitude tests to assess personality and emotional intelligence. 2) Exercises in both spoken and written communication. 3) Extempore speaking exercises and mock interviews. 4) Conceptual and general knowledge quizzes and 5) various tests for assessing communication and presentation skills. After the exercises, we were asked to provide the feedback so that depending on our learning process, further counselling could be provided, if the need arises.

Conduct of aptitude tests, communication exercises, extempore presentation and quiz therapy seem to be followed by Bank A in developing the soft skills of its employees.

Case 5.8: Bank B training manager on emotional intelligence

To me emotional intelligence and emotional quotient imply developing sensitivity to non-verbal messages, defining and understanding the skills used in recognising and articulating the emotional vocabulary of the participants and the application of those skills for the purpose of managing their functions more effectively. This enhances their communication behaviour in work, at the same time improving the quality of their response to work-related communication and presentation tasks. Our emotional intelligence training sessions provide the participants the skills to communicate at an emotional level as they perceive emotional vocabulary in others or as they manage their emotions or those of others or as they understand and apply the concept of you-attitude to communicate different tasks. This enables them to acquire better skills in effectively making or handling tasks through their verbal and written business communication.

The narrative exemplifies the criticality of emotional skills in fulfilling the communicative capability of the Bank B managers.

5.5.2 Emphasis of soft skills in oil companies

Although the oil industry has been in existence in Oman for the past twenty five years, its operations have remained for the best part of the time mainly in the hands of well trained and experienced expatriates. Inevitably this was necessary at the beginning, especially with the more technical and complex projects and operations. Approximately 50 percent of this work force is accomplished by expatriates. Jobs in the oil industry where contractors are employed vary from plant operators, mechanical and electrical technicians, welders, plumbers and carpenters. In the past, contractors and indeed most of the employers in the Sultanate complained that young Omanis shunned almost all industrial jobs due to high expectations of the young people. Moreover, the high expectations were well within reach of many of those young people, given opportunities to gain the necessary knowledge and skills. While those opportunities were plentiful there was little hope that young people would go into industrial manual work by choice. In order to give assistance to the contractors, an oil industry training board with the aim of developing the industry was established in 1994. It is composed of representatives from the contractors in order to serve the whole industry principally in training matters to Omanise semi-skilled and skilled personnel within the industry by the provision of effective training programmes using existing training institutes.

The administration section of the training board will assist companies in the recruitment of trainees. The focus is on the selection process which is considered to be a critical area of the whole project. Another function is testing and interviewing prospective candidates before streamlining successful ones into disciplines in accordance with the aptitude and capability displayed in the skill tests. The administration section will also assist in the training process itself. They will select appropriate institutes for specific training programmes. They will monitor the training programmes and assessments and provide feedback to the companies. They will monitor trainee progress and take appropriate action when performance is poor. The training board will assist companies in the development of their trainees including advice for on-the-job training and skill assessment.

A typical advertisement for junior managerial/technical position in oil marketing companies requires the following hard skills.

Case 5.9a: Job requirements for junior executives in oil companies

a) Minimum qualification is diploma in mechanical field.
b) Experience in oil related fields for a minimum of three years.

The soft skills requirements are:

a) Ability to speak and write Arabic and English
b) Excellent team member with a strong bias to assist others.
c) Excellent interpersonal skills and high learning ability
d) Self motivated and enthusiastic
e) Ability to work without supervision and make own decisions

Case 5.9b: Job requirements for senior managerial/technical positions,

The hard skill required is a minimum graduate or above and experience of 4-10 years. The prospective candidates have to demonstrate the ability to
a) Understand complex information and identify key issues
b) Make tough decisions while taking the long-term implications into account
c) Apply creativity and innovative thinking to produce sustainable solutions
d) Understand the diverse factors that affect the whole organisation
e) Adapt to changing circumstances
f) Deliver to meet strict targets and deadlines
g) Lead and motivate others to achieve ambitious personal and professional goals
h) Build trust and persuade others effectively
i) Involve people with diverse viewpoints in activities and decisions

In oil exploration and production, mainly technical skills are required, the soft skill requirement being minimal. Whereas in oil marketing the importance of soft skill is at a higher level than in oil production, though when compared to banking it may be at a lower level.

From the soft skill requirement, it is evident that senior managerial positions need a higher level, while the junior management is not expected to have that particular level. When recruitment is done, it may be that a minimal soft skill endowment is expected but as the responsibilities of the particular job increase over the years, training becomes essential to impart the necessary input to minimise the performance gap.

From the opinions collected by various other trainers, the sample institutions seem to place as much importance on soft skill endowment as they do on hard skills and in Bank A especially, the weightage given to soft skills is higher. In many formal interview sessions, more emphasis on attitude was accorded rather than on qualifications.

The following narratives by the executives and trainees in the oil companies outline the importance of leadership, teamwork and empowerment of local youth which are essential internal soft skills.

Case 5.10: Oil A executive on the leadership training:

I was assigned the task of training a batch of junior engineers in problem solving. I started the programme in the following sequence: 1) consider all factors involved in the project or process; 2) consider plus, minus and interesting aspects; 3) use creative thinking capability and ideastorming; 4) look for consequences and results; 5) play with ideas by substituting, combining, adapting, magnifying or minifying as the case may be to put ideas to other uses and 6) evaluate and choose from alternate solutions. As I understand, Omani youth lack good leadership skills owing to perceptual, emotional, cultural, language and interpersonal barriers. Hence, one of the basics has to be encouraging good conversation to culminate in effective communication. If the participants are really interested in the training programmes, they thoroughly immerse themselves into them and the result is astounding.

The above case narrates the essentials of leadership training like problem identification, analysis and alternative solutions that can be had from active participation by becoming what may be called 'poster children', wherein the enterprising participants assume the role of heroes and guide the rest.

Case 5.11: Oil A participant on teamwork and peer relationship:

In marketing oil products, teamwork is very essential. Some of the team members may engage in aggressive behaviour or exhibit higher degrees of loneliness and depression. One of my colleagues Mr. X was not cooperative in our team and it was left to me to mend him and see that his contribution to the team would be positive. My task was to promote social skills in Mr. X which included anger management, fairness and sensitivity. I drew him to my companionship through a discussion on literature, games, sports and music. I made him realise the importance of expressing his thoughts and emotions in socially acceptable ways. I made him understand that if he can succeed in acquiring empathy, he will be in a position to tutor other members who may exhibit uncooperative tendencies in the team. After a lapse of two months, I had the opportunity of witnessing his participation in a team and I was surprised that he was one of its cheer leaders and his contribution was very much appreciated.

The case demonstrates the crucial role played by empathy in anger management when working in teams.

Case 5.12: Oil B Senior executive on management style

I keep emphasising basic skills in the new recruits in addition to effective communication which is so much lacking now. Ours being a major oil distributing company in the region, coordinating between different market segments requires a combination of soft skills like empathy, communication and problem solving. However, the utility of these programmes has to be periodically assessed so that value-added courses are delivered. I have heard of master black belt certification for professionals and while abroad I have met a person with a six sigma black belt. I feel that similar certification programmes will have to be introduced in the region so that the local youth become internationally competitive and fit into any environment to perform very effectively.

The narrative illustrates the need for certification in training programmes so that like in martial arts, grading can be established to distinguish different skill levels and the impact thereon.

Case 5.13: Oil B participant on empowerment of local youth

The training courses and simulated exercises enable us to fully understand the ways and means of satisfying different types of customers. I am told that there is an online training course offering certification in customer care, customer relations, customer service on the telephone and positive customer care. Once I was to deal with an irate customer. In the beginning I was rather upset and was about to assign the task to another of my colleague but empathy prevailed and I was able to put myself in the position of the customer. The example of health care came into my mind and I thought that customer care is similar to that. I went in and brought the customer and in the lobby it took almost 15 minutes to convince the customer why the problem occurred and why the supplies to him were not made in time. I assured him that in about 24 hours the supply will reach him. Half-minded, he left the place but the next day he rang me up that the supplies have reached him and thanked me profusely. I consider such moments as really rewarding and value that much above the monetary rewards and bonuses I get from my company.

The above caricatures explain not only how internal soft skills in improving leadership qualities (through simulation and certification) are imparted and how the training sessions are conducted but also how the trainers and trainees feel about the different courses, besides the contents, the delivery system and utility of the programmes. Training to improve attributes of leadership, communication and presentation involve internal soft skills and training for customer care courses underpins the importance of external soft skills. Apart from training courses, mentoring and person-to-person coaching also assume importance though coaching and mentoring is equally favoured by higher age groups and also in oil companies especially for personal skill development. No course would be 100 percent fool-proof and no employee will be completely satisfied with the outcome of the course. The following are some of the issues which have been observed while studying the efficacy of the various training programmes conducted by the sample institutions.

5.6 Training programmes

The main objective of soft skill training is to improve the performance of the new entrants over the years so that the difference between their actual performance and the level of performance expected by the employer is minimised. By looking at the various training programmes conducted by the institutions, it may be possible to comment on the nature, content, the prospective participants and the impact of the programmes. The sample institutions have separate training and development divisions and regularly conduct courses for different groups of employees. When the new recruits join the institution they are usually given two to three weeks of induction training by all the institutions. In addition to in-house training programmes, the institutions outsource some of the courses and also send their employees overseas for specified training programmes like business strategy and application of IT. The institutions also have formal and informal coaching facilities wherein some outside coachers may also be brought in for the purpose. Mentoring junior staff is accomplished by the senior managers on one-to-one basis depending upon their expectations.

Particulars about training programmes have been collected from the annual reports, official documents and narrations of the training department staff and also from the participants as evidenced by many case studies presented. The consensus was that when compared to the past the number of soft skill training courses has increased in recent times showing their crucial role in organisation development. Over the years, the courses offered showed an increase first owing to increase in the number of employees and second owing to increase in the diversified products and regions. While the duration of hard skill training courses like business strategy, IT, accounting etc, take up to three weeks, soft skill courses are usually of 1-7 days duration. While presentation, time management, business coaching and emotional intelligence courses are of one day duration, effective communication, situational analysis and negotiation skills consume two days while customer care and team building consume three days each. A particular course can be repeated many times depending upon the need and requirement by the particular division. While staff members in departments like IT and accounts will require the least number of soft skill courses, others in the marketing and customer care divisions will be required to improve their competencies by attending regular courses. Customer care and effective communication courses are repeated to the highest number followed by team building, business coaching, leadership and situational analysis courses. From the viewpoint of intensity, leadership course assumes greatest importance followed by team building and customer care.

In Bank A, the average number of participants went beyond 30 in some courses and when there are lecture programmes the number may exceed even 50. The bank's training and development division had only two staff faculty in 2000, increasing to eight in 2006 from a mere 35 courses in 2000, the number of courses offered has increased to 281 in 2006. The different training courses are tailored to suit the requirements of senior as well as junior managers and hence for these two categories separate courses may be run though both the categories may participate in some of the courses like presentation, communication, emotional intelligence and customer care. The courses where most of the senior managers participated amounted to 30 while the courses intended for the junior managers amounted to 46. Leadership and negotiation skills followed by customer care and team building intended for senior managers were higher in number.

In Bank B, the training and development division has four staff members and occasionally the bank out sources some of the courses. Sponsorship of staff members outside the country for strategic training is not unusual. The duration of the different courses are similar to Bank A and in number customer care, communication and team building courses are more important. The average duration of the courses is slightly lower because the team building course had two days duration only. The average number of participants ranged from 17 to 31. While 18 courses were mainly intended for the senior managers, 23 courses were intended for the junior managers. Leadership and negotiation skills along with customer care were conducted mainly for the senior managers.

The oil companies by virtue of their operations emphasise more hard and technical skills but in oil marketing, soft skills are being required at a higher level in recent years. However, courses like time management and emotional intelligence were not conducted in them and in Oil B, in addition, negotiation skills were also not conducted in the reference year. In Oil A, customer care course had higher frequencies at five followed by others. The duration was lower in many of the courses so that for all the courses put together, the average duration was 2.1 days only. The average number of participants ranged from 15 to 30. While 10 courses were mainly meant for senior technicians, 12 were conducted for the junior technicians. Courses like situational analysis, leadership and presentation were mainly meant for the senior managers.

The average duration was 2.2 days ranging from one day in business coaching and situational analysis to six days in leadership skills. The average number of participants ranged from 18 to 25. Communication and presentation skill courses topped the list followed by coaching and leadership courses. Leadership and presentation courses were mainly intended for the senior technicians. The number of courses offered to the senior technicians amounted to eight while those offered to the junior technicians amounted to 11.

In the classroom itself some skill tests are given to evaluate the improvement in the particular skill by the employees. It is the practical competency that the employee shows that matters in delegation of work, deputation, transfer and on-the-job promotions. In one particular instance, the trainer used the Kirkpatrick (1994) framework wherein the participants begin by giving their immediate reaction to the particular training course. In the next stage, they were asked as to what facts and knowledge did they learn from the course? In the third stage of evaluation, an informal assessment was made as to what skills did the trainee develop and what information he is using on the job. The effectiveness of the programme was summarised as to how the new skills have been applied to the necessary tasks in the institutions and what results are achieved thereon. The participants were also imparted the necessary motivation to learn and improve their competency level. All this would make rate of return on the training programmes profitable to the particular institution (Cases 1 and 10).

It can be construed that the banking institutions give more importance to soft skill training than the oil companies. Though oil companies owing to high prices in recent years have higher productivity when compared to the banks (revenue per employee), they have lower profitability (profit per employee). One of the propositions of the study has been to see whether higher level of soft skill is related to higher productivity in the organisation. Other things being equal, between the two banks or oil companies the one which has a higher soft skill orientation should have a higher productivity. The revenue per employee has been RO 97,700, while profit per employee has been RO 30,800 in Bank A. As contrast to this, the revenue for employee in Bank B has been RO 32,300 while profit per employee was RO 28,200. This substantiates the hypothesis that higher soft skill orientation in an institution is accompanied by higher productivity.

Between the two oil companies, Oil A registered an employee productivity of RO 146,500 though profit was only RO 5,800 per employee. Oil B shows a lower level of soft skill orientation and revenue and profit per employee are lower when compared to Oil A. The fact that the sample institutions have started giving importance to soft skills in recent years suggests that soft skill is an important ingredient of human capital and plays a prominent role in employee and organisational effectiveness.

Table 5.2 summarises the weighted share of different training programmes wherein the share of the respective programme indicates the individual share in total multiplied by the duration of the course in days. From this perspective the banks accord importance to leadership, communication, team building and customer services followed by others. Bank B accords great importance to leadership, customer service, communication and team building skills. The oil companies on the other hand, accord a greater importance to leadership skills followed by customer service and communication. By this account, the common skill recognised as of great value by all the institutions happens to be empowerment of leadership skills followed by effective communication skills, customer care skills and team building skills. Other skills like presentation, situational analysis are less important and the oil companies do not accord recognition to skills like negotiations, time management and emotional intelligence unlike the banks. All this shows that while the banks' skill requirement converges on many, the oil companies are more selective and this explains the core difference between these two organisations – one being information-centred service entity while the other basically converges itself into technicalities demanding less of soft skills.

Table 5.2: Weighted share of individual training programmes during 2006 (%)

Nature of content	Bank A	Bank B	Oil A	Oil B
Leadership skills	26.2	28.3	36.8	42.9
Effective communication	12.8	16.3	12.2	19.1
Presentation skills	2.6	3.0	6.1	9.5
Negotiation skills	5.3	4.0	4.2	-
Team building	12.8	12.2	12.2	9.5
Time management	2.6	2.0	-	-
Situational analysis	7.5	4.0	2.0	2.4
Business coaching	4.2	4.0	6.1	7.1
Emotional intelligence	2.1	2.0	-	-
Customer care	23.9	24.2	20.4	9.5

Source: Compiled from information gathered from sample institutions

In the banks, leadership, communication and customer care skills are enhanced through intensive training courses as these are deemed to be essential for the functioning of both junior and senior managers. They also emphasise other soft skills which are required in both personal and organisational functioning. The periodic training courses to impart the necessary skills results in useful interaction between the junior and senior managers. Apart from regular trainers, many senior managers participate in the courses as facilitators, while personnel of other training institutes may offer strategic courses to the senior managers.

5.6.1 Approach to soft skill development

Table 5.3 summarises the differences among the sample institutions as regards training programmes and soft skill development.

Table 5.3: Soft skill training in the sample institutions

Indicator	Bank A	Bank B	Oil A	Oil B
Proportion of soft skill courses to total (%)	27	23	18	17
No of soft skill courses	76	41	22	19
Proportion of expenditure on soft skill training to total revenue (%)	0.3	0.17	0.1	0.09
Approach to soft skill development	Training, mentoring, coaching, case studies	Formal and informal, in-house	Formal and informal, case studies	Formal and informal, mentoring, guidance

Training and development is an important component of organisational performance and in the case of sample institutions, Bank A has conducted 76 soft skill training courses which accounted for 27 percent of all the training courses conducted by the bank in 2006. In Bank B, the number of soft skill training courses offered amounted to 41, accounting for 23 percent of all training programmes undertaken by the bank. In Oil A, 22 soft skill courses were conducted which accounted for 18 percent of the total number of courses conducted. In Oil B, the number of courses conducted were 19, representing 17 percent of all the courses.

The institutions spend between 0.5 to one percent of their total revenues on in-house training programmes, as revealed by their annual training reports. While Bank A allocated about one percent of its budget on training related programmes of which soft skill programmes consumed about 30 percent in 2006. Bank B allocated 0.65 percent of its budget on training and development of which soft skills programmes accounted for 26 percent. Oil A allocated 0.53 percent of its budget on training in which, the share of soft skills programmes was 19 percent. Oil B allocated 0.5 percent of its budget on training in which the share of soft skills programmes was 18 percent. Thus the share of soft skill training in total budget accounts for 0.3 percent, 0.17 percent, 0.1 percent and 0.09 percent respectively. Allocation to soft skill training is made based on the total number of training programmes and duration of each programme.

As regards training policy, Bank A conducts more formal programmes, sometimes going for simulated e-learning courses. When compared to other institutions, the focus on applied training courses on improvement of bottom line (productivity and competency levels) is high. Bank B concentrates on human resource and personal development aspects as in Bank A, in addition to needs analysis. In Oil A, training is very much focused, sometimes being outsourced. There is separate training board for the purpose of training Omanis in the oil industry. In Oil B, training is both formal and informal.

In respect of coaching and mentoring, the objective is to provide a common framework based on best practices to support in the design of new experience sharing and achieve staff and career development through confidential non-reporting relationship management. The oil companies adopt both formal and informal methods in coaching and mentoring in respect of staff development in the process of incorporating soft skills to business development.

Organisations are concerned that once trained, the employees may leave it before it has recouped the investment. Unless training pays off very quickly, organisations are reluctant to provide training to their employees according to the Kirkpatrick framework. Sometimes, institutions take advantage of training facilities of other institutions by deputing their employees by paying the necessary charges. Apart from the constraint of adequate returns, other problems faced by the institutions in implementing various training, mentoring and coaching programmes include less training demand owing to low skill requirement in certain jobs, but this may slow down the future intervention process when skill upgradation is required. In certain cases, adequate budgetary provision may not be made available owing to apathy of top management. This constraint may also result in lack of sponsorship of employees to undergo training elsewhere. When information asymmetry results in employees not fully conversant with what type of training or skill enhancement techniques are conducted, the programmes become less effective. Also, when some of the trainees act over-smart in grabbing the benefits from the intervention programmes all to themselves, the prospects of other genuine workers is affected, this may have negative impact on personal and company development. This type of development was observed in some measure in the sample institutions except Bank A and this could have been a reason for the latter's better performance in soft skill development.

The oil companies are implementing programmes to develop soft skills of their employees through both formal and informal means. While all the intervention programmes like training, mentoring, coaching, guidance, counselling and consultancy are more formalised in Bank A, in others informal development is also common. A formal approach standardises the impact mechanism in view of globalisation and results in problem description and solving. While on-the-job training is emphasised in the banks, mentoring has been touted as the major informal intervention in the oil companies (as in case 5).

Increasing global competition and quality demand have necessitated focus on soft skills in every aspect of human resource management – from recruitment, role modelling and identification of enterprising employee's to promotion and competency based performance appraisal. Recognition of soft or generic skills has become strategic in the sample institutions. This recognition may at times become firm-specific depending on the nature of activities and vision. For example, in the oil companies, customer care necessitates soft skills that are customer friendly and in the banks for the integration of technology with that of the skills.

There is not much difference in respect of rewards and incentives for soft skills among the institutions, the banks according special emphasis on giving additional responsibility to those employees excelling in soft skill endowment. The assessment mechanism consists of periodic monitoring and evaluation besides regular performance appraisals. Integration of soft skill with the overall business objectives of the concerned institution is characterised by the necessity to compete with others globally and establish competitive advantage in technology adoption and selling one's own image. In this, training assumes a critical role in the competitive process where Bank A is certainly the leader, followed by Bank B, Oil A and Oil B in that order.

5.7 Some critical issues in training

Due to the increasing number of training courses throughout the year, the staff of the training and development divisions and the experts invited to train feel that in recent years (especially after 2002) the focus of the banks and oil companies has shifted towards soft skills. The interaction between the trainers and the trainees facilitate the employees to learn new ideas and change their behavioural pattern in relation to co-workers, customers, family and friends. The concerned trainees can always approach the trainers as formal or informal coaching for further development. According to the trainers, not only their number has increased owing to an increase in the number of courses, also the focus of the courses is shifting more towards imparting soft skills to the employees. In almost all the cases the competency level of the employees who have attended the training courses has improved in the particular soft skill. The leadership and negotiation skill courses attract much interaction between the trainees and the trainers and of all the soft skill courses; the training managers view these courses as crucial for the development of the trainees. The increase in the number of participants over the years not withstanding the courses have undertaken such that each class does not contain more than 30 and less than 10 trainees.

Since the trainers feel that the performance of the trainees in absorbing the new ideas and behavioural patterns is satisfactory classroom evaluation is adequate. However, standard evaluation techniques and rate of return on investment in training procedures have not yet been standardised by the institutions. There are few repeat cases where some of the participants may attend the same course more than once if they feel that their absorption of the particular skill is not up to the mark.

The contents of the different courses are being revised over the years depending upon the demands for diversifying the economy, increasing number of products, customers and regions and increasing level of competition among the locals in entering into the job market. New courses like situational analysis and emotional intelligence have become popular with the participants. The participants are grouped according to common interest and are given work sheets and ideastorming exercises to work on the most critical issues in the courses.

Business reading, focus group discussions and use of SWOT (strengths, weaknesses, opportunities and threats) analysis has become quite common. When the participants acquire the competence to lead people and manage teams and are able to control complex situations and balance conflicting interests and objectives, the particular course is termed as successful. When the participant is able to solve problems which were unsolvable in the past and experiences less stress and loss of time, the trainers sometimes hold soft skill assessment interviews between the senior and junior managers so that the junior managers will learn not to make mistakes in the decisions and be creative in problem solving. Revealing integrity and honesty, personality and temperament and diplomacy in resolving conflicts are termed as crucial outcomes from any course.

5.8 Conclusion

Training and development, coaching and mentoring have been the important inputs in improving soft skills of employees at the organisational level. After introducing the Omani scenario, the sample banking and oil companies have been described with reference to their training and development efforts. They regularly conduct training courses in their own way in improving both hard skill based business operations and soft skill based competency development to facilitate the former. Propositions like banks faring better than the oil companies in developing soft skills, the positive relationship between soft skill endowment and productivity and emphasis on improving leadership, communication and personal skills have been documented by the analysis.

The finding shows that different institutions accord varying levels of importance to different soft skills depending on their focus and requirement and that between the institutions, those with higher budget and orientation perform well in terms of organisation development. Bank A has conducted the largest number of training courses mostly formal, whereas the other institutions (especially the oil companies) give more importance to informal training and mentoring. Training in soft skills like customer care, communication, team building, business coaching, leadership and situational analysis are important ones followed by presentation, negotiation, team management and emotional intelligence courses. These courses are being repeated depending upon the changing business environment and skill requirements. There are specific courses meant mainly for senior or junior management though both participate in common courses. In all the sample institutions, the number of training courses conducted specifically for the junior managers have been higher in number at 46 as against 30 for the senior managers.

Based on the training profile of the institutions, Bank A provides soft skill training to its employees at a higher level. Bank B comes next followed by Oil A and Oil B. This finding can be compared with higher revenue and profit per employee. Though the oil companies have higher revenue per employee (mainly due to recent high oil prices), profit per employee is higher in Bank A, followed by Bank B, Oil A and Oil B in that order. Similar would be the case as regards the profit ratio. Other things being equal, this is indicative of the positive relationship between soft skill orientation and organisational productivity. The different narratives of the trainers and trainees and cases illustrated explain the nature, role and efficacy of different training programmes conducted by the sample institutions, though the analysis is based on one year's information.

Chapter six will analyse the primary data relating to 120 respondents in the sample institutions as to their assessment of soft skills – personal, interpersonal and situational with suitable case illustrations.

6.1 Introduction

The various training courses and other intervention programmes like coaching and mentoring implemented by the institutions to enhance the soft skill endowment of their managerial staff revealed the differences in approach and impact of the programmes as discussed in chapter five. This chapter attempts to assess the soft skills of the sample senior and junior managerial staff as falling under different skill groups and compares the impact of soft skill along with hard skill in influencing the performance of the employees. The chapter seeks to answer research questions such as: how soft skills are grouped, whether there are differences in soft skill acquisition across different skill groups, what are the sources of soft skill acquisition, how soft skill is measured, what is distance travelled and how to construct a skill wheel, besides what is the impact of intervention programmes on soft skill endowment. The propositions to be tested include the relation between soft skills and productivity, the interaction between soft skill and hard skill components of human capital and the contribution of soft skills to human capital quality besides attempting the construction of soft skill index based on the individual scores of 31 sub-skills.

In the assessment of the various soft skills, though we have used a scoring system in the numerical scale 1-5 to elicit the responses and also a method wherein the response of the participants was one of: strongly disagree, disagree, neutral, agree or strongly agree, for convenience of comparison we have converted all the responses such that actual scores are in the numerical scale as explained in section 4.6. The Likert scale scoring system accords numerical scores in such a way that they can be compared across the different scenarios so as to assess the relative performance of the individuals or groups based on their actual scorings.

One may expect that when compared to junior managers, senior managers denoting a different skill group will have a higher level of soft skill endowment owing to their longer years of experience and higher level of training. Here, experience is taken as an intervention process. Senior managers by this virtue belong to higher skill category when compared to the junior managers. The analysis concentrates in assessing the soft skill between these two skill categories in two different institutions marked by an increased focus on soft skill requirement in banks when compared to the oil companies.

Section 6.2 introduces the profile of the sample respondents including their educational level, age group and experience besides their participation in training programmes. Section 6.3 assesses the soft skill endowment of the different skill groups (senior and junior managers) in the sample institutions and evaluates the soft skill endowment of those staff who had undergone recent training and those who have not. Further, the section analyses the impact of training according to the level of education, experience and mentoring and compares the training results with those of the before training scenario. Section 6.4 analyses the skill wheel of the different groups by suitable illustrations. Section 6.5 measures the distance travelled in all the senior and junior managerial categories making use of European Social Fund and the Hackney Strategic Partnership models. Section 6.6 analyses the statistical significance of each group vis-à-vis the overall sample in respect of pre and post training situations through confidence limit analysis. Section 6.7 discusses the impact of soft skills and hard skills (educational level) on employee performance through a multiple regression analysis before and after training effects. For particular skill groups like senior or junior staff, the scores were averaged and each employee's percentage share in the total score was linearly regressed on explanatory variables like percentage share of each employee in total hard skill and soft skill endowments. Section 6.8 compares the results of both bank managers and oil company technicians to highlight the differences in soft skill endowment across the sectors and this is achieved through a human capital development index. Section 6.9 concludes.

6.2 Profile of the sample respondents

This section presents an overview of the sample respondents selected from two banks and two oil companies. The analysis is based on the total sample of 120 respondents, selected through a method of both random sampling followed by purposive sampling as discussed in section 4.7. The questionnaires on the broad categories of hard and soft skills was distributed to 55 senior managers (the response rate being 55 percent) and 67 junior managers (the response rate being 45 percent) in two banks and 58 senior technicians (the response rate being 52 percent) and 70 junior engineers (the response rate being 43 percent) in the oil companies. The overall response rate has been 48 percent for the entire sample, the senior managers reporting a higher response rate of 53 percent when compared to the junior managers where the response rate has been only 44 percent. The response rate of the bank managers has been higher.

The total sample size is 120, distributed as 15 in each category-Bank A senior, Bank A junior, Bank B senior, Bank B junior, Oil A senior, Oil A junior, Oil B senior and Oil B junior managers. Senior managers include branch managers, regional managers, chief managers and assistant general managers in the banks and site engineers, section heads and marketing executives in the oil companies. The junior managerial staffs include probationary officers, assistant managers and deputy managers in the banks and training supervisors, junior engineers and assistant managers in the oil companies.

After adopting a random sampling method to identify the potential respondents from various divisions of the sample institutions, from a larger sample size, a purposive sampling technique has been adopted where adequate representation has been given to different levels of education (postgraduate, graduate and higher secondary), number of years of experience, recent undergoing of training and mentoring. Qualifications like M.A., M.Com. M.B.A., M.Sc., M.Tech and above is denoted by 'postgraduate', while higher diploma, B.A., B.Sc.,B.Com., B.B.M and B.E is denoted by 'graduate' throughout the study. The selection of 30 respondents per institution has been done in order to have significant results from the viewpoint of statistical analysis. All the 120 respondents were given the questionnaire and later contacted through personal interview so as to elicit the required information. They were asked to self-assess their soft skill endowment and how changes in them have taken place as a result of training and adequate care has been taken to cross-check with the employers and through a process of triangulation, the subjective bias in analysis is reduced to the minimum. Of course, in this the agreement of the respondents was important in arriving at the specific score. Care was taken to convince the participants by also not revealing the opinion of the employers and by citing the peer reviews. Individual information was kept confidential when cross-checking with the employers and though in few instances, there were objections to the scores, they were sorted out through objective cross analysis. It may be mentioned that the proportion of those who somewhat disagreed to the assigned scores at first, later consented to the scores since their colleagues also faired similarly. As mentioned in section 4.8.3, care has been taken to safeguard the privacy of informants and see that no bias enters into the assessment procedure besides upholding different ethical issues of research.

Table 6.1 summarises the profile of the respondents according to their age, sex, educational achievement and experience. Graduates account for the largest number in all the groups followed by postgraduates and secondary schoolers. The median age group is 36 to 40 years. The number of female managers varies from two in oil companies to seven in the case of bank junior managers. The mean age of experience of senior managers is more than 15 years in all the companies and it is less than five years for junior managers of oil companies and less than seven years for junior managers of banks. In each group two to five managers have been promoted during the reference period.

Table 6.1: The Profile of general survey sample respondents (N=120)

Indicator	Group	Bank A		Bank B		Oil A		Oil B	
		SM	JM	SM	JM	SM	JM	SM	JM
Sample size (No)		15	15	15	15	15	15	15	15
Education level	Sec.	2	0	4	1	4	2	3	3
	G	10	8	7	8	10	13	11	12
	PG	3	7	4	6	1	-	1	-
Experience (in years)	Total	16.5	6.3	17.2	6.1	17.5	4.8	15.7	4.5

Note: SM – senior management staff, JM – junior management staff
   Sec. – Higher secondary, G – diploma /graduate PG – Postgraduate
Source: Based on primary data collected by the author.

6.2.1 Female managers

The number of female managers was 31, the number being very high in Bank A and Bank B junior managers. The number is very low in the case of senior managers in both banks and oil companies. Preference for local youth and especially women in recruitment to banks has resulted in the number of females being employed in the sample banks. About 16 of them had undergone training courses during the reference year and among them, six senior managers (two each in Bank A and Bank B and one each in Oil A and Oil B) acted as coach/mentors to other female workers and assumed the role as trainers. All the female junior managers in the banks and oil companies started their career afresh in banks and oil companies and in their service have been benefited by promotions also within the junior level. Very little difference was observed in soft skill endowment between the male and female managers. One senior manager and three female junior managers in the banks have obtained their bachelor's degree from universities outside Oman (illustrated in Case 3).

Studies show that female workers do not lag behind male workers in acquisition of skills, though they may prefer non-technical jobs. Hence, the present study does not purport to analyse the soft skill endowment of female workers as such. Further, the sampling was not set up to study this aspect. Schneider and Holman's (2005) study on (migrant) workers in the UK found female workers faired better than the local workforce in acquisition of both hard and soft skills. This contrasts to the study by Du et al. (2007) wherein the major handicap for women's development was lack of opportunities. Another study also shows the preference of women for non-technical jobs (Ministry of Manpower, 2000) and in this study, a smaller number of female managers have been encountered in oil companies (technical jobs) when compared to the banks. Since male workers have longer years of experience, they tend to receive higher wages but in a few cases, the female managers felt that there is some discrimination in wages, supporting Skinner's (2002) findings. However, according to DePinto and Deal (2004), given the opportunities, female managers are as enthusiastic and enterprising as the male managers and exhibit characteristics such as leadership,

101

team building, effective communication and conflict management which improves their soft skills similar to the male managers. Kenney (2004) cited the cases of enterprising women entrepreneurs competing with their male counterparts in skill development.

6.2.2 Service and experience

The senior managers have an experience of over 15 years in their avocation and over 12 years in their present occupation. Senior managers in the oil companies have more than 12 years of experience in their present job, while those in Bank B have more than 13 years and those in Bank A more than 14 years of experience. The number of years of experience is around seven years in the oil companies, 10 years in Bank B and 11 years in Bank A for senior managers. In respect of junior managers, the mean is over 12 years in the oil companies and six years in the banks. The years of experience in the present job is slightly less than four years in Oil B, four years in Oil A, over five years in Bank B and six years in Bank A. However, the mean years of experience in the present company has been three years in the oil companies, 4.8 years in Bank B and 5.5 years in Bank A. It is found that the mean number of years of experience of the senior managers of the total sample is 16.7 years and only 56 percent of this is in the present company. The mean years for the junior managers are 5.4 years but 74 percent of this is in the present companies. This indicates that junior managers tend to stay longer with their employers.

When compared to the junior managers, the proportion of senior managers entering into the present jobs is higher, especially in the oil companies. Attractive perks and possibilities of higher salary (in the same grade when compared to other institutions) and other facilities are the pull factors, while employment in small institutions with low salary and perks are the push factors for this migration.

Both senior and junior managers have had a lower number of years of experience in the present institution when compared to the present job. That means some of them were inducted in to the particular institution as senior or junior manager as the case may be and continue so. However, it may be pointed out that junior or senior managerial position may consist of many grades in which case promotions can take place within the senior or junior managerial positions. For example, a person may be appointed in the branch manager grade (senior level IV) but subsequently may be promoted to other grades like regional manager, chief manager or section head, assistant general manager and so on. Likewise, there are different grades in junior managerial positions and a person who is appointed as a probationary officer (junior level IV) may be promoted as assistant manager, deputy manager and so on. Hence it does not mean that a person who is appointed as senior manager remain so forever because he would experience many periodical promotions. It may be mentioned that promotions are determined according to not only the years of experience but also soft skill endowment (as mentioned in section 5.2).

Senior managers in Bank A in their 11.2 years of service have had 4.2 promotions, five (out of 15) of them getting their last promotion very recently. With 10.5 years of service in Bank B, the senior managers have been able to get 3.8 promotions, four of them getting the next promotion recently. With a mean 7.8 years of service in Oil A, the senior managers have been able to get 3.6 promotions in Oil A while they have been able to get 3.5 number of promotions for 6.5 years of service in Oil B. Three out of 15 of senior managers in the oil companies have had their recent promotion.

In respect of junior managers, the number of promotions has been 1.2 for 5.5 years of service in Bank A, 1.1 for 4.8 years of service in Bank B, one for three years of service in Oil A and 1.1 for three years of service in Oil B. Two managers have had recent promotions in Oil B, Bank A and Oil A and the number was three in Bank B. On an average, a promotion takes place every 2.7 years in Bank A and Bank B senior managerial category and Oil B junior managerial category. In Oil A and Oil B senior category, a promotion is given every two years. In Oil A, junior managerial category, every three years an employee gets a promotion. In the junior managerial category in the banks, however, it takes more than four years to get a promotion.

Since in each of the group there are 15 in the sample, giving the proportion may sometimes be misleading and hence care has been taken to indicate the actual numbers wherever the analysis has to be precise.

6.2.3 Training profile of the respondents

In the previous chapter we saw how the sample institutions conduct regular training programmes, of which those on customer relations, communication, leadership, situational analysis, team building, presentation, negotiation and time management are important in enhancing the soft skill endowment of the employees. It must be mentioned that the major objective of the training programmes is to upgrade technical skills but nowadays the enhancement of soft skills is also on the agenda of the institutions. Though all the employees have undergone various training programmes in their career, we have segregated the trainees as those who have been recently trained and those who are not. In other words, the comparison is between those who have undergone a higher number of training courses and those who have not. Since our objective is to evaluate the impact of training on soft skill, we have treated pre-training sample as the control group, though strictly speaking the non-intervention group also would have acquired soft skill in their past training. Since soft skill acquisition is purely personal and subjective, we have considered only the recent training programmes which enable the employee to experience the 'distance travelled'. Though soft skills

103

may be acquired through experience over the years, the concept of distance travelled assumes relevance as a result of intervention. The sample distribution is given in Figure 6.1

Figure 6.1: Sample distribution

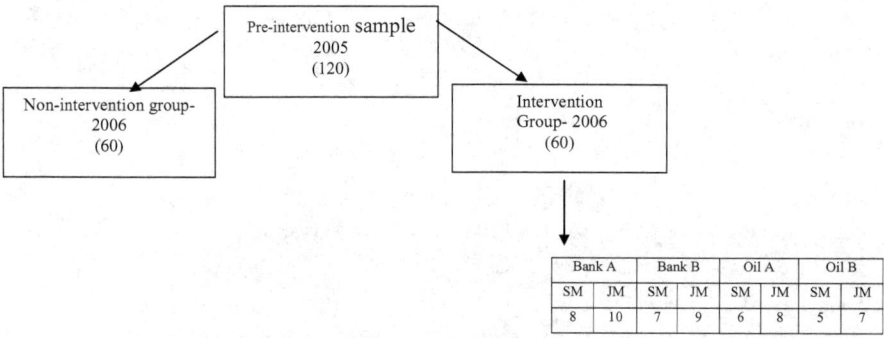

Bank A		Bank B		Oil A		Oil B	
SM	JM	SM	JM	SM	JM	SM	JM
8	10	7	9	6	8	5	7

Table 6.2 summarises the training profile of the respondents. Training programmes undergone by the senior managers include those on leadership, team building, negotiation and communication. The important programmes attended by the junior managers include customer relations, communication, team building, presentation and time management. Though a particular training programme may be common to both senior and junior managers, the content and approach are different and hence the programmes are offered distinctly in each category.

Table 6.2: Training profile of respondents during 2006 (N=60)

Indicator		Bank A		Bank B		Oil A		Oil B	
		SM	JM	SM	JM	SM	JM	SM	JM
Training	Number	8	10	7	9	6	8	5	7
	No of courses	3	4	3	4	2	4	3	3
	Days (per course)	3.5	2.2	3.0	2.0	2.5	1.8	2.3	1.6
Coaching/Mentoring - Personal	Formal	-	8	-	7	-	6	-	5
	Informal	-	10	3	9	4	8	3	7
Coaching/Mentoring - Interpersonal	Formal	2	10	3	8	2	5	4	6
	Informal	4	10	5	8	6	7	5	6
Coaching/Mentoring -Situational	Formal	2	6	2	5	2	4	1	5
	Informal	3	8	4	7	3	5	3	6
Coach/Mentor - Personal	Formal	6	-	4	-	4	-	3	-
	Informal	8	-	5	-	5	-	3	-
Coach/Mentor - Interpersonal	Formal	7	-	5	-	4	-	3	-
	Informal	8	-	5	-	4	-	3	-
Coach/Mentor - Situational	Formal	5	-	3	-	2	-	2	-
	Informal	5	-	4	-	3-	-	3	-

Note: Number = number of employees undergoing training; Duration = in days

The number of courses participated range from two to four in different categories. The duration of courses like leadership and situational analysis (strategy-oriented) averages more than five to seven days, while there are courses in communication and presentation which consume only one or two days. Along with training, the managers undergo coaching and mentoring also (seniors mentoring the juniors and being mentored by their seniors) so that the combination of training, mentoring and coaching results in a higher level of soft skill endowment. Though training is formal, mentoring and coaching is more informal than formal. Senior managers (especially section heads) act as mentors to the junior staff and every senior manager may be formally assigned a few junior staff for mentoring and personal coaching in different assignments. Whereas training may be for a particular duration of time, mentoring and coaching are a continuous process and assume a post-training assessment and improvement of the skills of the junior staff by the seniors. Over the years, the junior staffs also acquire the ability to mentor and coach their juniors.

The combined impact of the training programmes in addition to post-training mentoring and coaching, acts as an intervention enabling the employees to acquire and develop their soft skills in various areas. As the training programmes and mentoring may be in specific areas of hard or soft skill development and those who have had training recently would have undergone one or more programmes and hence are involved in mentoring and coaching in respect of many areas. However, the focus of the study is on the development of soft skill in the personal, interpersonal and situational contexts.

6.3 Assessment of soft skills

As characterised in section 4.5, the three types of personal, interpersonal and situational soft skills are assessed among the different categories of managers. In any institution, there will be different skill categories (high, medium or low) depending on the skill required for a particular function and job. The skill categories are not to be confused with the soft skills which vary according to the different skill categories. The institution will require a higher level of hard skill as well as soft skill for jobs (skill categories) which require higher skill. As mentioned in chapters two and three, personal, interpersonal and situational soft skills have been found as important among the senior and junior managerial positions.

Soft outcomes indicate the additional soft skill endowment the intervention group is able to acquire when compared to the pre-intervention group. Of the nine personal sub-skills, punctuality (including appearance) is most important soft skill in all the groups except in Oil B senior managers, where it occupies the third place. Self confidence which results also from positive attitudes, faith in oneself, good appearance and punctuality is second-most important, except in bank categories where it occupies third or fourth place. Next in importance is language (including numeracy skills), especially in the case of senior managers in both banks and oil companies. Self management is fourth followed by owning responsibility, positive motivation, enterprising quality, innovativeness and mentoring.

Leadership is the most important in interpersonal skills in all the groups except Bank A and Oil B junior managers where it is second. Teamwork is the next important soft skill followed by communication, respect to others, recognition of other's work, decision making, having diverse capacity, analysis, conflict management and creative thinking. In a study on university students, Motah (2008) found that stress management, conflict management and leadership were the important soft skills observed among the participants.

Cooperation with colleagues seems to be the major situational soft skill followed by exercising authority, time management, self reliance, goal setting, learning, adaptability, problem solving, planning, empathy, effectiveness and negotiation. Between the senior and junior managers, self confidence, self management, recognition, cooperation, reliance, learning, adaptability and empathy play a greater role in the latter categories. For the senior managers, language, creative thinking, decision making, conflict management, goal setting, planning, authority and problem solving skills have a significant role when compared to the junior managers. In respect of other soft skills, there is little difference between the senior and junior managers.

6.3.1 Soft skill endowment of the sample respondents

Though there may be individual differences in the sub-skills, punctuality, language and self confidence in personal; leadership, communication and teamwork in interpersonal and authority, goal setting and reliance in situational skills contribute to the soft outcomes. With increasing scores, the effectiveness of the particular skill also increases. If a manager assigns value of less than one to a particular soft skill, it has low intensity, whereas a score of four to five indicates a higher value. The self-assessed scores have been recorded for each individual soft skill based on the triangulation method as mentioned in section 4.8.1. When these scores are converted into indices as detailed in the methodology chapter (for the maximum value of five), the specific index shows the intensity of a particular soft skill in the specific group as to how satisfactorily the soft skill is being acquired.

Table 6.3 assesses the soft outcomes after intervention when compared to the pre-intervention scenario. The scores for overall and before intervention status is for the entire sample in each group, whereas the scores for the intervention groups refer to only to those who were subject to different intervention programmes during 2006. The situation at the end of 2005, i.e., pre-training scenario presents the base period soft skill score since this is the self-assessed scores of the respondents before undergoing training. The post-training scenario shows the scores of those respondents who had undergone training during 2006 and it shows skills augmentation in the case of the treatment group. When both the treatment and the non-intervention sample (who had not undergone training during 2006) is combined, the overall scores for the entire sample is obtained. For 2005 (pre) and 2006 (post) years, same rating procedure has been adopted, though the rating of the scores for those who had undergone training (60 in number) and for those who had not (60 in number) has been done with assumption that those without training do not develop their soft skills and the initial rating for those who were trained was the same as those who were not trained.

Since the time gap between the pre and post training situations ranges up to only one year, we assume that but for intervention, no major change takes place in the soft skill endowment of the managers. According to Table 6.3, the pre-training sample consists of respondents as at the end of 2005. Not all of them underwent training during 2006 and hence the training sample numbers were lower in all the categories. Of the total sample of 120, only 60 have undergone training during 2006, the banks reporting a higher proportion. In the table, the column 'pre-intervention' indicates the total sample of 120 at the end of 2005 and the column 'intervention' shows the skill changes of those who had undergone training (60) during 2006. When improvement in soft skill scores due to intervention is assessed, those who are trained only are able to improve their soft outcomes when compared to their pre-training situation. In a quasi-experimental design, the performance of the intervention group is compared with the pre-intervention group and hence the non-intervention group is treated as such since in 2006 it did not have any skill enhancement. It is reasonable to assume that those without intervention may not improve in their scores in such a short span of time.

Table 6.3 Soft outcome scores- pre-intervention (N=120) and intervention (N=60)

Status	Skill	Bank A		Bank B		Oil A		Oil B	
		SM	JM	SM	JM	SM	JM	SM	JM
Pre-intervention	Personal	3.1	2.5	3.0	2.0	2.8	2.1	2.6	2.1
	Interpersonal	2.6	1.8	2.5	1.4	2.7	1.6	2.5	1.7
	Situational	2.6	1.5	2.3	1.3	2.4	1.2	2.1	1.3
	Arithmetic mean	2.8	1.9	2.6	1.6	2.6	1.6	2.4	1.7
Intervention	Personal	3.9	3.0	3.6	2.8	3.2	2.7	3.0	2.6
	Interpersonal	3.1	2.2	3.0	2.0	2.9	2.2	2.8	2.1
	Situational	3.4	2.0	3.1	2.0	2.9	1.9	2.8	1.8
	Arithmetic mean	3.5	2.4	3.2	2.3	3.0	2.3	2.9	2.2
Percent increase	Personal	26	20	20	40	14	29	15	24
	Interpersonal	19	22	20	43	07	38	12	24
	Situational	31	33	35	54	21	58	33	38
	Arithmetic mean	25	26	23	44	15	44	21	29

It is seen that the self-assessed scores are open to subjective judgements as related to the particular age group and skill category of the manager, but this has been made more objective through triangulation. Since we are dealing with the managerial cadres who possess more or less the same educational qualifications, the same scale has been adopted for the skill assessment. Due to intervention, in respect of all senior managers in Bank A, the mean score is 3.5, indicating that these managers are endowed with 70 percent of the target (3.5 divided by 5) of the required soft skills. The score is higher in respect of punctuality, language, responsibility, self confidence, motivation and self management, average in mentoring and is low in enterprising and innovativeness. In Bank B, the senior managers score 64 percent, mentoring, enterprising and innovativeness having lower scores. In respect of Oil A, the score is 60 percent (3.0 divided by 5). In this group mentoring, enterprising and innovativeness have lower scores. In Oil B, the mean score is 58 percent and here again mentoring, enterprising and innovativeness skills are the least important ones.

It is evident that the personal soft skill endowment is at a higher level in the banks when compared to the oil companies. As seen, this is the case for interpersonal and situational soft skills as well. The nature of banking activity which demands better motivation, customer relationship and teamwork necessitate a higher soft skill endowment among the banking senior managers when compared to those in the oil companies. However, the difference between the banks and oil companies in respect of senior managers' pre-training scores is only marginal as shown in Table 6.3. In Bank A the mean score is 2.8 (56 percent), whereas it is 2.6 in Bank B, 2.6 in Oil A and 2.4 in Oil B. The mean score of the banks is higher than in the oil companies. Not only that the banks have a higher level of endowment when compared to the oil companies, the senior managers score high when compared to the junior managers. Further, there exist inter-bank and inter-oil company differences, wherein Bank A has a higher score than Bank B and Oil A has a higher score than Oil B. This arrangement yields the highest score for Bank A senior managers and lowest score for Oil B junior managers.

6.3.2 Soft skill endowment with and without intervention

The skill endowment of all sample respondents in the base period (pre-training 2005) is taken for comparison with the training scenario at end of 2006. When compared to the pre-training score, the score for those who have undergone training shows how far skill enhancement has taken place as postulated in chapter 4. From Figure 4.2, it is seen that only 43 percent of senior managers have been recently trained, the proportion being higher in Bank A. In respect of junior managers, 57 percent have recently been trained, Bank A having a higher proportion. Post-training skill enhancement is assessed by comparing the averages for those without recent training (before training) and for those with recent training.

Table 6.3 shows that the rate of enhancement in personal skills of senior managers when compared to pre-training score is 26 percent in Bank A, 20 percent in Bank B, 14 percent in Oil A and 15 percent in Oil B indicating a higher rate of increase in banks. The rate of increase in interpersonal skill has been 19 percent in Bank A, 20 percent in Bank B, seven percent in Oil A and 12 percent in Oil B. In respect of situational skill enhancement, the increase is substantial in all the groups indicating the effectiveness of the training programmes in the enhancement of the situational skills in particular. Any improvement in the exploitation of the situation, post-training certainly improves the personal characterisation as well the company image. On average, the senior managers in Bank A have been able to enhance their overall skill endowment by 25 percent post-training, while the rate of increase has been 23 percent in Bank B and 15 percent in Oil A and 21 percent in Oil B.

The skill enhancement seems to be high in respect of junior managers in all the institutions, especially in Bank B and Oil A (Table 6.3). The rate of increase in skill endowment has been 26 percent in Bank A, 44 percent in Bank B and Oil A and 29 percent in Oil B. In this case also, the rate of increase in situational skill is higher than in personal or interpersonal skills in all the groups. In personal and interpersonal skills, Bank B and the oil companies have a higher rate of increase than Bank A. The rate of increase has been 33 percent in Bank A in situational skills, whereas the increase is higher in Oil A at 58 percent and Bank B at 54 percent and in Oil B it is 38 percent. The analysis shows that while the junior managers in Bank B, Oil A and Oil B have enhanced their skill substantially, in other cases the level of enhancement is moderate, but nonetheless significant.

We can see the rate of skill enhancement for the senior as contrast to the junior managerial cadres irrespective of their affiliation. As indicated in Figure 4.2, of the total 60 training samples, 26 belong to senior and 34 to junior manager cadres. This can be compared with the pre-training sample of 60 each for the respective categories. This type of grouping is adopted for the regression analysis in section 6.7. Table 6.4 shows how when the overall scores as shown in Table 6.3 are decomposed into seniors and juniors scores separately irrespective of the institutions, the juniors fare better. When compared to pre-training scores, junior managers are able to realise 35 percent increase in soft outcomes, whereas the rate has been 21 percent for the senior managers.

6.3.3 Educational level and training impact: senior managers

The pre and post training stages may be compared for different educational levels. Though the comparison is based on small sample size for each of the education group, it is worthwhile to assess the ratings since this gives an idea of skill enhancement in different human capital endowments. The actual sample size is indicated in brackets. In our sample, the postgraduates have a higher score than graduates, though between high schoolers and graduates the difference is not much. In respect of senior managers of Bank A, the average skill endowment of the trained postgraduates (2) with a score of 3.75 which shows 75 percent of the target level, though those with no mentoring have a slightly lower average. Any rating between 75 to 100 percent of the target can be termed as satisfactory (UNESCO, 2007), while 50-74 percent is partial achievement and less than 50 percent is below expectations. Postgraduates without training (1) register only 62 percent of soft skill endowment, the difference of 13 percent being enhanced due to training. The average level for the postgraduates (trainees and non-trainees put together) is 71 percent. In all these cases personal skills score high followed by situational for the trainees and interpersonal for the non-trainees. All the senior mangers (PGs) are experienced.

As regards graduates with training (5), the average is 67 percent (slightly higher for mentors) and for the non-trainees (5) the average is 66 percent, indicating about 12 percent augmentation due to training. Experience without training has an average, higher than those without training and experience indicating a marginal contribution by experience. The arithmetic mean for both trainee and non-trainee graduates is 61 percent, which is over nine percent lower when compared to that of postgraduates. Between the postgraduates and the graduates, the difference between trainees and the non-trainees is 12 percent lower for the latter. The higher secondary schoolers have a lower mean of 62 percent scores for trainees (1) and 50 percent for non-trainees (1), though the difference between training and non-training average is higher.

In Bank B, the trained employees with postgraduate degree (2) have a lower score at 66 percent and when compared to the non-trainees (2), the difference is only 6 percent higher. The mean for the trained graduates (4) is 63 percent and that for the non-trainees (3) 51 percent. However, the higher secondary schoolers without training (3) but with experience have a higher average when compared to those with training (1). This is a case where experience counts more than training.

In Oil A, postgraduates with training (1) perform similar to that in Bank B (the average soft skill being 66 percent). The graduates with training (3) however, have a lower average (59 percent) but for those without training (7), the difference is very minimal. The high schoolers with experience fare better than those with training as in Bank B, indicating the superiority of experience over training for that group.

In Oil B, the postgraduate average with training (1) is slightly lower at 62 percent but the graduate training (2) average is similar as in Oil A; this is true for the non-training (9) averages also. The training average for higher secondary schoolers (2) is 53 percent higher than that of non-trainees (1) where the level is 44 percent. In Oil B, it is training and not experience which matters in all the education levels.

110

6.3.4 Educational level and training impact: junior managers

The average level of skill endowment for postgraduate junior managers in Bank A with training (5) is 53 percent indicating a big difference (75 versus 53 percent) between the senior and junior managers and this may be due to differences in age, experience and participation in increased number of training programmes. For those postgraduates without training (2) the skill level declines to 43 percent indicating the contribution of training to the extent of 10 (53 minus 43) percent. The average for the graduates with training (5) is lower at 43 percent which however is higher when compared to the non-trainees (3) by eight percent. There are no higher secondary schoolers amongst the junior managers in Bank A. In all the cases, the scores have been converted into percentages by dividing them by five which is the maximum score.

In Bank B, the average skill endowment for junior trained postgraduates (4) is 47 percent lower when compared to that of Bank A and the non-training (2) average is very low at 35 percent. However, graduates with training (4) have a higher average with 42 percent comparable to those in Bank A but those without training (4) have a lower average (30 percent). The average for the higher secondary schoolers with training (1) is 38 percent, which is higher not only than that of graduates with training but also postgraduates with training.

In Oil A and Oil B there are no postgraduate junior managers. The graduate trainee (3) average is 43 percent in Oil A and 44 percent in Oil B (6), which are higher than that in the banks. The graduate non-training (7) average is 32 percent in Oil A and 35 percent in Oil B (6), higher than in Bank B and comparable to that in Bank A. In Oil A, all higher secondary schoolers have training (2) with a skill level of 50 percent which is higher when compared to either training or non-training average of the graduates, indicating the significance of experience. In Oil B also the higher secondary schoolers with training (1) have a better average than postgraduates without training, though higher secondary schoolers without training (2) fare poorer of all the groups. The analysis shows that the impact of training is substantial in skill enhancement and experience also counts along with mentoring in skill augmentation, though at a lower level.

6.4 Skill wheel of the participants

The skill wheel represents the change in soft skill endowment before and after the training process as explained in section 4.6. This pertains only to those who had undergone training during the reference year and had realised skill enhancement thereon. The skill wheel depicts the skill enhancement process when compared to the pre-training characterisation. The European Union study (EC, 2003) made use of a task wheel wherein the assessment of employees was done according to their social skills, work skills, approach to work and personal issues in a graded system. The profile enabled the construction of hard and soft skill development plan based on the

111

inadequacies under these four categories. In a study on social and soft skills (Hillmer, 2007), about 20 percent of engineering curriculum concentrated on soft skills such as language training, self-management, personality development, communication skills and economics.

Though the duration of the training programme may be a few days, the impact of the training programme is assessed over a period of time which may run to two to three months after the particular programme is over so that proper feedback and appraisal can be made. Usually, the scores have been assigned based on the interviewee's self-assessment, though facilitation has been provided in explaining the significance of the particular questions and the issues. The intervention scores explain the level of skill enhancement and the distance travelled which indicates the progress made by the participants in achieving soft outcomes that lead toward sustained employment and associated hard outcomes. Hard outcomes are clearly definable and quantifiable outcomes such as promotion, reward and incentives that show the progress a participant has made, though there could be some subjectivity in their assessment, owing to overlapping with soft skills. Soft outcomes are intangible and hard to measure directly and represent intermediary stages on the way to achieving the hard outcomes. An increase in scores in any of the 31 sub-skills represents soft outcomes. For example, an increase in enterprise score indicates a higher level of soft outcome as a result of personal skills enhancement and so on. If hard skills describe how far an employee is professional, soft skills explain the effectiveness with which this professionalism is translated into achievement of goals (Dewson et al., 2000a).

The profile of a particular skill category – either senior or junior managers will provide the strengths and weaknesses of the different skills, wherein points nearer to the centre of the circle require intensive development. In the figures all the skills (within the broad categories of personal, interpersonal and situational) are profiled clockwise, wherein before training, the profile curve is in pink and the profile curve after the training period is marked in blue. The development in the particular category skill wheel is illustrated with specific cases of importance and impact of soft skills so as to highlight their significance as related to the participants and the institutions.

6.4.1 Skill wheel of Bank A Senior Managers

From the scores indicated in Tables 6.3 and the assessment of the skill wheels for all the categories, the movement (skill enhancement and soft outcomes) in the skill wheel is explained. As shown in section 3.4.1, the skill wheel measures the scores according to five ranges (circles). In the case of Bank A senior managers (Figure 6.2), the enhancement in respect of situational skill is higher at 31 percent followed by personal skill (26 percent) and interpersonal skills (19 percent). The skill gap in various groups (difference between actual and maximum score) as shown in section 4.6.1 is very high in respect of creative thinking, negotiations, innovativeness, enterprising, self management adaptability, decision making and problem solving. The skill gap turns low in most of the personal and interpersonal skills and it is in situational skills that the gap persists. It may be due to difficulties in acquiring situational skills when compared to personal or interpersonal skills. Intensive training programmes in creative thinking, innovativeness, negotiations, decision making and problem solving are required.

Figure 6.2: Skill wheel of Bank A Senior Managers

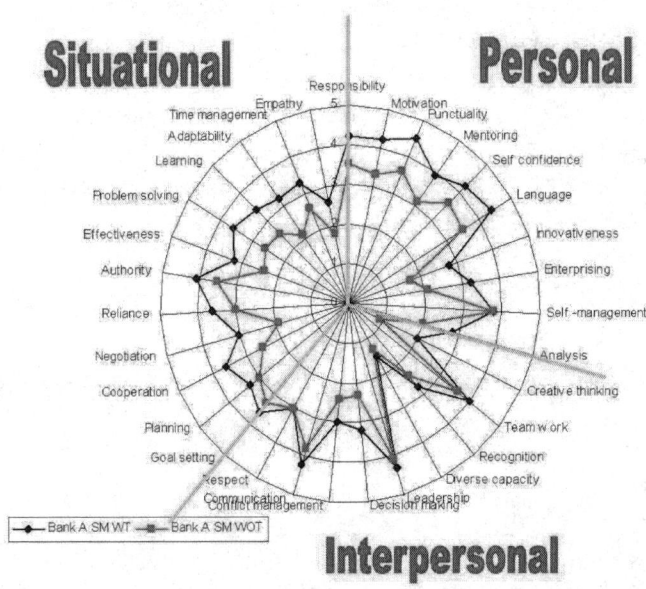

Case 6.1: On motivation and mentoring

I can vouchsafe that the different training courses I have attended and also where I have been a trainer have changed my perspective on work ethics and motivation. Before training, I was not motivated especially in effective negotiations concerning my department. Improvement in personal skills has had its positive impact on my interpersonal and situational skills as well. For example, during last year, I used to listen to others' arguments regarding expansion programmes. I would be feeling that my ideas would matter better than them, but was hesitant to express myself boldly and convincingly. At times, I would be telling something which may not be understandable to others. Now, I am one of the starters in any negotiation deals and my views are enthusiastically received by my seniors. Though my ideas sometimes may not be very practical, they are received for their positiveness and I do not have any problem to convince the top management to adopt any ideas which I feel are in the right direction. For all the development which I have experienced in these skills, I was able to get an additional increment besides obtaining a foreign visit to negotiate a deal with a multinational bank (Training Manager, Bank A).

The narrative explains the advantages of active participation in training programmes and how the participant was able to imbibe ethical qualities and was transformed from a mentee to mentor and from a passive listener to active cheer leader and how he has been able to improve his personal qualities. This is a case of improvement in internal soft skills which is recognised by the bank in according additional increments.

6.4.2 Skill wheel of Bank A Junior Managers

When compared to before training scenario, junior managers in Bank A (Figure 6.3) realise a 26 percent enhancement, similar to that of the senior managers. However, there is wide variation among the different types of skills. While situational skill distance increases by 33 percent, the increase is 20 percent in personal and 22 percent in interpersonal skills. Mentoring, innovativeness and enterprising skill gap in respect of personal, leadership and decision making skill gaps in respect of interpersonal skills and goal setting, negotiation, authority and learning skill gap in respect of situational skills are higher. As in the case of the senior managers many situational skills show a huge gap before and after training.

Figure 6.3: Skill wheel of Bank A Junior Managers

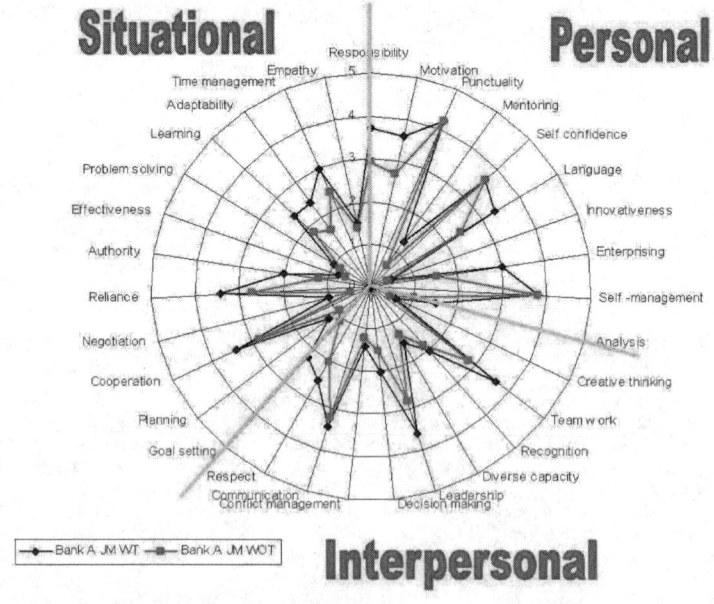

In Bank A, bulk of the training programmes concentrate on customer care, communication, leadership, presentation, team building and business coaching. While skills related to these programmes have to travel a longer distance, skills which have a noticeable gap require either incorporation in the existing programmes or separate treatment so that the distance travelled in respect of them increases. The analysis shows that even though the distance travelled by the situational skills is longer, it is in many situational skills that the gap persists.

Case 6.2: On self-management

The trainer deliberated on the impact of both 'soft spoken' and 'hard spoken' outcomes of the proposed introduction of e-banking facilities. He pointed out that the 'hard spoken' argument was that the bank required a huge investment and expertise for the purpose. However, the 'soft spoken' argument of inducting the existing personnel to a workshop on e-banking convinced the Board and immediately it was implemented. That highlighted the important role of anything soft and I began to understand the meaning of soft skill as that one which makes a person a better person whether he is lowly or highly educated.

In another training course, I learnt so many things about cultivation of innovative ideas and to be enterprising (in the sense of being ever proactive and taking on-the-spot decisions) and I started reading contributions by smart businessmen as to their success. I extensively read materials about e-banking and other modern banking technologies and was soon started practising new management styles in organisation and helped my section head in drafting important documents relating to the bank's e-banking. I also began to organise my work-related activities in such a way that there was no overlap and I avoided answering useless calls while at work (Junior manager, Bank A).

The narrative brings out the conflict between hard and soft outcomes and how reconciliation may be attempted in arriving at a consensus for effective decision making. In the case of e-banking, the question arises as to the need to invest on the hard (equipment) as well as on the soft (training) component. Innovative ideas like smart business solutions and advanced business review help in the launch of the e-banking project of the bank, wherein soft skill training more than compensates for the hard investment.

6.4.3 Skill wheel of Bank B Senior Managers

The skill enhancement of Bank B senior managers (Figure 6.4) is 23 percent and the enhancement in respect of situational skills is higher at 35 percent when compared to a 20 percent increase in personal and interpersonal skills. Innovativeness and enterprising personal skills show a bigger gap and in interpersonal skills, it is creative thinking and decision making. The skill gap is higher in situational skills like goal setting, planning, negotiation and learning.

Figure 6.4: Skill wheel of Bank B Senior Managers

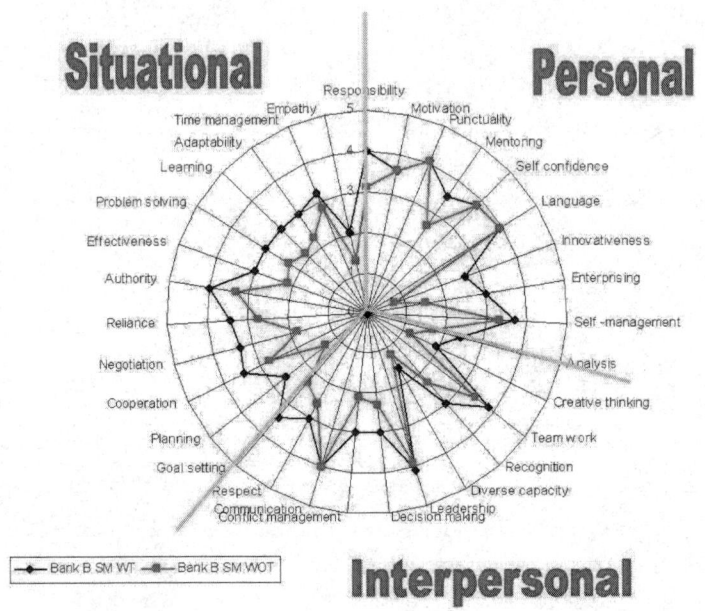

Case 6.3: On authority and problem solving

Getting a bachelor's in a UK University and having worked in banks outside Oman has enabled me to adapt to changes and to have ability to work in teams in a better way. To me, a leader is one who makes others work but does not take the credit. During the past three years I have given lectures on leadership and problem solving not only in my bank but also in other institutions. I was on a career break to undertake a professional diploma which had enabled me to acquire knowledge on human resources and organisational psychology. I am liaising with a number of divisions to provide support in aspects of recruitment, selection, restructuring, redundancy, discipline, training provision and continued professional development procedures. I give advice on routine HR issues. In my training sessions, I move away from a reactive method of working to a more project–focused approach which requires adaptation to many changes. New information and communication technologies have enabled people like me to lay greater emphasis on the ability to people-manage effectively with leadership.

Once HR manager was in a fix to shortlist applicants for the post of deputy manager in retail banking. All the 10 applicants had the required education and experience and a few of them had attached testimonials and documents in support of the claim for social responsibility and customer service. I cited the example of two airlines, one in which the customers would not get any definite answer from the airline staff for undue flight delay and in another airline, how the customers were informed one day earlier that due to inclement weather, the flight schedule will be delayed and how the customers were accommodated without they feeling cumbersome till the flight took off. In the interview, this question was put and the candidate who spoke well of the second airline opined that the staff in the first airline were not properly trained in customer service (Senior manager, Bank B).

116

The narrative demonstrates how the respondent female manager has been able to acquire soft skills to the satisfaction of her employers and how the manager's foreign education and work experience enabled them to adapt to the local banking conditions. Developing her soft skills, she has been able to master organisational psychology and lecture on the significance of leadership skills not only in the banks but also in other institutions. The case also shows how people with high soft skill endowment can assist the management in identifying competent persons at the time of recruitment or promotion as the case may be.

6.4.4 Skill wheel of Bank B Junior Managers

The junior managers in Bank B (Figure 6.5) have been able to augment soft skill by 44 percent higher after training when compared to the before training scenario. The situational skills enhancement is 54 percent higher, followed by interpersonal skills (43 percent) and personal skills (40 percent).

Figure 6.5: Skill wheel of Bank B Junior Managers

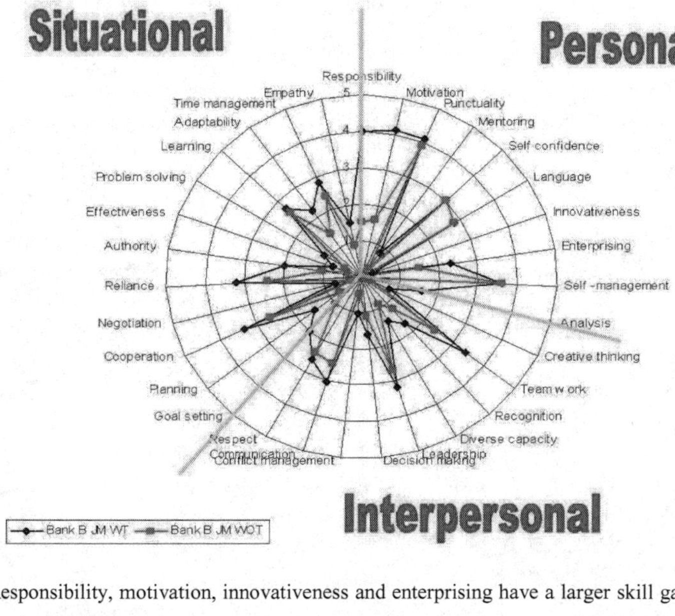

Responsibility, motivation, innovativeness and enterprising have a larger skill gap in respect of personal skills. The gap is very large in respect of analysis, creative thinking and conflict management in respect of interpersonal skills. Goal setting, planning, effectiveness, problem solving, learning and empathy are the major situational skills where the gap is substantial.

117

In Bank B also, most of the training programmes concentrate on business coaching, leadership, communication and team building exercises which necessitates proper treatment to those skills which have a larger gap.

Case 6.4: On transferable skills

My section head occasionally acts as my mentor and has been able to instil in me transferable skills and qualities like time management, efficiency in numbers and language, effective communication and problem solving. I am able to exhibit my ability in respect of the above skills drawing upon my experience as captain of my college football team. The team represents the bank I work for, while the opposite team stands for our competitors. The spectators are the customers and whichever team plays well will provide them the maximum utility. Playing a game requires utmost agility, workmanship, coordination, timing and proactive stance. A player will have the necessary skills but he has to effectively use them, otherwise it is a case of under-utilisation. In banking also, the entire team has to coordinate and time the decisions in such a way that the expected results are forthcoming. Even if one member of the team faults, the end result will be mutilated and the customers will go awry (Junior manager, Bank B).

The narrative speaks of the experience of the participant as a college football team captain and how that leadership quality has been further developed in the bank by his supervisor. The job description is allegorical wherein, its effective teamwork under able leadership that brings in the desired results.

6.4.5 Skill wheel of Oil A Senior Managers

The skill enhancement rate in Oil A senior managers (Figure 6.6) is 15 percent higher when compared to the before training scenario. The enhancement is higher in respect of situational skills, where the increase is 21 percent, but only moderate in personal skills (14 percent) and low in interpersonal skills (7 percent). Mentoring and innovativeness have a larger gap in personal skills while it is conflict management in interpersonal skills and planning, negotiation and effectiveness in situational skills. On the whole, the skill gap is smaller which is accompanied by smaller increases in skill endowment.

Figure 6.6: Skill wheel of Oil A Senior Managers

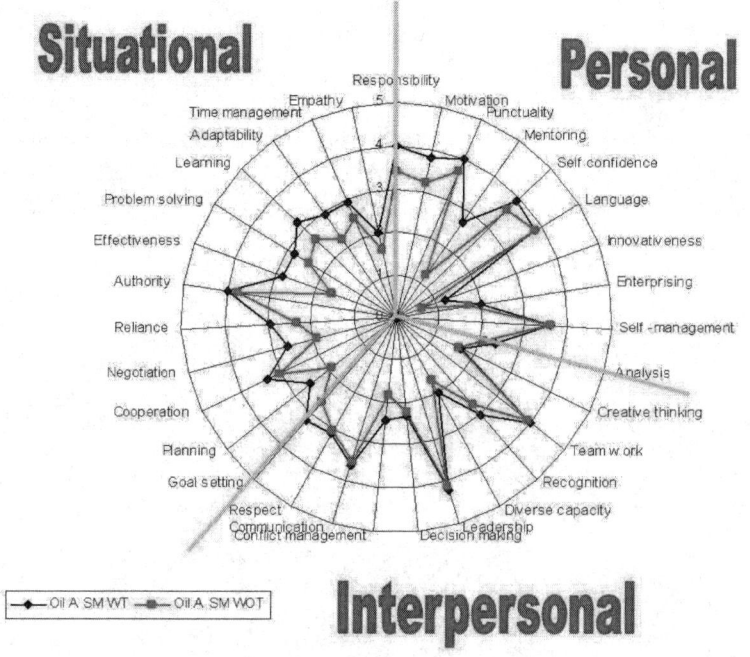

Case 6.5: On effective decision making

In 2003, our division had to make an important decision regarding opening a filling station in a less crowded area. The area besides being remote had no other enterprising units in and around it. Since some local customers and tourists desired the filling station to be set up in that place (nearest filling station was about 25 kms away) owing to the fact that when they reach that area, petrol was exhausted, we decided to give it a try. We collected information over a period of 25 days, discussed with the board but no conclusive decisions were taken. Again we spent another 10 days meeting travellers and asking them questions not only on fuel but on other facilities as well. We were able to convince the Board that once the filling station in that area was established, that will generate a series of new activities because of the mini growth pole. We estimated that we will be able to breakeven in less than two years. The Board reluctantly agreed to the proposal and in the next four months, that remote area began to undergo changes. Within three months of the installation, a coffee shop was opened and in the next year there were already a boutique shop, a restaurant and few houses sprang up. Now the area has become a mini-centre and we have doubled the capacity of the filling station and the Board has asked us to find out other similar areas for expansion. If we had backed out from the decision, there would not have been a min-centre now. Not only had the decision improved the status of the company and its profitability it also vouchsafed for its corporate social responsibility (Senior manager, Oil A).

The case illustrates business development that takes place because of quick and effective decisions in setting up of a filling station. Because the decision team was very effective in its

119

proposal, survey and breakeven analysis, the filling station was able to yield not only satisfactory rate of return but also effected business clustering in the original remote area. All this is because the team possessed high soft skill scores.

6.4.6 Skill wheel of Oil A Junior Managers

Unlike the senior managers, junior managers in Oil A (Figure 6.7) have been able to travel a longer distance, the increase in overall soft skill endowment being 44 percent when compared to before training. Situational skill registers the highest rate of increase (58 percent), followed by interpersonal skills (38 percent) and personal skills (29 percent).

Figure 6.7: Skill wheel of Oil A Junior Managers

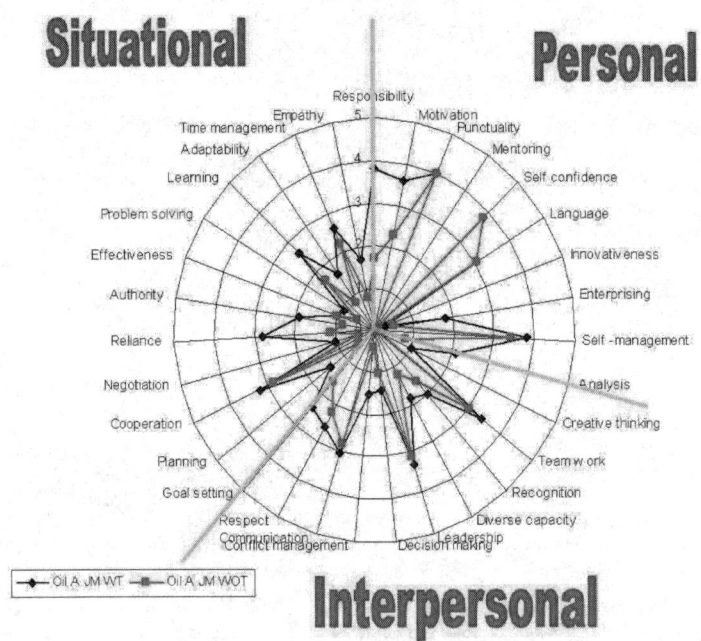

Though the rate of increase is substantial, there are many skills where the gap is very large – responsibility, motivation and enterprising in respect of personal skills, analysis, creative thinking, diverse capacity, conflict management and communications in respect of interpersonal skills and planning, negotiations, reliance, authority, problem solving, learning, adaptability and empathy in respect of situational skills. Here again, the problem skills are many situational skills, even though they register the highest rate of increase.

In Oil A, the training programmes concentrate on customer care, team building, presentation and the like and skills like mentoring, planning, empathy and others are not given that much importance, indicative of the fact that proper attention be given to set right the skill gaps.

Case 6.6: On situational skill development

The coaching sessions deal with the issue of effectiveness and we have identified the following as crucial for making the skills effective so that the competency levels of the workers would improve substantially.
a) Always to have an effective action plan wherein encouragement of accountability and problem solving techniques will be accomplished.
b) Integration of all action plans in various departments and self-sustaining and self-propagating drives wherein the entire interface is considered and not just the subsistence in problem solutions.
c) Learning from stories of famous leaders and infamous failures in order to understand the characterisation of influence, integrity, inspiration and improvement.
This process involves adapting to the situation and solving the problems in such a way that high risk failures are addressed through effective action plans which only capable leaders can achieve. Hence, I prefer the training course concentrate on improving leadership ability so as to manage the business environment effectively (Junior manager, Oil A).

Adaptation to the given situation and integrating soft skills to business development demands innovative leadership and effectiveness in decision making and coaching. The oil example illustrates how when soft skill development is transformed into an action plan, problem solving has to take into consideration various risks and how the training programmes can enable the participants to have a positive attitude in overcoming the bottlenecks.

6.4.7 Skill wheel of Oil B Senior Managers

Senior managers of Oil B (Figure 6.8) have been able to realise 21 percent higher skill enhancement after training, the increase being higher in respect of situational skills (33 percent) and low in personal (15 percent) and interpersonal skills (12 percent). The skill gap is high in respect of responsibility and motivation and in this group there is deterioration in enterprising skill augmentation. The skill gap is minimal in interpersonal skills. In many situational skills the gap is substantial – planning, negotiation, reliance, effectiveness and empathy.

Figure 6.8: Skill wheel of Oil B Senior Managers

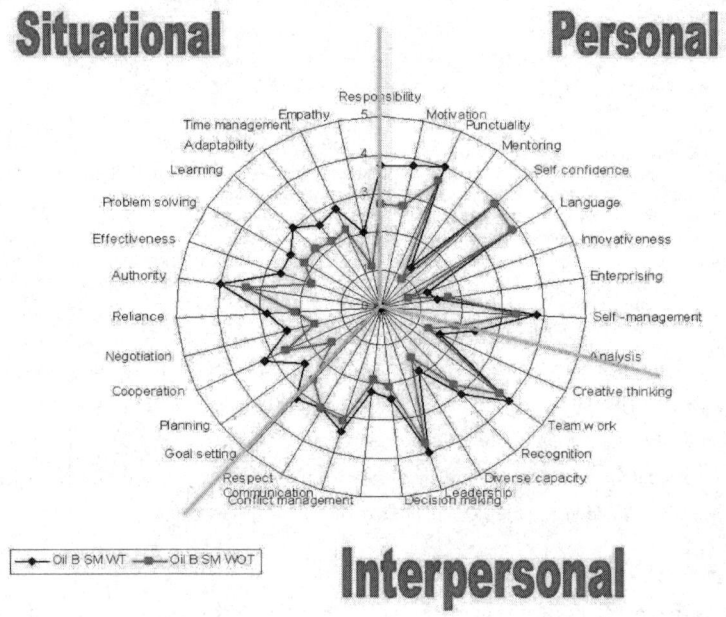

Case 6.7: On the importance of facilitation

Facilitation comes not only from superiors and peers but also from family members wherein comparisons are made between my growing up in the family and in the company. This comparison enables me to put traditional wisdom I gain from my family into the working of the company. To me, the company is like my family, more accepting and understanding. There have been instances where I had considered my peers' needs ahead of my own and I felt like reliving and understanding my life in a better way. Sometimes they chide their colleagues' habits or mannerisms which they say are annoying to them. Where the familial background is unhappy, there may be many cases prompting them to have negative attitudes. Hence, the facilitators have to inspire and guide the trainees such that only the positive aspects are ingrained into the process (Senior manager, Oil B).

Family's role in soft skill development and understanding of life enables the participant to overcome the risks and have positive attitude that transforms him into a facilitator to his peers. The informal relationship in the facilitation process makes the facilitator function as a developmental interventionist in guiding the juniors and enabling them to grow (Rich et al., 2002).

6.4.8 Skill wheel of Oil B Junior Managers

The junior managers of Oil B (Figure 6.9) have been able to realise 29 percent higher rate of skill enhancement in the post-training scenario, the increase being higher in situational skills (38 percent) followed by the other skills (24 percent). In respect of motivation, responsibility and self management (personal skills) and analysis, creative thinking, decision making and conflict management (interpersonal skills), the skill gap is higher. In almost all the situational skills the gap is higher, markedly in negotiation, problem solving and reliance.

Figure 6.9: Skill wheel of Oil B Junior Managers

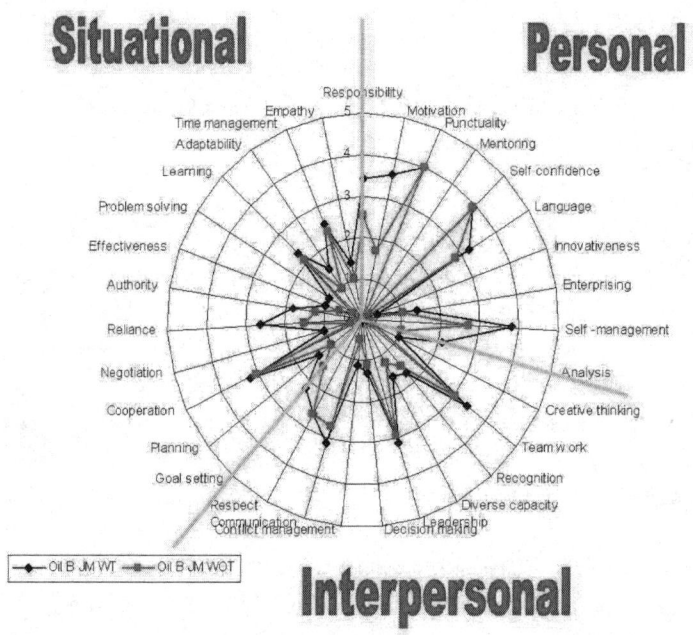

In Oil B, the training programmes concentrate on customer relationship, communication and presentation indicating a less than optimal treatment to those skills where the gap is large.

Case 6.8: Which soft skill tops the list?

Continuous quality improvement should be the objective of time management and this improvement has to take place with utmost care to workplace safety. I am informed that many thousands of man years are lost in workplaces due to absence, late coming, sickness and related factors. If only one can manage time effectively, the current productivity level can be improved substantially without any technological intervention.

On the other day, one of my colleagues was referring to team spirit as the most significant soft skill, while one of my senior colleagues emphasised on the crucial role played by problem solving skill. To me, there is little relevance in acquiring only one particular type of soft skill in the absence of others. What I have observed is that unlike hard skills, soft skills come in bunches and endowment of one skill prompts empowerment in the other. Though we may for convenience sake categorise these skills as interpersonal or intrapersonal, they are focused on improvement in one's behavioural attitude. It is common to find that in any selection process effective communication and presentation skills are emphasised. Problem solving skill requires good empathy, negotiation, learning ability, listening capacity, team spirit and also leadership qualities. Hence, I would prefer emphasis on one particular bunch of soft skills for given job requirements (Junior manager, Oil B).

The narrative is another example of development of internal soft skills wherein personal appearance and time management become crucial for quality improvement. Unlike hard skill, soft skill does not come in pieces but in bunches that a combination of various soft skills becomes the effective leverage. For example, some aspect of activity may require more of problem solving or team work skills but in the final analysis it is a mix of these skills that will provide the necessary solution. Further, the interaction between inter and intra personal skills not only demands personal development but also team development.

6.5 Distance travelled

The movement in the skill wheel due to intervention shows the progress made by the employee in acquiring soft skills which are essential for better employability. The purpose of acquiring soft skills has to result in not only personal skill development but also organisational development. As mentioned in chapter four, distance travelled indicates the growth in the performance of the individual because of intervention which has to be assessed in terms of achievement of goals like leadership and self-esteem and organisational goals like increase in productivity or image (Balgobin et al., 2004; Butcher and Marsden, 2004; Lloyd and OSullivan, 2003). Hard outcomes are clearly definable and quantifiable results that show the progress a participant has made toward achieving desirable outcomes by participating in an intervention programme. Soft outcomes are intangible and hard to measure directly and represent intermediary stages on the way to achieving the hard outcomes. Distance travelled is the progress made by the participants in achieving soft outcomes that lead toward sustained employment or associated hard outcomes, as a result of participating in the intervention programme and against an initial baseline set on participating in it.

When intervention takes place toward skill enhancement and organisational development, acquisition of soft skills becomes the major outcome. Soft outcomes indicate the acquisition of leadership and problem solving skills which ultimately enable the employee to perform better and exhibit better qualities when compared to pre-intervention stage. Hard outcomes are accomplishment toward better employability like higher educational qualifications which result due to acquisition of soft skills (Lloyd and OSullivan, 2003).

Soft outcomes have been described as those having a qualitative character, that try to capture any changes to the behaviour of the participants before the achievement of the actual training targets, expressed by hard, statistically based outcomes. Soft outcomes may be seen as those referring directly to features improving the personal skills and psychological state of the participants, such as self-esteem, initiative to do something or interest in anything. Soft outcomes are also seen as things that encourage the participants to achieve something in their career, allow reintegration to the mainstream and encourage them to get involved in learning or work. The focus is on personal development and improvement of well-being. The hard outcomes would be learning an actual qualification, gaining the qualification, getting a job or achieving a particular piece of work. Soft outcomes indicate what sort of benefits they get from participating in that, as an improvement of their attitude. Distance travelled by the participants within the time of the training programme may be described as soft outcomes, which make the participants able to complete the next step on their way to training or employment. If the participant is put in the right direction, he makes a next step and this will be a soft outcome, whereas in the training case, the issue would centre on acquiring some level of skills. By developing soft skills the participants improve different aspects of their career and fulfil their needs and increase their capabilities. Ultimately, training and soft skills lead to widening opportunities and help the participants to improve their employability (Lloyd and OSullivan, 2003).

The assessment of distance travelled is based on the self-assessed scores as given and triangulated by the respondents in the pre and post training scenarios. In the European Social Fund model, distance travelled has been measured as the difference in soft and hard outcomes which result after intervention takes place. That model has considered not only third party assessed but also self-assessed scores for the measurement of distance travelled. In the ESF study (EU, 2003), both hard and soft outcomes from social fund projects were assessed in different categories of workers through work appraisal procedures wherein before and after project assessment was carried out to measure the distance travelled by them. These appraisals were used as reference for employees when the workers move on to take up responsibilities. The appraisal also enabled the employees to identify the areas where the workers require strategic training for improving their hard and soft outcomes. Our model uses only self-assessed scores and hence largely conforms to that model.

Hard outcomes are the ultimate goal of skill enhancement and the realisation of them indicates how far the participants have their distance travelled. As already mentioned, hard outcomes result from the impact of soft outcomes and hence they proxy the distance travelled measure. Table 6.4 presents the transformation of the employees over successive scores, indicating an increase in the distance travelled and also an increase in the higher score distance travelled. Some of the hard outcomes are transfer to a preferred place or division, promotion, foreign visits, participation in seminars, publication of papers, appointment as a coach or mentor or trainer, awards and rewards, incentives, membership in committees, obtaining new qualifications and being given more responsibility and accountability. In many cases, they seem to be not identical with soft outcomes resulting from skill enhancement. Preference for nationals in employment, extension of project period and organisational inertia in recognising and rewarding skill enhancement are some of the reasons for hard outcomes being less intensive when compared to those of the soft outcomes.

Table 6.4: Number of managers distance travelled under different scores*(N=120)

Outcome/DT	Score	Period	Bank A		Bank B		Oil A		Oil B	
			SM	JM	SM	JM	SM	JM	SM	JM
Soft outcomes	4-5	I	0	0	0	0	0	0	0	0
		II	2	4	2	3	1	0	1	0
	3-4	I	3	4	3	3	3	4	2	3
		II	5	6	4	5	4	6	4	5
	2-3	I	3	2	3	3	4	3	3	2
		II	6	2	4	5	6	5	5	4
	<2	I	9	9	9	9	8	8	10	10
		II	2	3	5	2	4	4	5	6
Hard outcomes/ distance travelled	4-5	I	0	0	0	0	0	0	0	0
		II	2	3	2	2	1	0	1	0
	3-4	I	3	4	2	3	2	3	2	2
		II	4	5	3	4	3	5	3	4
	2-3	I	3	3	3	3	3	3	3	2
		II	5	3	4	5	5	5	5	4
	<2	I	9	8	10	9	10	9	10	11
		II	4	4	6	4	6	5	6	7

Note: * indicates the number of frequencies against each score.
  I = baseline (2005); II = post-training (2006)

Due to intervention programmes, the participants realise many soft outcomes and resulting hard outcomes indicate the distance travelled. This realisation has to be assessed with reference to a baseline representing the scores with their corresponding frequencies at the end of 2005 for comparison with 2006 to evaluate the distance travelled during the period due to intervention. Table 6.4 follows the HSP model (section 3.4) and compares the before and after intervention scores. The baseline (2005) information has been obtained by discussing with the participants and HR and training managers of the respective institutions and the post-training (2006) scores have been assessed based on survey triangulation in respect of the trained managers in respect of assessing both soft and hard outcomes. Scoring for soft outcomes shows two senior and four junior managers in Bank A, two senior and three junior managers in Bank B, one senior manager each in Oil A and Oil B have moved over to 4-5 score because of intervention. In the baseline, there were none with that score. In respect of other scores, the number of employees under higher scores has shown an increase, though there were two to six managers still under less than two score in 2006.

As mentioned in section 4.6.2, soft outcomes such as better work conditions, personal development indicators and situational skill acquisition determine the nature of distance travelled. Soft indicators signify improved time keeping, effective team building, improved communication and presentation skills, low sickness and absence from work, positive attitude and so on. These

126

indicators will in turn improve the hard outcomes such as promotion, awards and more responsible assignments. Respondents were asked to list the outcomes such as increasing confidence and self-esteem, time management, developing communication skills, increased motivation, improving relationship with others and building team-working skills. These were indicated as helping them to move towards better employment. The pre-training scores have been compared with the intervention scores for assessment of distance travelled.

6.6. Analysis of pre- and training performances

In order to assess the statistical significance of the small sample size of each group analysed, confidence limits have been calculated at 95 percent level for the individual groups for comparison with the larger sample analysis pertaining to pre and post training situations. The confidence limit is a range of values in which the population parameter will likely fall and is calculated using sample mean and best estimate of standard error. The proposition is that the spread of individual groups has to be much smaller than the difference between pre and post-intervention situations for the results to be significant. It is the range within which we would expect the value of the statistic to fall, if we were to repeat the study with a very large sample. It is the likely range of the true, real or population value of the statistic. In a two-group comparison of means, if we observe a mean difference of 10 units with a 95 percent confidence interval of 6 to 14 units (or lower and upper confidence limits of 6 and 14 units), the true difference between groups could be somewhere between 6 and 14 units.

Table 6.5 summarises the results wherein the t-test is significant at 95 percent in all the cases and the mean difference of individual samples is smaller when compared to the pre and post training situation for the entire sample. The significance is assessed by whether the confidence limits overlap as the pre-training and training samples are not the same people. However, the range of difference for the individual groups is higher when compared to the overall situation as should be the case for small sample size. Since the difference in spread between the pre-training or training sample and the individual groups is not very much, it can be presumed that the results of the individual groups are significant. The analysis shows the goodness of fit for the small samples when the confidence limit is at 95 percent, when pre and post training scenarios are considered. If the mean difference of a particular individual group is larger than the overall mean difference, then the goodness of fit does not exist. With respect to this, save a few cases in oil companies, all the individual groups exhibit the significance of the models. For example, the mean difference for senior managers (all sample) is 3.84. The mean difference for all the bank and Oil seniors is lower than this and hence is significant. Similarly, the mean difference for all the junior managers is 2.95 and it is lower than this in each individual cases. This clearly establishes the small sample mean difference less than that of the overall mean difference, confirming their significance. When the individual mean is lower than the overall mean difference, it indicates significance of the groups as shown in the last column. Where the confidence limits are significant, it indicates the individual mean differences do not exceed that of the overall mean difference of either 26 (seniors) or 34 (juniors) respectively. However, in the oil cases, there are little differences which make the results not significant. In many cases, there has been no overlapping between the training and pre-training mean differences. However, there may be overlapping- 2.54 to 3.0 pre-training and 2.88 to 3.32 training in Bank A senior managers, which indicates that these two are not significantly different, but the mean difference of training is quite higher than that of pre-training. In Bank B junior managers, the pre-training confidence limit is between 1.38 and 1.76 when compared to training difference of 1.8 and 2.19, indicating significant difference.

Table 6.5: Confidence limits for pre and post training samples

Sample group		Sample size	95% Confidence Interval of the difference		Mean	Significance of the small sample
			Lower	Upper		
SM	training	26	3.71	3.98	3.84	significant
	pre- training	34	2.86	3.03	2.94	
JM	training	34	3.65	4.04	3.85	significant
	pre- training	26	2.81	3.08	2.95	
Bank A SM	training	8	2.88	3.32	3.10	not significant
	pre-training	15	2.54	3.00	2.77	
Bank A JM	training	10	2.03	2.41	2.22	not significant
	pre-training	15	1.80	2.14	1.97	
Bank B SM	training	7	2.62	3.04	2.83	not significant
	pre-training	15	2.39	2.81	2.60	
Bank B JM	training	9	1.80	2.19	1.99	significant
	pre-training	15	1.38	1.76	1.57	
Oil A SM	training	6	2.46	2.88	2.67	not significant
	pre-training	15	2.37	2.76	2.56	
Oil A JM	training	8	1.76	2.14	1.95	not significant
	pre-training	15	1.44	1.84	1.64	
Oil B SM	training	5	2.47	2.70	2.59	not significant
	pre-training	15	2.31	2.53	2.42	
Oil B JM	training	7	1.77	2.08	1.92	not significant
	pre-training	15	1.57	1.87	1.72	

The analysis presented above arrives at the following conclusions. The emphasis on soft skills is at a higher level in Bank A when compared to Bank B owing to better motivation and mentoring besides, increased number of training courses. Oil A places a greater emphasis on training and development, whereas in Oil B coaching and mentoring are as important as training. Oil A has a higher number of courses and is slightly ahead of Oil B in soft skill development. There seems to be no one-to-one relationship between hard and soft outcomes wherein hard outcomes is slightly lower than that of soft outcomes. Distance travelled in Bank A > Bank B > Oil A > Oil B. The junior managers, especially in Bank B and Oil A have been able to realise a higher rate of skill enhancement than the senior managers, since in their case the increase in skill endowment is 32 percent higher whereas it is only 21 percent in the case of the senior managers. Senior managers in oil companies have been able to travel a shorter distance when compared to those in the banks. The rate of increase in situational skills is the highest in all the eight skill groups, especially junior managers. The rate of increase is low for personal skills especially in the case of senior managers of oil companies and the rate of increase is very high in the case of Bank B junior managers. The rate of increase in interpersonal skill is very low for senior managers in the oil companies and Bank A and also for junior managers in Bank A. Innovativeness and enterprising skills have a larger skill gap when compared to other skills. In interpersonal skills, analysis, creative thinking, decision making, negotiation and conflict management show a larger gap. In situational skills, the skills having a larger gap are goal setting, planning, negotiation, reliance, authority, problem solving and empathy.

6.7 Soft skill development and employee performance

In section 4.4, one of the objectives of the study relates to the contribution of soft skill to the improvement of human capital quality and another objective is to compare the relative roles of hard versus soft skills. Hard skills indicate educational qualifications whereas soft skills as discussed in the study complement them and in the process assume significance in human capital growth. When the institutions adopt various intervention programmes, the main objective is to enhance the soft and hard skill endowment of the employees and thereby improve the productivity level. Hence, soft skill plays a crucial role in improvement of productivity. Intervention in the form of training improves the soft skill endowment of different categories differently. The fact that the banks require employees with a higher level of soft skill than in the oil companies suggests that banking sector owing to its service and customer orientation, places high premium on the soft skills. However, for particular jobs, the required hard skill is also crucial and it is the interaction between hard skill and soft skill that enables a particular employee to perform in such a way that it helps in one's own development and the company's development. In recent years, the importance given to soft skill in recruitment, transfer and promotion has increased considerably and hence the employers spend considerable amount on training so that its impact is positive bringing in adequate rate of return to the organisation.

While soft skill enhancement takes place owing to training, mentoring and also due to longer years of experience, the contribution of soft skill before and after training to the improvement in human capital quality and also productivity assumes crucial role.

The extent of contribution to one's own or company's development denotes the hard outcome and is measured on a scale of one to five, where a score of less than one indicates very low contribution, between one to two low, between two to three moderate, between three to four high and between four to five very high level of contribution as explained in section 4.6. The assessment in respect of individual skills is done according to the perception of the employee with regard to own development and that of company since the purpose of acquiring soft skills is to effect these changes. Contribution to company's development is also from the perspective of the employee and may indicate the likely increase in productivity, proxied by earnings capacity. While development in soft skills is measured by comparing pre and post intervention scenarios, contribution to company's development is assessed by attributing suitable scores.

Increase in the level of innovativeness, creative thinking, goal setting, lifelong learning and problem solving skills to name a few certainly improve the performance levels of the employees. The performance which is reflected by the combination of own and company's development from the perspective of the participant may be regressed on soft and hard skills to assess which one contributes more to it. The individual scores are aggregated and the percentage share of each employee in the total is taken for regression before and after training for both senior and junior managers to arrive at a uniform measure. The ordinary least square regression considers the overall scores of the sample respondents and on this total each respondent's share is regressed with reference to the explanatory variables- contribution of soft and hard skills.

The sample selected for the regression analysis pertains to the decomposition of the training sample of 60 into seniors and juniors (irrespective of institution affiliation) as mentioned in section 6.5. Of the 60 training cases, 26 belong to senior and 34 to the junior manger cadres. Hence, we have separate scores for seniors and juniors in each category. This is compared to the pre-intervention sample of 60 senior as well as junior managers. Since our focus is to assess the training outcomes, we compare pre-training situation in the same senior or junior categories. Thus we have four equations– senior managers pre-training (60), senior managers after training (26), junior managers pre-training (60) and junior managers after training (34). The four equations estimate the coefficients of soft and hard skills with or without training. While the ANOVA (analysis of variance) specifies the statistical significance, the regression model specifies the positive or negative nature of the coefficients for each of the four cases. For the sake of statistical significance, the samples have been aggregated into only two categories –senior and junior managers. The soft and hard skill coefficients and their significance in the regression analysis are presented in Table 6.6.

Table 6.6: Regression coefficients for senior and junior managers

Indicator	Senior managers		Junior managers	
	Pre-training	Training	Pre-training	Training
Sample size	60	26	60	34
R^2	.898	.960	.934	.962
ANOVA- F value	134.4	277.4	166.4	390.1
Significance level	1%	1%	1%	1%
Constant – coefficient	.309	.194	.321	.240
- t value	1.692	1.243	1.266	2.397
- significance level	10%	>10%	>10%	5%
Soft skill – coefficient	.319	.505	.322	.404
- t value	2.835	2.839	1.930	3.509
- significance level	5%	5%	.10%	1%
Hard skill – coefficient	.574	.445	.593	.514
- t value	6.545	2.455	2.775	4.159
- significance level	1%	5%	5%	1%

6.7.1: Skill endowment and productivity of senior managers

Pre-training performance of the senior managers is assessed by the result

a)   SMPERWOT = .31 constant + .32 SMSSWOT + .57 SMHSWOT where,

SMPERWOT = percentage share of a senior manager in the total performance score of all
sample senior managers (pre-training sample size 60)

SMSSWOT = percentage share of a senior manager in the total soft skill score of all senior
Managers (pre-training)

SMHSWOT = percentage share of a senior manager in the total hard skill score of all senior
managers (pre-training)

The regression fit and the high R^2 (coefficient of determination) are significant at one percent level according to ANOVA test. The R^2 is 0.9 indicating that both hard and soft skill together influence performance to the extent of 90 percent. In this case, the standard error of the estimate is very small at three percent of the mean of the dependent variable. Since the SMSSWOT (soft skill of senior managers without training) coefficient is .319, an increase of one percent share of soft skill increases productivity share by .32 percent, while in the case of hard skill, it is .57 percent, indicating a higher level of impact by hard skill on productivity. When both the skills take zero value, constant is positive indicating that there will be a certain level of performance without these skills.

This scenario can be compared with the result of after training where,

b) SMPERWT = .194 constant + .51 SMSSWT + .45 SMHSWT where,

SMPERWT = percentage share of a senior manager in the total performance score of all
sample senior managers after training (sample size 26)
SMSSWT = percentage share of a senior manager in the total soft skill score of all senior
managers after training
SMHSWT = percentage share of a senior manager in the total hard skill score of all senior
managers after training

Post-training, the R^2 increases to 0.96 showing that 96 percent of variation in performance (dependent variable) is explained by the combination of hard and soft skills (independent variables). The higher value of R^2 by six percent when compared to the pre-training situation indicates the specific contribution of training in variations in performance. The result validates the positive contribution of intervention programmes. The standard of error of the estimate is very small when compared to before training. The regression fit is significant at one percent level according to ANOVA. Post-training, the enhanced contribution of soft skill and the reduced contribution of hard skill to productivity can be seen. As regards the regression coefficients, that of hard skill declines to .45 whereas that of soft skill increases to .51. In other words, one percentage share increase in hard skill induces only .5 percent increase in the performance share post-training, which is lower when compared to that of before training.

The impact of soft skill on the other hand has become quite substantial and even higher than that of hard skill in the training scenario. The changing influence of the two skills is primarily due to training. Training in the case of senior managers also indicates a cumulative effect of all the training programmes and mentoring undertaken so far. The increased level of impact by soft skill clearly supports the hypothesis that increased level of soft skill resulting from training induces a higher increase in productivity. Between the banks and the oil companies, the former have a higher level of soft skill endowment and also productivity.

6.7.2: Skill endowment and productivity of junior managers

Unlike the senior managers, the junior managers would not have undergone many training and mentoring programmes and are having a lower level of experience also. But when compared to the senior managers at their recruitment time, the soft skill endowment of junior managers has been high. Now-a-days, enhancement of hard skill and various soft skills are so essential for employability that the employers specifically demand particular soft skill development appropriate to the given jobs.

In the pre-training regression result

c) JMPERWOT = .32 constant + .32 JMSSWOT + .59 JMHSWOT where,

    JMPERWOT = percentage share of a senior manager in the total performance score of all
               sample junior managers (pre-training sample size 60)

    JMSSWOT = percentage share of a senior manager in the total soft skill score of all junior
               managers (pre-training)

    JMHSWOT = percentage share of a senior manager in the total hard skill score of all junior
               managers (pre-training)

both soft and hard skills put together influence variations in performance to the extent of 94 percent and fit is significant at one percent level.

For every one percent increase in the share of hard skill, the resulting increase in performance is .59 percent whereas in the case of soft skill, it is .32 percent indicating a greater influence of hard skill. When these two skills take zero value performance is positive and also significant.

Post-training, the regression equation is as follows

d) JMPERWT = .24 constant + .4 JMSSWT + .51 JMHSWT where,

    JMPERWT = percentage share of a senior manager in the total performance score of all
               sample junior managers after training (sample size 34)

    JMSSWT = percentage share of a senior manager in the total soft skill score of all junior
              managers after training

    JMHSWT = percentage share of a senior manager in the total hard skill score of all junior
              managers after training

Training has increased the value of coefficient of determination by three percent which is lower when compared to that of senior managers. The standard error of the estimate has a lower value under training than under before training.

It is observed that hard skill is still the dominant variable influencing performance, though soft skill has shown an increased level of contribution after training. In the case of senior managers, the rate of increase in soft skill contribution has been much more than the rate of decline in hard skill contribution. However, for junior managers, the rate of increase in soft skill contribution equals the rate of decline in hard skill contribution. This may be due to the fact that the junior managers have not undergone many training and mentoring programmes and also have shorter period of experience and hence the change in soft skill endowment is not substantial as in the case of senior managers, though when compared before training, the post-training scenario shows augmentation in soft skill and also its enhanced role in influencing productivity.

The analysis shows that not only the importance of soft skill vis-à-vis hard skills improves in the post-training scenario; its contribution to performance enhancement is also validated. Further, the role of soft skills is more visible in the case of senior managers. Whereas the increase in soft skill share has been 58 percent in them (.505 divided by .319), the increase in share has been only 25 percent in the case of junior managers (.404 divided by .322). Decline in hard skills share is higher in the case of senior managers (23 percent, from .574 to .445) when compared to the juniors (13 percent, from .593 to .514). The results show that intervention programmes result in a greater distance travelled and a greater level of job satisfaction and organisational development for the senior managers. Some of the narratives (cases 2, 5, 6 and 7) mentioned in chapter 5 highlighted the importance of soft skill orientation of the recruits and new entrants and how they had contributed to personal development besides job achievement at the workplace. The improvement in the quality of human capital stock resulting from soft skill enhancement due to intervention is captured by analysing the increase in the stock keeping higher secondary schooling as the baseline.

Since the purpose of the study is to point out the relative changes in the significance of hard versus soft skills due to intervention, adding both the skills in the regression equation (as above) may give wrong information that soft skill has an upper hand and so on. So, the regression is run separately for hard and soft skills to see the relative changes in the respective skills due to intervention. Intervention certainly enhances soft skills but at the same time, soft outcomes have their impact on hard outcomes and hence indirectly hard skills may also undergo changes as a result. Table 6.7 captures this aspect. Both hard and soft skill improve their coefficient of determination (changes in performance is largely explained by variations in the respective skills due to intervention), but the rate of increase in the soft skill coefficient in respect of junior managers due to intervention is quite substantial.

In the regression Table 6.6, when both hard and soft skills were combined in the equation, the post-training situation showed that the rate of increase in the soft skill coefficient is much more that the rate of decline in the hard skill coefficient, implying that there has been a total enhancement of skills. In table 6.7, we find that the coefficients of both the skills improve in scale due to intervention and though both hard and soft skill enhancement take place for the senior managers, in the case of junior managers, actually hard skill coefficient show a decline, whereas that of soft skill coefficient shows a substantial increase, indicating a positive impact of soft skills on the juniors, which slightly differs from the results of Table 6.6. From this can be speculated that the very high value of the correlations may in part be explained by the self-assessment of both soft skills and contribution to own and company development.

Table 6.7 Regression coefficients for hard and soft skills run separately

Indicator	Senior managers		Junior managers	
	Pre-training	Training	Pre-training	Training
Sample size	60	26	60	34
HARD SKILL				
R^2	.869	.946	.925	.947
ANOVA- F value	211.9	472.5	297.5	567.3
Significance level	1%	1%	1%	1%
Constant	.632	.297	.043	.201
HS Coef	.785	.946	.989	.932
SOFT SKILL				
R^2	.752	.950	.914	.940
ANOVA- F value	97.0	455.7	255.8	505.5
Significance level	1%	1%	1%	1%
Constant	.215	.269	.859	.397
HS Coef	.927	.930	.777	.865

6.8 Human capital stock in the sample institutions

Human capital traditionally is measured as the ratio between the wage earnings of a worker with zero level of education and the wage which an employee earns for a given level of education. The longer the number of years spent in schooling and training, higher would be the wage level. Since the measure requires a baseline for comparison and indexing, the higher secondary schoolers with or without training (lowest educational level in the sample institutions) has been treated as the baseline and weights have been given cumulatively for subsequent levels of education and training as in section 4.7. The proportion of employees of different levels of education is treated as another weightage to average the hard and soft skill development. The baseline index is taken as 100 as explained by the ILO norms as mentioned in section 4.8.2 and depending on the skill enhancement in different education levels, the increase in skill index is paired with that. The analysis pertains to the two skill categories for the two banks or oil companies combined. Accordingly, senior managers in banks are given a weight of 0.4 in respect of higher secondary schooling (which is taken as the baseline), the weight increasing to 0.5 in the case of graduates, 0.6 in the case of postgraduates with training.

Following the ILO methodology and as mentioned in sections 4.6 and 4.8.2, the improvement in quality of human capital stock is assessed keeping high school as the base (for both hard and soft skills) and calculating the hard and soft skill indices for different education levels. Each education level with or without intervention component is given weightage (different for senior and junior managers) and corresponding achievement of soft skills is ascertained to view the improvement in the human capital stock in the banks or oil companies. The computed hard and soft skill indices indicate the extent of soft skill development to a particular level of hard skill.

135

As per Table 6.8, in the case of junior managers higher secondary schooling has a lower weight indicating their smaller proportion. However, in the case of oil companies for both senior and junior managers, the weight increases to 0.5 indicating a higher proportion. The cumulative weight stops at postgraduate with training and mentoring in all the cases except junior managers in oil companies where the weight stops at graduates with training and mentoring. Depending on the relative position of the particular education level like postgraduate or graduate, the hard skill index will change. Corresponding to the hard skill index, the soft skill index is constructed to indicate its overall augmentation during the reference period. When both the indices are averaged, it denotes the improvement in human capital stock for that particular period as a result of the interaction between hard and soft components. However, the calculation of the indices ignores the error margins in the figures in view of the very small numbers in some of the categories.

Table 6.8: Improvement in human capital stock (in percentage) (N=60)

Education level	Banks						Oil companies					
	SM			JM			SM			JM		
	Weight*	HS	SS	Weight*	HS	SS	Weight*	HS	SS	Weight*	HS	SS
High Sec (base)	0.4	100	100	0.3	100	100	0.5	100	100	0.5	100	100
G	0.5	115	104	0.4	115	104	0.6	120	102	0.7	120	116
G+T	0.6	120	132	0.6	120	110	0.7	125	104	0.8	125	116
G+T+M	0.7	125	136	0.7	130	113	0.8	130	121	1.0	130	122
PG+T	0.8	135	144	0.9	140	126	-	145	-	-	145	-
PG+T+M	1.0	140	148	1.0	145	134	1.0	150	143	-	150	-
Overall	-	**120**	**131**	-	**126**	**116**	-	**123**	**116**	-	**121**	**114**

Note: * indicates cumulative weights
High Sec= higher secondary schoolers; G= graduates without training; G+T = graduates with training; G+T+M =
Graduates with training and mentoring; PG = postgraduates without training; PG+T = postgraduates with training;
PG+T+M =postgraduates with training and mentoring SM= senior managers; JM= junior managers; HS = hard skill;
SS = soft skill
Weight = proportion of the respective education level

Thus the increase in human capital stock over subsequent levels of education when higher secondary schooling is treated as base shows that in respect of bank senior managers, hard skill development index is 20 percent higher when compared to the base whereas in soft skill the increase has been 31 percent as in Table 6.7. This shows that human capital stock index has increased by 25 percent which is the arithmetic mean for both hard and soft skills in 2006 when compared to 2005. Between the different educational levels, the increase has been quite substantial especially for those graduates and postgraduates with training. The rate of increase in human capital index is 25 percent higher in its hard component and 36 percent higher in its soft component in respect of the graduate senior managers with training and mentoring capabilities. In respect of postgraduates with training, the rate of increase is 35 percent in hard skill and 44 percent in soft skill. When mentoring is added to training, the rate of increase has been 40 percent in hard skill and 48 percent in soft skill. In respect of junior managers in banks, the average rate of increase has been 26 percent in hard skill and 16 percent in soft skill. Graduates without training fare poorer when compared to higher secondary schoolers. The rate of increase in soft skill is substantial only in the case of postgraduates and is moderate for the graduates.

In respect of senior managers of oil companies, the soft skill increase is quite visible only in the case of postgraduates and in both the companies the soft skill endowment of the senior managers increases only slightly. In Oil B, graduates fare poorer when compared to the higher secondary schoolers. The average increase in soft skill is only 16 percent higher when compared to the base in respect of senior managers and 14 percent higher for the junior managers. This shows that between high schoolers and graduates, there is little difference in the oil companies, whereas it makes a big difference in the case of banks. The type of hard skill and the soft skill requirement is different in the service oriented banks and market-driven oil companies and hence the focus of the bank groups is different from that of oil companies. Human capital development is very marked in the postgraduates and graduates with training though the higher secondary schoolers through their experience and training have been able to improve their human capital.

As a result of the interaction of hard and soft skills, the improvement in the human capital stock in 2006 when compared to 2005 has been 25 percent higher in the case of senior managers and 21 percent higher in the case of junior managers of banks and 19 percent higher in senior managers and 17 percent higher in junior managers of oil companies. This suggests that the hard skill contribution is still larger than that of soft skills as revealed by the regression results.

6.9 Conclusion

The results of the general survey on soft skill assessment covering pre-intervention and 60 intervention respondents have been discussed with reference to their personal profiles and participation in training programmes. The nine personal sub-skills, 10 interpersonal sub-skills and 12 situational sub-skills have been assessed as before and after the training programmes in terms of a skill wheel and on that basis soft outcomes the personal skills have a higher score when compared to others. The impact of the training programmes is very marked on situational behaviour. Based on pre and post training situations, distance travelled by the different skill groups has been measured to point out the skill gaps and the necessity for attitudinal changes for better performance. Multiple regression analysis has been employed to assess the contribution of soft skill vis-à-vis hard skill in productivity increase wherein post-training, the influence of soft skill considerably increases and even over-shadows that of hard skills. Finally, based on the results an attempt has been made to assess the increase in human capital stock index in the different skill categories.

The descriptive and regression analyses have validated the following objectives and propositions.

o   The importance of soft skill orientation is more in the case of banks than the oil companies.

o   Soft skill orientation of the senior managers is at a higher level when compared to those of the junior managers.
o   The grouping of soft skill into personal, interpersonal and situational is empirically validated in the sample institutions.
o   By giving scores 1 to 5 in the Likert scale, all the 31 soft skills have been aggregated to yield a soft skill index before and after intervention to indicate the level of soft skill endowment in different skill groups.
o   Intervention in the form of training, mentoring and experience enhance soft skill endowment, especially those belonging to the situational skills.
o   Human capital, both in its soft and hard contexts, determines productivity in a micro level also and intervention enhances the contribution of the soft skills over that of hard skills.
o   The distance travelled in respect of the different skill categories range from 16 percent in the case of Oil A senior managers to 42 percent in the case of Bank B junior managers.
o   When compared to the base education level, the human capital development index increases by three to 24 percent in the different institutions.

The other objectives are analysed in the next chapter, wherein the soft skill profile of 40 respondents (five each in the eight skill groups) along with the results of the in-depth survey is analysed.

Impact of soft skills in the
reference groups

7.1 Introduction

What the study points out is that soft skill enhancement takes place due to training and other intervention programmes and in a given period may be subject to a particular measure which may undergo changes depending on the changes in skill endowment. The score may reach the maximum level theoretically but not in actual practice due to changing dynamism of the organisation and work culture. If the actual score is say 80 percent of the maximum in two different time periods or in two work environments, it does not follow that both are same. A particular score has to be assessed with reference to the specific skill category, time period or work environment. If the institutions find any discrepancies in skill endowments, they may bridge the skill gap through appropriate intervention programmes. The important thing to note is that owing to interventions, skill score would improve toward reaching the maximum.

When compared to the pre-training, the post-training situation results in skill enhancement and thus enables the employer in bridging the observable skill gap. The base endowment has been low for interpersonal and situational skills especially in the oil companies for both senior and junior managers. But post-training, the difference in interpersonal and situational skill endowment is reduced in almost all the cases. This showed the effectiveness of training programme in enhancing the soft skill endowment of the respondents, the increase being higher in situational skills. Mentoring, innovativeness and enterprising personal skills, analysis, creative thinking, diverse capacity, decision making and conflict management in interpersonal skills and goal setting, problem solving and empathy in situational skills have been identified as those skills whose endowment and enhancement are at a lower level and hence seem to be the difficult skills to be imparted. The objective of this chapter is to showcase the skill endowment of the in-depth survey respondents so as to evaluate the above proposition. The narratives from the in-depth interview aptly demonstrate the focus of this chapter in analysing aspects of soft skill development at the individual, group and institutional levels. Research questions such as what are the sources of soft skill development, what are the crucial intervention tools, which type of soft skill develops faster, the role of different sources and what will be the impact of various intervention programmes on their own and company's development are answered in this chapter. Since the numbers involved are very small (five in each group), the results pertain only to the specific cases and need not be generalised.

Section 7.2 outlines the skill endowment of the reference group identified for in-depth analysis. Section 7.3 compares the performance of the reference groups (corresponding to eight sample cases) with the general (all post-training sample) and pre-training (non-intervention) groups through self-assessed scores in respect of individual soft skills. The skill endowment level of the reference groups is demonstrated through various skill acquisition sources (family, school, colleges and workplace) in section 7.4. The assessment of different intervention programmes at the workplace is accomplished in section 7.5, while section 7.6 examines the outcome of these programmes on personal and organisational development. Section 7.7 showcases the contribution of the reference groups with suitable illustrations and narrative documentation. Section 7.8 provides an evaluative summary of performance of the reference groups, while section 7.9 concludes.

7.2 Soft skill endowment of reference groups

The concept of focus group is used to indicate a reference group in this study. Having presented the caricature of a larger sample in the sample institutions as to the assessment of soft skills, the cream of that sample is analysed to see how far this reference group differs from the overall sample and in what way it affects the performance of the entire sample. When the questionnaire was filled in by the respondents, a choice was given to all of them to offer to take part in further interviews to probe deeper aspects of soft skill development which not all the sample respondents were in a position to provide. Though more than 50 responses were received, after cross-checking and particularising the various issues required, 40 respondents were selected (five in each group, giving the response rate of 40 out of 120) to be the reference group for the respective bank/oil managerial cadre. Hence, the reference group indicates only the in-depth respondents in whose case the particulars about acquisition, sources and impact of the programmes were available and who willingly provided the information. The reference group exhibits specific characteristics like high soft skill score which are not to be found in others.

A reference group of five respondents was identified from each of the general groups based on high scores obtained in different soft skills, especially in those where the skill gap for the general sample showed significance, besides undergoing of recent training programme. A comparison of soft skill endowment shows that the reference group has three to 12 percent higher level of performance when compared to the overall sample.

Table 7.1: Performance of reference group (N=40)

Skills	Group	Bank A		Bank B		Oil A		Oil B	
		SM	JM	SM	JM	SM	JM	SM	JM
All	All	62	43	56	40	54	39	51	37
(Scores in	Pre-training	55	38	51	31	51	32	47	33
percentage)	Intervention	69	47	64	45	60	44	57	42
	Reference	73	53	67	49	62	49	59	47
% change	Intervention: Pre-training	25	24	25	45	18	38	21	27
	Reference: All	18	23	20	23	15	26	16	27
	Reference: Pre-training	33	39	31	58	22	53	26	42
Share (%)	Personal	34	24	26	26	30	23	26	24
(Reference: Pre-	Interpersonal	28	21	31	33	19	34	22	30
training)	Situational	38	55	43	41	51	43	52	46

Since a score of five is like a benchmark for a particular reference period, the percentages shown in Table 7.1 indicate the skill differences among the different groups and how the reference group fares when compared to others. In Bank A, the increase in interpersonal skill level is higher than that in the other two skill groups. In respect of Bank B reference group, the score shows an improvement of five percent over the general group with intervention. Here again, the increase has been higher in the case of interpersonal skills than in others. In Oil A reference group, the score increases from 60 to 62 percent, the increase being uniform in all the three skills. Oil B reference group also registers a similar increase when compared to the general group, the score however being lower than in Oil A.

In the case of junior managers, Bank A reference group registers the highest level of increase over 12 percent, especially in interpersonal skills. Bank B reference group has nine percent higher performance level than the general group, the increase being higher in interpersonal skills. In Oil A reference group, the score increases by 10 percent, the increase being higher in situational and interpersonal skills. In Oil B, the reference group has a score of 47 percent, which is higher by over 10 percent when compared to the general group. The increase is higher in interpersonal and situational skills. Overall the reference group shows higher scores in skills like innovativeness, enterprise, creative thinking, diverse capacity, effectiveness and empathy in which the general group has low scores. In other words, the reference group performs better than the general group in almost all the skills thus making the skill gap less apparent.

The following illustration showcases how employees with special skill endowment can play a dominant role in facilitating and motivating other employees in improving organisational performance.

Case 7.1

Last October, one of our moderators was facilitating a group in a project for an international company. They had to do a very important advertisement test before an international campaign for a new product line in refined oil. It was a very visual work task to do in the group with lot of advertisements to look at and a collage to be made. When the facilitator entered, in the group were two blind people and he was really shocked and did not know what to do. The group started and he tried to act as natural as possible.

When he came to the part where every group member should express their feelings about the advertisements those with sight started to explain for the blinds what the advertisements really were about and in great detail expressed their feelings about them, to help the blind to visualise them. This type of transfer spillover may be applied in the realm of skill development also. Those with a high skill endowment can motivate those who want to learn new skill so that the latter can visualise the importance of being skilled. Like technology transfer, skill transfer can also take place and it may be possible to generalise the transfer process just like there is transfer of energy from high energy sources to low energy sources and not otherwise. In this way skill transfer is a downward process and our group is an ideastorming group (Senior manager, Oil A).

7.3 Comparison of reference with general group

The reference group is endowed with high scores when compared to other groups. In personal skills, it has 13 to 17 percent higher score when compared to the post-training sample of 120, while when compared to the pre-training group (120 in number), its performance level is higher by 18 to 45 percent. When compared to the intervention sample (60 in number), itself faring better than the pre-training group by seven to 35 percent, the reference group performance is substantially higher especially in Bank A and Bank B junior managers.

In respect of interpersonal skills, the reference group performs better than the average group by nine to 26 percent and when compared to the pre-training group it is higher by 11 to 57 percent. This increase again is higher in the case of bank junior managers. Situational skills register the highest percentage increase in the reference group when compared to others, especially in Bank and Oil junior managers. The overall change indicates 17 percent higher performance in Bank A senior manager group when compared to the average group. The intervention group has 25 percent higher endowment when compared to the pre-training group but in the case of the reference group, the increase is 32 percent. In Bank B senior managers, the intervention group has a 25 percent higher soft skill endowment when compared to the pre-training group. However, this increase is 31 percent for the reference group. The intervention group has 17 higher performances when compared to the pre-training group in Oil A senior manager group. The increase in reference group is 21 percent and in Oil B it is 25 percent as against 21 percent for the intervention group.

In the case of junior managers, the performance of the reference group is quite high when compared to that of intervention group vis-à-vis the pre-training group. In Bank A, while the intervention group has 23 percent higher endowment when compared to the pre-training group, it is 39 percent in the reference group. In Bank B, while the intervention group registers 45 percent higher soft skill endowment over the pre-training group, the reference group is able to mark 58 percent. In Oil A, the intervention group performs better by 33 percent over the pre-training group whereas it is higher for the reference group at 53 percent. In Oil B, the scores are 27 and 42 percent respectively.

While the reference group has been able to experience the highest skill enhancement level for all the skill groups in the post-training scenario, situational skill accounts for the highest share in that increase. When compared to the pre-training group, the reference group has 21 to 58 percent higher performance. When compared to personal and interpersonal skills, the share of situational skills is higher, especially in Bank A junior managers and Oil A and B senior managers (over 50 percent). The share is less than 40 percent in Bank A senior managers and over 40 percent in Bank B senior and junior managers and Oil A and B junior managers. The high share of situational skills in post-training skill enhancement for the general group has already been explained in section 6.3.1.

7.4 Sources of soft skill acquisition

Soft skill development takes place through different avenues. The type of social environment in which an individual passes through different stages of his life and the individual's biological maturation provides the type of behaviour management he or she has to adopt throughout life. In this, the influence of parents, siblings, peers, teachers, the type of education and work environment all generate the required behaviour systems. The individual relies on them for guidance, nurturing and development of the skills for better employability and or lifelong learning. Local cultural norms and religious beliefs fortify the behavioural patterns thus formed. Many members of the reference group have been influenced by their parents especially in goal setting, obedience to rules, orderliness, ethical work values and involvement in crucial decision making process. Where parental style has been authoritative (normal case for the reference group), it has resulted in a better level of pre-training and responsiveness. On the contrary, an authoritarian style resulted in a higher level of pre-training but a low level of responsiveness. An indulgent style resulted in a low level of pre-training but a high level of responsiveness whereas a neglectful parental style results in low levels of both pre-training and responsiveness.

The reference group feels that (information collected from the group as a whole) the parents were able to interpret and explain events in which they were involved besides establishing regular routines in family life like negotiation, information search and communication. The skills which are acquired by parental guidance become the basic skills on which further skill development takes place. The effectiveness of parent coaching is exemplified in holding children's attention, asking questions, interacting with comments and providing feedback. Literary and numeracy skill development through bedtime stories, help in homework, listening and fostering enable their children to have a positive attitude in life. Similar effect may be imparted by other elder members of family and relatives whereas collaboration with junior members and peers will be more or less similar to social interaction with peers and friends in the external world. The peer group may be identified by distinct dress, language or conformity code and if the group does not result in a deviant culture, the individual learns good team spirit and crisis management skills.

Schools and higher education institutions in which the individual passes through for his education, skill development takes place through different means. The type of curriculum standards and their assessment, the type of teaching and mentoring and the type of social morality and physical education that are imparted define an individual's technical and personality features. The fact that social competence, risk management researching skill development, application of learning to real world situations, interest in the content, organisational skills etc, which are developed in the learning institutions result in the acquisition of problem solving, high order thinking and job preparation skills as an indicator of the influence these institutions generate on the students.

Table 7.2: Sources of soft skill acquisition (%age contribution) (N=40)

Skill	Family	School	Higher Education	Work-Place
Personal	08	10	26	56
Interpersonal	05	09	20	66
Situational	06	07	14	73
Overall	**06**	**09**	**20**	**65**

When the share of family, schools, higher education and workplace in soft skill acquisition of the reference group is considered, it is the workplace which turns out to be the dominant source of soft skill acquisition, i.e., of skills needed for work. However, its contribution is very high in the development of situational skills when compared to that of interpersonal or personal skills. The influence of family is more marked in personal skill development than in situational and interpersonal skills. The influence of school is evident more in the case of personal skill development than in interpersonal and situational skills. The share of higher education institutions in personal skill development is 26 percent as against 20 percent in interpersonal and 14 percent in situational skill development. This shows that the influence of family, school and higher education is relatively stronger in the development of personal skills. Family influence is evident in development of personal skills like taking responsibility, being self-confident and punctuality (and appearance); interpersonal skills like recognition of merit in others, leadership qualities, respect to others and better communication and situational skills like goal setting, learning and empathy. In a New Zealand study (NZME, 2005), the influence of the family in children's achievement at school and elsewhere was documented wherein collaboration between parents and teachers was of critical value. In the UK, family influence on children's sports (Kay, 2004), verbal communication (Buck et al., 2002) and decision making (Mantle et al., 2007) illustrate the critical role of family in early childhood growth. Studies by Peters (2007) and Michael (2004) points out the crucial role of family in the development of young students especially linked to their social and emotional development.

Development of situational skills becomes the major objective of workplace training, mentoring and collaboration, though development of interpersonal and personal skills takes place in the process. Family's influence is evident more in the case of personal and situational skills, while that of school in personal and interpersonal skills mostly. Similar trend is visible in respect of higher education also where its focus has been more on personal and interpersonal skill development than that of situational skills. Workplace is more focused on situational and interpersonal rather than personal skills. This shows that at least one third of the skill endowment of an employee is influenced by external forces, while the work environment accounts for the rest. The contribution of workplace is higher for the senior managers in all the institutions when compared to the junior managers. Hence, it can be concluded that the influence of family, school and higher education is relatively more on the junior managers. Since workplace is the major skill developer, a discussion on the different interventions implemented at the workplace and how they contribute to the skill development of the reference group indicates the relative importance of training and other programmes.

7.5 An assessment of intervention programmes

Many intervention programmes are responsible for soft skill development in the workplace, prominent among them being training, mentoring, experience and experience-based coaching, business meetings, ideastorming sessions and keeping abreast with latest information and technology in the functional areas. Training programmes not only include on-the-job-training being provided by the employer and sponsored external training but also prior training. Where the employees had prior experience before they entered the banks or the oil companies, they have been trained in their previous jobs and where there was continuity between the previous job and the current job, prior training has been beneficial in enabling the new entrants to adapt to the situation. Each senior manager is given the task of mentoring the juniors formally or informally depending upon the team or group to which they belong functionally or spatially. Over years, there is spillover effect of this type of mentoring and in some institutions, there are designated mentors whose function is to see that the new entrants and junior staff are made to realise their functions in the right direction so that they can be accomplished efficiently.

In the corporate world, experience is losing much of its charm in developing technical skills owing to the insistence on fresh graduates of cutting-edge technology; it does have sheen at least in developing the soft skills of employees. Experience counts in making the employee more resilient and persevering and this in turn shapes the employee towards better technicality. Another advantage in this regard is the experience-based coaching which enables their junior staff to learn many of the soft skills which in turn may augment their basic skills. As pointed out in section 3.5.1, ideastorming sessions (including electronic), quality circles, nominal group meetings and demonstration of facilitation capability also enable the employee to learn new ideas and put them into practice for effective development. The ideastorming sessions may be conducted by specialists in specific management tools and in the sessions ideas are generated, modified, reviewed and implemented in the business process.

Table 7.3: Share of intervention programmes in the workplace (in %age) (N=40)

Skill	PT	OJT	SET	PBR	MENT	EXP	IS
Personal	20	16	08	10	24	16	06
Interpersonal	16	16	07	11	23	18	09
Situational	07	18	08	09	19	20	19
Overall	14	17	08	10	22	18	11

Note: PT – prior training; OJT – on-the-job-training; SET – sponsored external training;
     PBR – Publication and business reading; MENT- mentoring; EXP – experience;
     IS- ideastorming

As soon as the new recruit joins the institution, on-the-job-training is given for a specific period but on-the-job-learning process continues forever. Whenever new technologies or procedures or methods are introduced to equip the employees in these fields on-the-job-training is provided. Also, whenever promotions are made or new assignments are conferred, on-the-job-training is implemented. Oman being a technologically developing country, the organisations usually depute their staff to overseas training programmes besides deputing them to strategic training programmes conducted within the country and also by outsourcing some of the difficult programmes. Many nationals are sponsored to undergo these external programmes so that their technical skill along with soft skill may improve so as to benefit the organisation.

The share of the soft skill training in overall training programmes (constituting prior, on-the-job and sponsored external training) at the workplace is 38 percent for all the organisations put together. In this, the share of on-the-job-training is 17 percent, closely followed by prior training and distantly by sponsored external training. Prior training has a higher value in development of personal skills, shares equally with on-the-job-training for development of interpersonal skills and plays a minor role in development of situational skills. On-the-job-training has a higher share in Bank A seniors, Bank B juniors and Oil B seniors; it has a higher marginal contribution in Bank A juniors and Bank B seniors and Oil B juniors. In Oil A juniors and Oil A seniors training has a higher share. Overall, on-the-job-training contributes to skill development, though prior training is equally, though not more important.

Next important intervention is mentoring. Whether junior or senior, the managers would have been mentored or being mentored and even mentoring others. For all the institutions, the average share of mentoring is 22 percent but its share is higher in respect of personal and interpersonal skill

146

development. Like training, the role of mentoring is relatively subdued in the development of situational skills. The contribution of mentoring is very high in all cases of junior managers indicating a greater influence on them. When compared to this, the contribution of experience is very high for the senior managers indicating interplay between these two factors. Experience and experience-based coaching and mentoring augment soft skills (especially situational) that arise distinctly in the workplace.

Keeping abreast with the latest trends in the functional areas results in the reference group browsing through the internet, e-books and business magazines and news and other literature besides, being well-equipped in banking procedures, laws and norms and oil and gas technologies as the case may be. In certain cases some of the faculty group members bring out publications also. The senior managers allot a larger amount of time for information searches as indicated by its higher contribution in their cases.

Ideastorming sessions contribute a major part of skill development. It is in these sessions that situational skills are augmented more than personal or interpersonal skills. From this, it can be concluded that apart from on-the-job-training and experience it is ideastorming sessions and discussion groups which result in situational skill enhancement. This also shows that the reference group has benefited more than the rest of the sample in respect of situational skill enhancement and also in other skills. In one of ideastorming sessions in Bank A, the discussion centred on macro objectives of skill development and their contribution to education. A facilitator introduced Bloom's (1984) taxonomy of education objectives and the group had a lively debate on the application of the model to their situation (as mentioned in section 2.2). The following case illustrates the discussion as to how the group feels about following the typology in improving its performance. This shows that the group is adopting such best practices which are theoretically grounded toward better performance.

Case 7.2

Given the intricacies of training, some of the trainers give due importance to the balanced impact of the programmes so that the participants' post-intervention stage consists of an augmented level of knowledge in the particular field that the participants are able to demonstrate their capabilities in observation, understanding information, predicting consequences, use of concepts, new situations, better organisation and problem solving values based on reasoned argument and verification. Some have acted as facilitators in many courses and have been able to infuse and order proprietorship in the participants. This all started when one of us participated in an international training programme a few years ago in a neighbouring country wherein the participants had an opportunity to learn new theories and concepts and how to apply them in real life situations. As managers in this reputed bank, we feel that any banker has to know not only the basic banking theory but also the ever changing technology of banking and the competence required to deliver the competitive results to the clientele. The analysis of the different goals results in prioritising the objectives and adopting a stage-by-stage process to fulfil the demands of not only the staff members but also other stakeholders (Training manager, Bank A).

7.6 Outcome of the intervention programmes

The information relating to the reference group analysis has been obtained by both questionnaire and interview methods. The narratives as told by the participants have been suitably edited for language and clarity. Because of the different intervention programmes, the reference group has been able to realise soft skill enhancement and thereby increased competency by acquiring such abilities like better authority, punctuality, time management and others. When compared to the overall sample, the reference group has been subject to a higher level of intervention and hence specifying the outcomes of the programmes shows how far this group has been able to augment the soft skills and exhibit competency in various spheres. For example, a score of four out of the maximum score of five would indicate a participation rate of 80 percent but the participation rate has to be assessed cautiously owing to the incidence of small numbers.

Bank A senior group realises the core skills of decision making, motivation, negotiation, enterprise and mentoring much more than others. The participation rate is high in leadership and time management training sessions and the group is able to realise 61 percent (ranging from 50 to 68 percent) of the expected results, which can be termed as partial achievement. Similar is the case with the Bank A junior group which realises 59 percent of the expected results in motivation, leadership, time management and are able to enhance skills in respect of conflict management, enterprise and leadership.

Bank B senior group is able to realise 61 percent (ranging from 56 to 68 percent) of expected results from programmes like leadership, time management and problem solving. This group is able to acquire many value added skills like the other members of the reference group. The Bank B juniors realise 58 percent (ranging from 52 to 62 percent) of the expected results from programmes like self management, customer relationship and communication. Putting hard skills to better use, emotional intelligence, team spirit, efficient resource use and motivation are some of the skills they have been able to realise higher value addition.

The Oil A senior members are able to realise 57 percent of the expected results from programmes like customer relationship, time management, leadership and problem solving. They are able to realise skill development in respect of attracting customers, organisational efficiency, besides being role models and problem solvers. The percentage of Oil A juniors undergoing mentoring related programmes is higher and their able to realise 59 percent of the expected results from this and other intervention programmes. They realise skill augmentation in respect of building customer base, cause and effect analysis, personality development and resource use efficiency.

Oil B senior members have undergone leadership, problem solving and team management programmes and in which they realise 57 percent of expected results by acquiring value added skills in decision making, mentoring, organisational efficiency, speeding up end results and being role models. The Oil B juniors are able to realise 60 percent of the expected results from programmes like time management, motivation, self management, leadership and communication. Enterprise, motivation, self confidence, emotional intelligence and customer care skills are augmented by these members.

In all the above cases, the achievement of the different groups has been partial, indicating that in the next level of soft skill enhancement, the reference group members may aim at 'satisfactory' level of achievement, when they would aim to obtain at least 75 percent of the target competency level. In the case of junior managers, the impact consists of emerging enterprise, empathy and self confidence skills. In Bank B senior managers, the impact of motivation results in creative thinking, enterprise, self-confidence and adaptability, while in junior managers, responsibility, self-confidence, creative thinking and enterprising abilities emerge. In Oil A, goal setting, innovativeness and leadership qualities sequester from motivation in senior managers and in the case of juniors, the result is in learning, goal setting, language and punctuality. In Oil B, motivation results in emergence of authority, creative thinking and goal setting in senior managers and innovativeness, learning and goal setting in junior managers. The regression results in chapter six showed how soft skills imparted through intervention programmes contribute to the overall performance of the individual. For the reference group members, the contribution is much more than in the pre-training group owing to their higher soft skill endowment and abilities in improving their competence. All the skills and innate abilities improve the competency levels and thereby has resulted in personal and company's development.

In respect of decision making, the impact results in motivation in all the cases; diverse capacity in Bank A juniors and Oil A seniors; enterprise in Bank A juniors, Bank B seniors, Oil A seniors and Oil B seniors and juniors; planning in Bank A seniors, Bank B seniors and juniors Oil A seniors and juniors and Oil B juniors; learning in Bank A seniors and Oil A juniors; adaptability in Bank A juniors; analysis in Bank B seniors and Oil B seniors; creative thinking in Bank B seniors and empathy in Oil B seniors.

Leadership skill is associated with mentoring, conflict management, recognition, authority and communication abilities in Bank A seniors, while in juniors authority, conflict and time management are the results. In Bank B, goal setting, time management, mentoring, teamwork and problem solving abilities result in senior managers, while authority, recognition and conflict management capabilities emerge in the case of junior managers. In Oil A, goal setting, time and conflict management and problem solving skills occur in senior managers while authority, planning, responsibility and learning result in the case of junior managers. In Oil B conflict management, diverse capacity, goal setting and teamwork are the major outcomes while goal setting, authority and communication feature in the case of junior managers.

149

Teamwork skill is associated with cooperative spirit, innovativeness, punctuality, recognition, problem-solving and leadership qualities in Bank A seniors and in respect, negotiation, conflict management, communication and leadership in junior managers. In Bank B, teamwork resulted in creative thinking, decision making, motivation, negotiation and mentoring while in junior managers the emerging skills were problem solving, punctuality, recognition, reliance and respecting others. In Oil A, negotiation, conflict management, communication, innovativeness and mentoring in the case of senior managers and cooperative spirit, decision making, analysis, enterprise, effectiveness in the case junior managers were the outcomes. In Oil B, self confidence, time management, negotiation, reliance, leadership and mentoring in senior managers and cooperative spirit, reliance, negotiation and time management in junior managers was the offshoot of teamwork.

Adaptability, innovativeness and enterprising skills resulted from communication skill in Bank A seniors, while in juniors, language and adaptability were the major outcomes. In Bank B, learning, motivation and problem solving skills in seniors and self confidence, self management and language abilities in juniors were the outcomes. In Oil A, language, self confidence, empathy and problem solving in seniors and motivation, decision making and effectiveness in juniors were the outcomes. In Oil B, language, adaptability and innovativeness in seniors and self confidence, language and leadership qualities in juniors were the outcome.

Innovativeness, self management and analysis resulted from higher learning capability in seniors, while enterprise, adaptability and problem solving skills emerged in the juniors in Bank A. In Bank B, self confidence, self management, analysis and creative thinking were the outcomes in seniors while enterprise, innovativeness and self management emerge in respect of juniors. Language, adaptability and innovativeness in seniors and time management, innovativeness and adaptability in juniors in Oil A and enterprise, self confidence, self management and analysis skills in seniors and innovativeness, enterprise and self management skills in juniors in Oil B indicated the diversified nature of the impact of different soft skills.

When the reference group performance was compared with that of the pre-training group, the change in the outcomes of different skills mentioned above was rated medium (by data triangulation) in Bank A and Bank B seniors and Oil B juniors in respect of motivational skill. In the rest, the rate of change was low and in Bank B juniors, it was negative indicating very little difference between the reference and pre-training groups in motivation.

In decision making, all the groups (except in Bank B juniors where the rate of change is high and in Oil A seniors where it is low) had medium rate of change and this is repeated in leadership also in Bank A seniors and juniors and Bank B seniors. Bank B juniors and Oil A seniors and juniors and Oil B juniors had a high rate of change while Oil B seniors had a low rate of change.

150

The performance in teamwork was at a lower level in Oil A seniors and Oil B seniors and juniors, while Bank A juniors and Bank B seniors and juniors and Oil A juniors had a medium rate of change. In communication, Bank B juniors and Oil B seniors had a medium rate of change while Oil A juniors had a high rate of change. In all other cases, it was low rate of change. In learning, Bank B seniors and juniors and Oil B seniors registered a high rate of change while Bank A seniors, Oil A seniors and juniors and Oil B juniors had a medium rate of change, Bank A juniors having a low rate of change.

When compared to the pre-training group, the reference group registered zero to 80 percent improvement in various skill endowments. Bank B juniors and Oil B juniors in motivation, Bank A seniors and juniors and Bank B juniors in decision making, Bank A juniors in leadership, Bank B juniors and Bank A juniors in teamwork, Bank B juniors in communication and Oil A juniors, Bank B seniors and Bank A seniors in learning have a higher rate of improvement when compared to the pre-training group. The improvement is very small in Bank B seniors in respect of motivation, Oil A seniors in respect of decision making in many groups in leadership, the oil companies in teamwork, in most of the groups in communication and in Oil B juniors in respect of learning have low improvement levels. In all others the improvement is moderate.

The reference groups fare better than the pre-training groups in almost all the skills and acquiring sub-skills through them, they are yet to realise the maximum scores ranging from 14 (Bank A seniors in motivation) to 54 (Oil B juniors in learning). If we benchmark the improvement, where maximum could be a score of 5 (100 percent), the overall expected performance in decision making and learning is better than in other skills. The performance of Bank A seniors and Bank B juniors in motivation, Bank seniors and Oil A seniors in leadership had low levels of improvement. However, this type of evaluation has its own limitations because of the fact that for the individual employee, even a one percentage improvement would be satisfactory. On the whole, the analysis showed that the reference group excelled in all the skills when compared to the pre-training group and that is the point.

7.7 The impact of the reference group

The reference group stands apart from the pre-training group in better work accomplishment because of its acquisition of high scoring soft skills through exposure to intervention programmes. This section showcases a few narratives pertaining to skill development approaches of the different reference groups. The section presents the views of the in-depth respondents on the role of select soft skills and situational aspects that have been found to have strategic importance in organisational development. When the contribution of the reference group to own and company's development is measured in the 1-5 scale as mentioned in section 4.6, the scores in respect of critical 14 of the 31 soft skills and three hard skills (qualification, acquired qualification and training) are transformed into percentages. The senior manager reference groups scored more than the juniors and between the institutions, Bank A scored better than Bank B and Oil A scores better than Oil B. In all the cases, qualification followed by training and other skills contributed most to one's own and company's development. Between own and company's development, however, there was very little difference in the groups, indicating that the reference group felt that one's own development was synonymous with company's development.

In Bank A seniors, qualification, training, leadership, motivation, planning, communication and team spirit were the major contributors to one's own development while qualification, training, planning, leadership and problem solving contributed most to company's development. In respect of juniors, training, qualification and communication were the major contributors to own development while qualification, training and communication contributed to company development.

In Bank B, the contribution of qualification was at a higher level and along with training, motivation and leadership, it contributed to own development while in the case of company development, the major variables were qualification, training, leadership and motivation. In Oil A, the contribution of qualification was still higher followed by training and planning in both own and company development. In Oil B also a similar trend was noticeable and planning and enterprising skills assumed importance in the juniors.

Acquired qualification is relevant only in few cases and negotiation along with time management had low contributory value in many cases. The analysis showed that though the managers were assessed in respect of many soft skills, only a few of them really mattered. On those skills which the reference group felt as important, the next section discusses their relevance and crucial roles.

The reference groups understand the training needs in a better way which enabled them to develop soft skills more than others, as evidenced by Beryl (2001). The need analysis prompts the reference group to obtain necessary information on skill development which is then put into practice. von Seggern et al. (2003) point out the importance of gathering information in skill development. In the one-to-one in-depth analysis, pre and post group briefings indicate the nature of skill development the group has made because of interventions (Thomas, 2002). This is similar to our analysis of pre and post-intervention scenarios.

7.7.1 Problem solving skills

An employee possessing problem solving skill recognises crucial problems to be solved and is able to generate new ideas and devices and implements plan of action. For this, the employee has to observe and record information accurately and define the problem and articulate it. The information gaps have to be identified along with the constraints and limitations. Once this is done, the employee will be able to create, test and modify solutions as required for implementation. Generalisation can be made through training in new situations by documenting systematic decision making processes using techniques like ideastorming, probing and analysis. The impact of the solutions and resources has to be identified and evaluated as to their accuracy, relevance and importance. In Bank A, four senior and three junior respondents felt this skill was very crucial while in Bank B; the number was three each in the two groups. In the oil companies, it was three senior and two junior respondents respectively. The following narrative in Oil B explains how coaching is intended to sustain good results in problem solving and other issues.

Case 7.3

When we were coaching, the participant reviewed the results by himself or herself with the supervisor and with the in-house coach or external consultant. In this case, the feedback meeting provided the quantitative and qualitative results along with a discussion of future plans so as to sustain good results and increase the scores in the specified skills. The results of the feedback were used to focus on problem solving, leadership or decision making analysis as the case may be. We have suggested that this system apart from being used as a coaching tool can be used as a factor in determining incentives and promotions. The participants who were identified as better leaders or decision makers were given incentives commensurate with performance. However, care has to be taken so that the seniors do not suggest to the juniors that they will give good ratings and peers do not agree to give each other good ratings (Senior manager, Oil B).

7.7.2 Communication and negotiation skills

The following case exemplifies the development of negotiation and communication skills, besides exploring the relevance of soft skills simulation. Simulated training through images, 360 degree performance reviews, self assessing SWOT analysis play crucial roles in soft skill development and work performance.

Case 7.4

Through interactions with employees and managers and deliberating on aspects like empowerment and participative management, the bank has instituted reward system and 360-degree performance appraisals which enable de-bureaucratisation. In the negotiation process, managers undergo a personal transformation on a large scale. The course starts with a video-taped presentation by individuals and the participants are encouraged to take part in group simulations and giving feedback to others. Each participant addresses the audience for about two minutes picking up exactly where the previous speaker left off. There is no preparation for this exercise and the participants must think instantly and critique their performance in writing. Before there was videotape, somebody would say 'you were scratching your nose' and they would deny it. Now they see themselves scratching their nose and write a memo about it. The denial problem disappears. This is the first stage in negotiation- accepting the truth as it is.

We encourage the participants to self-assess their performance through a SWOT analysis wherein hiding their strengths, they can focus on their weaknesses so as to convert them into opportunities through active involvement in various intervention programmes. YX, a team member was not that communicative in the negotiation table. We showed him a video clip of about 25-minute duration wherein in six successive stages; a worker is able to prepare his presentation successfully. The participant at first expressed his reservation in mastering the technique in one session but we let him go in his way and in about 15 days time, he was back at the table. This time his performance in the team was far better than in the past and we wondered what could have made him this drastic change.

He narrated how he got help from another senior colleague and how he practised the presentation till he achieved the goal. Now-a-days he rather makes impromptu presentations to the satisfaction of all the team members. This is the type of change we expect from the participants in whichever field they are trained or coached. YX opined that a good coach understands the developmental needs of the less experienced colleague and strengthens his achievement quotient. In this way, the junior member is able to acquire such of those skills which himself can transfer into his junior colleagues in the course of time. Coaching plays a very important role in persuasive presentation and communication, besides negotiation (Senior manager, Bank B).

7.7.3 Interpersonal skill

An employee possessing oral skill receives, attends to, interprets and responds to verbal and non-verbal messages and other cues, besides organising ideas and communicating orally. To excel in this, one has to ask questions to find meaning and use active listening techniques and summarising conversations. Oral instructions have to be given one-to-one and use of telephone, email etc., and has to be for exchange of information in a courteous and efficient manner. The job description has to be explained and an issue has to be reasoned or argued very clearly and tactfully. Participation in tele and video conferences, organisation of meetings, formalising speech, impromptu presentations and use of conversation strategies, effective voice mail communication and use of modern languages to communicate are some of the steps taken to improve the skill performance of the employees of the sample institutions recently. Further, reading skill, visual literary skills, mathematical skill and IT skill are related to effective communication and presentation. In certain circumstances, development of software packages and troubleshooting equipments has been witnessed. In the banks and the oil companies three each of junior and senior managers regard communication skill as very crucial.

Interpersonal skill enables an employee to work with others effectively. To achieve this, the employee has to work within the culture of the institution following the standard practises of appearance and hygiene. Rapport with other employees has to be developed with appropriate feedback and responses have to be made effectively by using general sense and empathy. An appropriate level of confidence has to be demonstrated to create a mutually beneficial work climate. The attitude toward personal change has to be open-minded to enable resolution of conflicts that may arise because of varying assumptions and traditions. Interpersonal skills also require working well with employees from diverse backgrounds by respecting individual preferences.

The following narrative illustrates the crucial role of listening and empathy in respect of interpersonal relationships and how the reference group in Oil A intends to motivate the employees through an approach consisting of empathy, self effectiveness and motivation. The case can also fit in appropriately in respect of communication skill.

154

Case 7.5

Our group does not like to use the term soft skills because we feel that it diminishes their importance. It is essential that every employee in the oil company possesses these skills and the first one that we typically think of as important is communication, followed by listening. However, we find that there are no courses to help an employee to become a good listener. Good listening capacity requires empathy which enables the team members to understand each other and then extend the empathy towards others. We have come across cases where employees who are held back in their professions lose confidence, leading to a diminished feeling of self-worth at work. With clear vision and awareness of what to achieve, an employee when he listens and communicates properly, can achieve better leadership qualities also. As an informal group, our members in one way or other have been instrumental in effecting a change-over in the attitudes of other members of our division. In the past year, we have been able to motivate and change the attitude of more than 14 employees in this way (Senior manager, Oil A).

7.7.4 Leadership and teamwork skills

Active and productive participation is required for establishing cooperative working relationships with the team members. Constructive feedback has to be solicited and responded with win-win strategies. Goals and priorities have to be set and the schedules followed so as to resolve conflicts and build consensus besides, positively reinforcing the contribution of others. A motivational climate has to be created and leadership provided to the team when appropriate. Coaching and mentoring the team members and others, fair treatment of subordinate staff and evaluating personal and organisational characteristics so as to accomplish the set goals turn out to be significant leadership qualities cherished by most of the in-depth respondents.

As a case in point to substantiate the leadership skill of the reference group in Bank A, the following narrative illustrates how the bank has been able to introduce a new product like mobile banking and how it has been able to successfully implement it owing to the leadership and innovative team spirit of some of its employees.

Case 7.6

Recently, our bank celebrated the launching of a new value added service (m-banking) and an international certification for implementing information security, management systems on par with global standards. The new service will allow the bank customers to access their bank accounts and conduct banking transactions and enquiries using their mobile phones. We have opened separate m-retail banking for this purpose. By this service, our customers have a flexibility to receive alerts as and when the selected transaction takes place or requests for alerts whenever they want by sending an SMS in the specified format, the alerts may be push or pull, wherein in the case of push alert facility, the bank sends the messages to customers with they asking for, in the event of transaction taking place. In the case of pull facility, customers can perform query-based transactions from their mobile phones and view their account information and carry out transaction by sending text messages, the response of which will be received by the customers on their mobile phone screen from the bank within a short period of time. Because of m-banking, the importance of security assumes great significance. Our group is fully prepared to tackle any problems that may arise in this context and we realise that empathy is a major component of our relationship with the customers who are anxious to protect their mobile accounts from hackers and the like (Senior manager, Bank A).

7.7.5 Personal management skill

An employee adept in this skill displays adaptability, sociability, resource management and qualities of personal ethics in taking responsibility for one's own actions and decisions. Honesty and integrity are demonstrated, goals and priorities are set in work and personal life and time, money and other resources are planned and managed in such a way as to achieve the set goals. Most of the respondents felt that employees having the skill were able to promote and market his or her talents and skills and adapt to new situations by updating knowledge. Setting performance standards and working to satisfy the expectations of the clientele, the employee ably handles any tense situation by demonstrating initiative, motivation, energy and persistence to get the job done. Further, the employee is able to understand how social, organisational and global issues are interrelated with personal and local concerns and assess one's skills and attitudes in relation to organisational and global standards. Behavioural skills like punctuality, entrepreneurship and self management have been rated as important in three bank senior and junior managers, two oil senior managers and one oil junior manager respectively.

In performance evaluation, the banks have been practising different procedures, one such being 360-degree (multi-rater) review as in cases three and six. The reference group of Bank A is quite familiar with the system and feels that any intervention programme has to be reviewed as to its impact on the employees and also on the organisation and in this regard, the 360-degree review will enable assessment of not only the contribution of different soft skills development emanating from the programmes but also in motivating the employees toward higher contribution to their own and company development.

Case 7.7

Our company follows 360-degree evaluation which relies on multiple sources providing a more balanced and objective approach to measure performance. This type of approach results in higher levels of productivity besides better customer service and enhanced organisational performance. We understand that in many large corporations like Coca-Cola, bulk of the employees prefer appraisals that include both co-workers and supervisors. We identify a few high priority training or coaching goals and obtain feedback about the perceived strengths and development areas of the participants. Sometimes a confidential profile is prepared and goals are set for each individual participant and are shared with the group. This effectively creates interlocking accountability. This type of coaching provides an opportunity to the team to align soft skills to improve rapport, communication and teamwork. Feedback from only the supervisor enables the target to act on limited information whereas in 360-degree feedback, the targets gain a more complete picture of performance (Senior manager, Oil B).

7.7.6 Accomplishment of work

Though most of the managers seem to have accomplished their work within the prescribed time limits, when cross-checked, this was found to have some inconsistencies. What one thinks within the prescribed time limit sometimes becomes overstretched in the view of the management. Hence, what really matters is how effective is the work accomplishment given the time limitation. This calls for time management skills involving prioritisation among different tasks in and out of the institution and also how the prioritisation is changed to reflect an individual's personal development. Mr Y, a senior manager in Bank B was assigned to complete a project on modifying particular banking software to meet the needs of institutional customers in the area of corporate finance.

Case 7.8

Once the package was developed and used, it would reduce the risks involved in online financial dealings by the institutions. I had three months time and was working with a team consisting of both local and external experts on the package and was also deputed for a training programme in a neighbouring country for about 18 days. The time limit of three months being over, the management was anxious for the new package. However, I was only midway through the process and it seemed that another two to three months might be required for the package to be completed. At this juncture, I contacted an IT expert in a multinational bank and got the solution in a matter of few hours. The next week the package was ready for trial running. The project was completed two months in advance (Senior manager, Bank B).

How do we judge the work accomplishment skill of Y in this particular case? This can be explained either through structural or conceptual approaches. Given the type of technical expertise in local banks, the best policy would have been to outsource the development of software to a software company elsewhere. But the management had a different view. Having witnessed the IT skills of Y and his claim that he can develop any banking software package needed in the region prompted the management to given him a try. They assigned the work to him with the condition that he can seek assistance from others. The main reason for this in-house development was to protect valuable information which the management thought as not communicable to others. At the end, the work which could not be completed in more than three months was finalised in about three hours. This instance showcases the importance of proper identification of the problem and taking necessary urgent assistance in its solution, otherwise several man-days are lost along with additional cost expended on time and resources. Also, it might be possible that Y has had some learning over three months.

Three senior oil respondents felt that work accomplishment should mean no duplication and only introduction of value added products and services. If a particular product has no value addition to it, it has to be discarded. Hence, before a project for introduction of new products or services is initiated, time management demands that the project is conceived in its proper perspective and implemented from the viewpoint of the stakeholders. It may be common to come across wastages and non-value additions, but the same can be overcome by supplementing hard skills training like total quality management (George and Weimerskirch, 2007) and six sigma, indicating practically no mistake situation (Yang and El-Haik, 2003). Effective project management requires leadership and problem solving skills. Organisations require excellence in management and very well motivated employees to ensure excellence in implementation. Further, there is the need to evaluate the skills and their impact on organisational performance and customer requirements. These improvements could be from employee suggestions and better team management which are included in the above quality improving techniques (Brey, 2001).

A reference group member narrated an instance of a new entrant and how his managing the case turned out to be highly satisfactory. For any new entrant, orientation and adaptation to the existing work schedule of the institution becomes a challenging one. For those with zeal experience, it is a question of adaptation whereas it will be more of orientation for the new recruits. In many instances, the reference group members opined that the initial relationship with co-workers and supervisors had a long-term standing. In the induction stage, the orientation training programme helped the new recruits in a great way and by the time the programme is over, they were able to feel as members of the organisation like other workers.

If a new recruit already knows a person in the institution, that person acts as an introducer and even as a facilitator for the incorporation of the new recruit into the system. In the absence of that, the new recruit has to seek the help of his supervisor or his immediate neighbour for the socialisation process. Coffee and lunch breaks are as important as working hours because during this time the acclimatisation process takes place. Once the foundation for interpersonal relations is laid with the facilitation of the reference members, the new workers are able to fortify this relationship which over the course of time develops into an effective team. However, three to four managers in each group were not new to the job when they joined the present banks. The business coaching classes by the reference groups gave an opportunity for the recruits to interact with their co-workers and seniors not only in respect of banking or oil matters but also regarding the augmentation of their soft skills as is illustrated by the following example.

Case 7.9

When Z joined as a junior engineer in Oil A, he was just 22 fresh from a foreign university and much less conversant with local marketing practices. He reported to the head of marketing department who immediately convened a staff meeting to introduce the new engineer to others. The recruit was asked to say a few words to the gathering. Z stood up, glanced at the other members looked at the roof and for a couple of minutes was wondering how he would sweep the floor. Some murmurings started and suddenly with flowery English he thanked the company and the co-workers for the opportunity to work with them and learn many things. This later part of the speech was enough to convince the audience that here he was a man to reckon with. Z went on to highlight the importance of resilience especially when oil prices were on the rise. The company was to be on the vigil since oil was a risky venture and its price may collapse anytime. In his initial presentation itself, Z had demonstrated his interpersonal skills along with that of resilience which impressed his co-workers very much that he did not have any hard time with any of them after that (Senior engineer, Oil A).

7.8 Development of soft skills

The above analysis has shown that the reference group has been engaged in development of some specific skills, besides overall skill development. Since skills refer to competencies and abilities to develop particular learning methods and acquire specific soft skills, a competent manager has to operate effectively in both technical and soft skill domains. Learning becomes an organisational initiative and a collaborative venture. The managers have to share knowledge and other learning capabilities with others and arrive at a consensus of performance appraisals. This section purports to discuss the effectiveness of leadership qualities, criticality of soft skills in the learning process and challenges faced in the development of soft skills. When there is a mention of personal abilities, it may be that the end result of that is to become an executive. Acquiring specific skills would make that position effective and performing specific tasks would make the institution also effective.

An example of how decisional, conceptual, relational and ethical competencies of soft skill endowment can develop an institution is illustrated by the example of Reynolds and Reynolds of Dayton, Ohio (Business Wire, 2001). In the early 1990's, the company was a supplier of paper forms and promotional products to the automotive industry mostly to dealerships and independent auto shops. When Dave Holmes took over as Chairman and CEO, he boldly declared to take the company's sales from $600 million a year to over one billion dollars by 2000. Holmes leveraged the company's present position while reflectively theorising the impact of his actions. The result was a calculated decision that went through an iterative and transparent process of action and evaluation by both management and the workforce. What Holmes created was an environment that fostered workplace learning to acquire new skills and increase the productivity level. In this, Kolb's learning model has been the contributor to Holmes's success. Kolb (1984) advocates a learning style model that depicts a cycle of action, reflection, theorising and experimentation. All these appeared evident in Holmes's corporate strategy. Holmes first instituted action to transform the company from a mere paper forms supplier for the auto industry into a solution and information partner of its clients. He then taught the workforce to think introspectively and become possibility thinkers. Holmes further theorised that by leveraging the company's strong corporate features he can offer business know-how to help clients run their enterprises better. He created a sense of pragmatism by integrating organisational and personal development aspects by combining performance parameters with rewards and individual goal setting aligned with corporate vision planning. Holmes did all these while adhering to humane and ethical standards that for years endeared the company to its workers. The process involved development of specific soft skills like creative thinking and emotional intelligence. Such case studies are usually used by the training managers to stimulate the learning process of the employees, especially the reference group members on whom the burden of organisational development rests.

Adhering to ethical standards requires confiding oneself to others especially in strategic issues so that it does not result in one becoming an informant to the management. In such circumstances, conflicts do result and the same have to be resolved amicably and ethically. This is true in the case of divulging critical information of bank customers to others. Once in Bank B, a conflict management case occurred involving a junior manager's specific suggestion on his promotion (which can be useful in any promotion) with the condition that his identity was not to be revealed to other employees. Since it was just one employee's suggestion and pertained to a single incident, it was argued as to whether it should be considered at all. If it were to be ignored, would it not amount to ignoring a valuable suggestion? Or, if the incident were to be reported vaguely to protect the identity of the manager, what if it becomes unclear and not helpful? Finally, it was decided to report the issue with the consultation of the junior manager in which case it was included as general guideline in conflicts involving promotions. It was suggested that the employees are to be careful not to say anything derogatory which might reveal their identity especially at times of performance evaluation.

Training, mentoring, ideastorming and keeping one up-to-date with theory and practice in one's field have the common characteristic of improving the competency levels of the participants. The interaction processes in all these intervention sessions enable them to learn more from others and learn better outside one's own domain. Further, these interventions improve the perceptions of the trainees to such an extent as to broaden their horizon of understanding and conceptualising things. Experience plays an important role in synthesising the different intervention programmes to standard Kolbian learning styles. For example, in any intervention programme, based on the absorption of knowledge, the participants may be grouped into the following types. In learning a particular programme, the activists jump in and do it, whereas the reflectors think about what they first performed that assignment. As regards mentoring or coaching, the activists use their soft skills with what they have learned to achieve their coaching styles. The reflectors on the other hand observe how other managers coach. Theorists read through different manuals to get a clear grasp on what was performed. They try to find out the pros and cons of different coaching methods in the process. Finally, the pragmatists use the help of trainers to get some insights into the affair. They prefer to have a coach to guide them in coaching someone else. The reference group envelops all of these types of learners. The members of these groups grow and develop owing to integrating the knowledge with the existing social process. They treat concrete experience and abstract conceptualisation to acquire experiential learning capability while making use of reflective observation and active experimentation to transform that learning. In this, they integrate knowledge obtained through the above intervention programmes into the work culture and reinforce their competencies.

In cases where conflict management has to be sorted out, such as dealing with a talkative manager, one way is to ideastorm the talkative manager such questions which he may not venture to answer or to point out the time which has been wasted in mere talking. Since the major focus of soft skill enhancement is to initiate new work patterns and better job satisfaction. The various benefits accruing thereon have to be emphasised so that the supervisor or the colleague understand the significance and change their attitude. In other circumstances where, the supervisor or colleague will be indifferent or rude, the same strategy has to be worked out. If a widespread skill deficiency is observed, the ongoing intervention programmes have to be aligned to skills audit. As the purpose of the intervention is to impact on end behaviour, an audit has to be accomplished as to what behavioural changes are required in different skill groups and accordingly the training or coaching sessions have to be conducted. An essential aspect of this skill audit is 360-degree review.

To cite an example: There was one Mr XX who very recently started to spend lot of time taking personal calls and chatting with customers and others about non-work subjects. He had a good performance rating but now the situation had to be handled in such a way that it did not affect the productivity of the organisation. The supervisor met other staff members to get specifics on the effect XX's talkative behaviour was having on the office needs. XX was reminded that he was a valuable team member and what were his expectations and why he should balance his personal and work time so that he is not a nuisance to others. He was impressed about the trade-off between chatting and work time and the importance of productivity of the organisation. It took several days for the micro manager (manager who specialises in supervising those committing mistakes and who never exhibit leadership qualities) to coach XX to see the pitfalls of talkativeness and finally XX realised his mistake and now he behaves diligently as though nothing had happened. To be a micro manager, it demands great effort on the part of the supervisor or colleague to understand and change the behaviour of the employee quite similar to parenting.

The following paragraphs deal with the means of soft skill development in the reference groups. Reference group members in banks feel that as students, they had the opportunity of having business interaction through vocational and cooperative classes during their school and college education. Besides, they were taught about career and interest exploration. They were informed and in certain cases counselled as to the importance of "what you are doing now will pay off later and if you get behind, you probably will not catch up to stay in your career". In their college days, basic skills and work place skills necessary for careers were discussed and in some curriculum, incorporated. Skills like stressing the importance of deadlines, communication, study skills and ethics were taught until they understood the implications. Study guidance was given in three cases to prepare them to pursue their interests. Business exposure was through mentoring site visits, guest lectures, information fairs, employer seminars and through exposure to literature. In many cases there were student internships, which enabled them to understand the reality of workplaces.

Summer camps to explore career fields of interest, career days, field trips and guest speakers from business motivated them to choose the career interests.

Actual instruction in the classroom, according to the reference group has to be related to employment. However, they feel that over emphasis to employment will kill the instinct for lifelong learning and hence balance has to be struck. Instead of memorising, hands-on contextual learning was encouraged and the situations have to consider what they learn and what they expect to become and how it relates to problem solving for everyday life. Whenever students are involved in these deliberations, as in their case, an amicable situation is created for informal guidance and the teachers discuss with the students and their parents about their career options and also studies. The group pointed out that some of them had individual counsellors who were quite helpful in pursuing their studies and also in their career interests. If this practice were followed and vocational training in schools and colleges were tuned to take into account the dual interaction of study and career options, the labour market would become less imperfect.

Home is the place where seeds are sown for the acquisition and promotion of life and social skills and stand reinforced in schools and colleges. Starting from how to distinguish right from wrong to basic ethics and advanced skills, the family plays an important role. The skills learnt in the family and educational institutions have enabled the reference group members to utilise the opportunities in the workplaces to have recourse to interactive learning, portfolio building and effective teamwork. Work ethics, workplace communication and self esteem have been the planks on which the members start their careers, which are followed up with orientation, mentoring and challenging motives.

Given the modalities of work culture, it is for the members to respect their co-workers and strive toward personal management. Personal development involves cultivating positive attitudes and having self-confidence. Leadership and team skills develop the personal skills to be an effective executive. Team approach has been touted as an effective way of interacting among the managers and to solve a problem. Team approach also helps in conflict resolution in a smooth way, the managers feel. The reference members feel that when they realise job satisfaction through effective involvement in the decision making process which leads to organisational development, they are able to achieve a higher level of personal development that has to be viewed more crucial than any monetary benefits.

Logical thinking and problem solving abilities become essential ingredients of the life-long learning process and facing of frequent challenges becomes unavoidable in some places. For example, in solving a particular problem, the crucial issues under consideration stem from how the problem has to be solved and in what duration of time. It is not that a problem is allowed to creep in and only when its magnitude increases that some action will be initiated to mitigate it. Leadership qualities expect the manager to be proactive in foreseeing future conflicts and problems and avoid them effectively by devising such measures that may capture the essence of competency and entrepreneurship. As a senior manager remarks, *soft skills refer to a particular level of competency and ability to learn and acquire further skills.*

Many managers feel that ICT-enhanced skills improve their professional skill, at the same time to work on specific work situations and solving the problems. An oil reference group member has this to say: *information sifting is so essential in understanding the basics of ICT and conflict resolution.*

Working in small groups is another strategy, the reference group members feel as an effective tool in clearly understanding the problem and espousing collaborative spirit among the workers. Group feedback, loyal team support, conflict resolution and taking responsibility are the qualities which result in further skill development and improvement in performance levels. Any problem solving exercise has to be coordinated with a good presentation skill in selecting the correct design and use of effective media in interacting with the target population. As Bank B junior reference group member put: *the perception of the intervention programmes rests on the belief that along with personal skills, organisational skills of an individual can also develop such that the company feels that the employee is a knowledge asset.*

7.9 Summary indicators

We started with the propositions that different skill groups will have different skill endowments and depending on the skill requirements of the institutions and skill endowment of the employees, their performance can be evaluated. Various intervention programmes have the capacity to enhance the skill endowment through specific training, coaching and mentoring sessions as a result of this, the skill portfolio undergoes a change and when this change is evaluated in its contribution to personal and organisational development, the other hypothesis on the crucial role of human capital can be tested. When compared to the overall average, the reference group has additional endowment of soft skills, the juniors in all the institutions registering a higher growth. When compared to the pre-training group, the juniors have a higher rate of growth. This suggests that though the junior managers originally were endowed with a lower level of soft skill development in relation to the seniors, they have been able to achieve faster rate of enhancement. To this extent, the intervention programmes have been successful in narrowing down the skill gaps between the seniors and juniors. Mention may be made about Bank B juniors, where the level of enhancement has been substantial in all the three soft skills, though in all the groups situational skills register the highest growth rate. If the overall difference between the total sample and pre-training sample is 16 percent for seniors and 24 percent for juniors, there is little difference between the banks and the oil companies. This is indicative of the fact that though there may be differences in skill group, the overall skill endowment of different institutions remains more or less the same. Though total skill endowment may be similar between two institutions, within each there could be many differences and it is up to the institutions to bridge the skill gap to be competitive. The intervention programmes have been able to reinforce this pattern.

When the reference group performance is compared with that of the pre-training group, the differences seem to be somewhat glaring. While the seniors have been able to achieve 27 percent increase in skill endowment when compared to the pre-training group, the junior have been able to achieve an increase of 48 percent. However, the banks have been able to register a growth of 40 percent, whereas in oil companies it is only 35 percent. This suggests that the reference groups in the banks are able to realise a higher level of skill enhancement.

In skill acquisition, family plays a larger role in the development of personal skills and higher education institutions give prominence to personal and interpersonal skills. The workplace places greater emphasis to the development of situational skills across the different groups. In the workplace, training, mentoring and experience assume great importance. The proposition that family contributes to personal skill development and training is the most important skill development mechanism at the workplace is shown by the analysis. The share of prior training (in overall interventions) has been 14 percent for seniors and 15 percent for juniors, while in banks, the share is 14 percent and in oil companies 15 percent, showing the greater emphasis on this variable in the oil companies and especially in the case of junior managers. Since the numbers involved are small, the differences have to be interpreted with caution.

The relative contribution of on-the-job training is 16 percent for the seniors and 17 percent for the juniors while in banks it is 17 percent and in oil companies 15 percent suggesting a greater emphasis in banks and among the junior managers. The share of external training is higher in the case of seniors (10) as compared to six for juniors, while in banks the share is seven percent, the oil companies having a higher share at eight percent indicating a greater emphasis in the latter case. The contribution of publications and business reading is similar (10 percent) for both seniors and juniors. While in the banks, the share stood at 10 percent and in the oil companies nine percent, suggesting a relative readiness of the bank managers in updating their knowledge.

The contribution of mentoring is very high for the juniors (29 percent) when compared to the seniors (16 percent), while in banks it is 22 percent and in oil companies indicating little difference between the institutions. Experience many a time substitutes for learnt skills and its contribution to skill enhancement process is 23 percent for the seniors and 12 percent for the juniors. In banks, its share is 18 percent, while in the oil companies it is slightly higher. The share of ideastorming sessions in skill development has been 11 percent for the seniors and 13 for the juniors, the share in banks being 12 percent and in oil companies 12.2 percent respectively. Taken as a whole, training and mentoring are the major sources of workplace intervention for the juniors, while in seniors they are experience and training. Between the banks and the oil companies, training is more important in the latter while other programmes have similar contribution.

The impact of the training and other intervention programmes have resulted in many skills to be acquired ranging from 16 in Oil B juniors to 24 (of the total number of skills) in Bank A seniors and Oil A seniors and juniors. While all the groups have realised skill enhancement, the rate of improvement when compared to the pre-training group has been 21 and 36 percent in Bank A, 28 and 39 percent in Bank B, 30 and 42 percent in Oil A and 31 and 44 percent in Oil B in seniors and juniors respectively. The overall improvement for juniors is higher at 40 percent as compared to that of seniors (27 percent). The average growth in the oil companies has been higher at 37 percent when compared to the banks (31 percent), suggesting a greater level of impact in the case of junior managers and in the oil companies.

As regards contribution to own and company development, the score of senior managers is greater than that of juniors, the banks performing better than the oil companies. Qualification contributes at higher level in the oil companies, while soft skills have a higher level of contribution in the banks

7.10 Conclusion

Though the overall sample respondents and the members of the reference groups in both the banks and the oil companies view soft skills similarly, their conceptualisation differs owing to own experience, attitudes and the type of intervention undergone. In this regard, the reference group has been better placed to represent the reference among all the participants, given their initial skill endowment and the higher level of acquisition they have made. This is evident when the scores they have achieved show a substantial increase over that of the non-intervention group, but also the general group. Their approach to the different skills is aimed at achievement of professional development and increase in competency levels and ethical attitude.

The senior reference group members have been found to have higher qualifications and experience and have demonstrated differential attitudes from that of others from the beginning. They have been possible to take part in decision making functions in their institutions and influence their junior colleagues in a positive way. Respect for the customers and improving their communication skills for this have been the hallmark of skill accentuation in the oil companies, while teamwork and problem solving capabilities have been judged as crucial in the banks. In a way, the reference group positions itself as a benchmark for other employees to develop their soft skills.

The narratives and cases presented in the chapter spotlight not only the awareness of the respondents about different soft skills, but also knowledge about which soft skill to employ for specific purposes and how this practice has to be imparted to the employees. The lessons learned about the importance and development of soft skills is discussed in the next chapter which also summarises the major findings of chapters five, six and seven and their implications.

Contribution of knowledge and lessons learned
about the importance and development of soft skills

8.1 Introduction

The reference group analysis in the previous chapter showed how soft skill endowment can serve as the benchmark for other employees to acquire the skills in order to achieve not only personal but also institutional development. From the general sample, the reference group has been segregated for detailed study wherein apart from the soft skill scores; sources of their acquisition and the efficacy of different intervention programmes have been assessed. This chapter justifies a case for soft skills and assesses the type of treatment meted out to them by select higher education institutions in Oman. After presenting the major findings of the study, its implications in terms of experiential learning process are explained to showcase the necessity for imparting soft skills through intervention programmes. Section 8.2 presents an empirical account of soft skill presentation in select higher education institutions in Oman. Section 8.3 summarises the major findings of the study. Section 8.4 discusses the development of soft skills in terms of experiential learning, illustrated with narratives. The soft skills which need to be developed at the workplace are assessed in section 8.5, while section 8.6 concludes.

8.2 How higher education institutions in Oman view soft skills?

With universalisation of education owing to globalisation, the impact of education on economic development is immense in many countries in the UN Decade of Education for Sustainable Development. In their struggle to maintain a strong economy and develop good jobs, economies are increasingly turning to higher education institutions for innovative, flexible, and timely assistance. In Oman, over the past ten years, there has been a significant increase in the involvement of these institutions in its economic development. Recently, colleges and universities across the nation have stepped forward to meet the challenge of growing jobs and to develop the workforce. While most colleges began with a mission to serve the community with low-cost, accessible educational programmes, they often found that their mission was tied not only to the academic and educational goals of their students, but also to the health of the economy. Many of the technical colleges, which were founded to help meet the explosion of new technology in the workplace, saw this connection earlier than some of the more broadly structured general colleges. Meeting the needs of the students is one part besides meeting the needs of business and industry.

What policies and programmes can help or hinder a college in becoming more involved in economic development? The answer lies in the development of soft skills that have assumed great importance in recent times. The Transferable Skills Project in the UK (Harkonen, 2008) has found that soft skills score over hard skills in many respects and in order of importance, the following skills do matter in the workplace- oral communication, time management, team work, presentation skills, coping with multiple tasks, managing one's own learning, written communication, planning, ICT skills and decision making.

When Omanisation is the driving force in employment in key sectors, soft skill development becomes focused mainly on improving the skill endowment in different ways. The government has been following a policy of 'education for all' wherein free access to literacy, numeracy, language and social skills is being encouraged (section 2.5). Recently, the basic education system has been introduced aimed at teaching, communication and learning skills, modern technology and traditional school subjects (Goodliffe, 2004). Personal development planning is a learning skill (section 2.6) which is being implemented by some private engineering colleges to enable the students to acquire skills required by the employers. The modules cover areas like nature of higher education, personal development, reflective learning, critical thinking and communication skills, problem solving, case studies of local issues, professional writing, interview preparation, ethics and professional practice, entrepreneurship, leadership skills, emotional intelligence, team building and collaborative skills (Goodliffe, 2004). In this way, the students are motivated and self directed to be responsible learners and competent workers. While undergoing the personal development planning course, the students are assessed periodically especially through peer reviews.

In the traditional curriculum, formal lectures and teaching activities on soft skills were part of the teaching time allocated to various disciplines. In the new curriculum, these activities are much more varied and spread out including role-players from a variety of disciplines. Two forms of ob-servation that contributed to the development of soft skills have been observing teachers (as role models) and observing the interplay between what had been taught formally and what was being practised. In both instances, observation could either reinforce the values that students subscribed to and that had been taught formally or students could distance themselves from particular unprofes-sional behaviours and practices. Soft skills are developed and constructed through interaction with others. With regard to their working environment the situation had been shaped by their interactions with educators, fellow students and others. In addition to learning from role models, interaction with customers was considered the most important way of developing soft skills. Peer discussion is

168

an important means of developing soft skills. Most of the recent curriculum reforms include emphasis on non-cognitive factors such as communication skills and teamwork in the selection process.

On the lines of recommendation of the Dearing Report (National Committee of Inquiry into Higher Education in UK, 1997), UK and other students should be able to monitor, build and reflect upon their personal development. The Spiral Induction Programme (rather than short cramming sessions) is designed to be an integral element in implementing that recommendation. This induction programme introduces students to the Kolb Learning Cycle (as mentioned in section 2.6) establishing through suitable student-centred, individual and group learning activities, notions of self-assessment, action planning and reflection. The aim is to give students the skills necessary for them to begin to take responsibility for their own learning and to enable both staff and students to proactively identify if and what additional support is required.

All the Oman universities and colleges are affiliated to either to UK, USA or other foreign universities and hence have to follow the curriculum of those universities. In addition to those courses where the soft skill component is already included in the original syllabi, local adaptation in the shape of language and communication skills have been incorporated into the teaching and training modules of higher education institutions in the country. This becomes pertinent under the Omanisation policy and given the soft skill endowment of local youth which is not at the level witnessed by students of the affiliated universities.

Higher education has become more of a supply provision and hence it is for the higher education institutions to meet the demands of the labour market on the one hand and Omanisation on the other as per the Seventh Plan document (MONE, 2007). In skill improvement, soft skills (section 3.2) play an important role and upgrading training and vocational education have been the cornerstones of higher education in Oman. The reference to the select higher education institutions revolves on imparting new knowledge through organisation of skill enhancement programmes.

There are four kinds of knowledge according to Lundvall and Johnson (1994). 'Know-what' refers to knowledge about facts and consists of what is called 'information' that is capable of being broken down into bits and communicated as data. 'Know-why' refers to scientific knowledge of principles and is organised in terms of technological change, usually by HEIs like universities. 'Know-how' refers to skills and capability to do something and this knowledge is developed within the individuals. 'Know-who' refers to social and soft skills, involving information about who knows what and who knows how to do what. The sharing of know-how creates social networks and when these networks are formed between different teams and companies, 'know-who' involves information about 'who know-what' and 'who know-how to do what' (OECD, 2000). The process of know-how knowledge development through skill enhancement is discussed in section 8.4. It is

169

the distinction between 'know-what' and 'know-how' that enables the managers to understand that specific skills are required in the learning process so that the required competency levels may be achieved. For example, in order to acquire leadership qualities, an individual has to demonstrate qualities like effective decision making, authority, goal setting and innovativeness. To practise these qualities it is essential then to learn the appropriate skills. Since the institutions have different knowledge bases and different methods to impart skills (through programmes like personal development planning as is discussed below), these skills and abilities are to be learned through training, mentoring and coaching. The knowing of how to do something is a matter of knowing that something is the case and know-how requires theoretical knowledge also (skill theory). Knowing that something is the case requires a prior knowledge of know-how and centres on the relationship between knowing how to do something and having the ability to do it. Acquiring the required ability is necessary for knowing-how, which is demonstrated by the following cases of problem-based learning case studies.

8.2.1 Higher Education Institution 1

This university was established in 1986 and has different colleges offering graduate and postgraduate degrees in engineering, science, commerce and economics, agriculture and marine sciences, education, medicine and health sciences and arts and social science, besides having research centres. Its engineering college has the objective of preparing highly qualified engineers in various specialisations. The engineering curriculum consists of technical English and communication teaching to equip the students with effective speaking and listening skills in languages and to develop generic and people skills so that they could be fitted into the workplace. Also, the syllabus includes such performance enhancement procedures to enable the students to excel in presentation, time management, teamwork, stress management, interview skills and the ability to appreciate the ever-expanding knowledge. Most of the training programmes conducted by the sample institutions (section 5.6) have been conceived by institutions like HEI 1. Some faculty members have argued that competence with explicit knowledge or know-what is no longer sufficient and an element of know-how is necessary which is developed through experience. However, current programmes are poorly equipped to accommodate periods of practice and hence engineering graduates have to be equipped with necessary skills which employers consider essential in knowledge-driven organisations.

The science college of HEI 1 offers many courses and its objective has been to help the students develop their competencies in critical thinking, problem solving and analytical reasoning. There has been a shift from content-oriented to skill-centred approach to science education in the university, wherein the following three conditions have to be fulfilled according to the faculty- what the

170

student is able to do, situation under which the student is able to do it and how well the student is able to do it. This type of learning outcome becomes the guideline for teaching and learning. The teacher is able to select course content, test measurement of learning and evaluation besides periodical reviews. Learning outcomes help the students to be focused on self-assessment and decision making. In all the degree courses, basic language and numeracy skills have been incorporated into the syllabi.

Its commerce and economics college has incorporated in its courses soft skill development; there have been specific courses on business communication which focuses on producing graduates who are adept in critical thinking, public speaking and technical writing. As stated in the college brochure, its mission is to educate, train and continuously develop local youth in providing the labour market with highly qualified business ethic professionals who would be able to contribute to society's development needs. The courses are so organised as to develop the skills, personalities and leadership qualities of the students. A faculty member felt that the course materials intend to enhance the learning and teamwork skills of the students of the college in combating the current crisis of business ethics.

The agricultural college of HEI 1 delivers variety of courses and believes in training the students in action learning, goal orientation and problem solving and to fulfil these objectives, the courses have been so developed as to include the basics of languages and local history besides having emotional intelligence. The other colleges of medicine, education and arts have similar objectives of equipping the students with people skills and social skills in combating the problems faced by the society.

HEI 1 runs special summer internships in many disciplines to enable the students to gain real-world experience. During these specialised treatments, qualities like self-confidence, leadership and motivation are developed through accepting challenges, stretching the limits and achieving success. The summer internship (another type of learning experience) is a flexible course to provide opportunities to the students to link between textbooks with real-life practices, and to develop employability skills in preparation for future employment opportunities. Besides this internship, student counselling is offered to make them psychologically and socially fit candidates. Since HEI 1 charges no fees till the bachelor's degree level (unlike the private colleges), there is stiff competition to enter its colleges wherein the soft skill component assumes importance in selection of the students. Afterwards, the focus on soft skills extends to that of research also. The university is trying to develop a site with an objective of integrating soft skills with life-long and self-directed learning so that the same may be incorporated into the curriculum. It is felt necessary to develop an explicit soft skill policy so that soft skill development is addressed by all the programmes of HEI 1.

Higher Education Institution 2, established in 1996 is affiliated to a UK university and follows the University's model of personal development planning (PDP) at each level of study in the degree and diploma programmes developed on the above lines with the objective of improving the capacity of the students to understand what and how they are learning and to review, plan and take responsibility for their learning. PDP is an example of soft skill development through learning (section 2.6) and is being offered as a 20-credit module out of 120 credits at each level of study (Goodliffe, 2004).

Module 1 of PDP discusses the nature of higher education, personal development planning, reflective practice, critical thinking skills, learning strategies and core communication skills. The students of the college are given in-house entrance test in English, mathematics and science. They are asked to produce their reflective learning experience and the programme provides an opportunity for developing the communication skills of the students. Module 2 introduces theories of learning, organisational behaviour, understanding human personality, research strategies and problem solving skills. The focus is to encourage the students to have awareness of the functioning of the workplace and understanding the organisational culture. Module 3 pertains to study of labour market, networking, case studies of local issues, analysing success and personal goals, professional writing and interview techniques and preparation. The students have to show an understanding of the employment nuances in recruitment and opportunities available for engineers through self-appraisal methods. Module 4 teaches professional ethics, entrepreneurship, leadership skills, emotional intelligence, team building and collaborative skills. Once the students learn, they will be able to work not only as team members but also as leaders by carrying out in-depth review of life skills toward personal development.

The PDP is intended to improve the motivation and maturity of learning among the engineering students of the college and toward this, it advances integration of soft skills in the curriculum. The teachers are introduced to PDP in many subject areas through reflective learning and case studies. However, caution has to be exercised so that the focus on soft skills does not dilute the importance given to the technical aspect of engineering education. In each year of engineering degree, a 'professional and personal development' module is introduced to involve the students in personal development planning, student-centred learning and reflective practice in the core skills. The PDP modules are assessed continually through presentations, workshops, reflective logs, case studies and project work. The outcome results in the ability to reflect, show self-awareness and to plan ahead which otherwise is not possible under normal study conditions. The teachers of the college are unanimous in saying that through PDP, it has been possible to identify oral communication skills, team work and listening as the core soft skills among their students.

8.2.3 Higher Education Institution 3

HEI 3 has been conducting human resource development courses since 1991, later to be followed by MBA and graduate studies. It is affiliated to three UK universities and has the objective of developing students with creative and proactive thinking who are equipped with effective decision making and problem solving skills. The International Foundation Programme which prepares the students for further diplomas and degrees incorporates modules to provide generic and English language skills and also application and integration skills. The programme is intended to equip the students with skills, competencies and communication abilities as suggested in section 2.6. The generic module focuses on the development of essential personal and communication skills, practical numeric skills and information technology skills. The English language module provides a systematic approach to general and academic English. The module which relates to application and integration skill focuses on developing the understanding of the business environment and the factors influencing the businesses through necessary skills on identifying project planning, conducting and presentation. The bachelor's degree programmes have in them the essentials of business and employable skills to make the students fit into the workplaces. The master's outreach programme in business administration focuses on developing critical thinking skills of the managers toward managing better relationships, knowledge and processes. Business communication, presentation, decision making and problem skills are in-built in the syllabus so that the students acquire the sustainable soft skills required for their jobs. A few of the faculty opined that the main drawback of students is the inadequate exposure to soft skills which has to be corrected by suitable teaching and training methods.

8.2.4 Higher Education Institution 4

HEI 4 is the first private college established in 1995, having affiliation with noted UK universities in both bachelor's and master's programmes. A survey carried out in 2006 with 45 major employers of its graduates showed that the core transferable skills and performance have been rated very positively (Anon, 2008) Areas which the college has identified for further enhancement have been leadership skills, creativity and innovation and the ability to manage information effectively from a variety of sources. The college is exploring opportunities to provide free training in the corporate sector to add value to students that enables accelerated career growth and to develop and enhance a career in business and management by developing skills at a professional level, besides developing the ability to apply knowledge and understanding of business and management to complex issues and enhancement of lifelong learning skills and personal development. The student service and placement department sets a time schedule for training college students during the first and second semesters or during the summer vacation. The department maintains good relations with various public and private sector companies and prepares the students in better interview techniques.

The faculties of business, business administration, information technology, marketing and finance all have incorporated English language and personal development, employment and communication skills in their syllabus at the bachelor's level. At the master's business administration level, leadership skills and managing people skills have been incorporated in the curriculum, besides imparting practical counselling in these fields. As a matter of fact, during the recent years when competition among Omani graduates is increasing in the labour market, soft skill syllabus and summer training in core soft skills have been much appreciated by the out-going students as they help them to get good jobs with the skills acquired in the college. The faculty believe that owing to its exemplary performance, the college has been able to obtain international quality standardisation.

What has been the experience of the above institutions, other colleges also seem to nourish in according due importance to the soft skills owing to the background of Omani youth in preparation for the labour market. In addition to soft skill component of curriculum in many disciplines, the institutions have been emphasising human resource development so that the local youth can be globally competitive. Hence, it is found that emphasis on soft skill has been not only to prepare the local youth for the job market but also to make them competitive in the long-run global labour market. The baseline standard they adopt is that which is prescribed by the affiliated universities plus their own adaptations. When we consider the sample institutions and impact of their training programmes, it is evident that the efforts of both the institutions and workplace bear fruits in improving the soft skill endowment of the students and the employees. The training programmes as mentioned in section 5.6 extend those introduced by the above HEIs, suggesting a close link between the HEIs and business establishments in pursuing soft skill development. The achievement of the reference group alludes that the group would have had students recruited from institutions like HEI 2 and those that give special treatment to soft skill development.

8.3 Major findings of the study

The institutional analysis of the fifth chapter outlines soft skill orientation and distinguishes among the different institutions as to the efficacy of various training programmes conducted by them (especially section 5.6). The sixth chapter examines the soft skill endowment (Table 6.3) and development of the entire sample, while the seventh chapter focuses on the reference groups and case studies. The banks have a better soft skill orientation than the oil companies owing to their dealing with public at large whereas the oil companies deal only with the oil distributors. A few banking departments like accounts and audit may not have direct dealing with the public but certainly employees in those divisions would have had interaction with people in some capacity or other. Between the banks or the oil companies, higher levels of capital investment, revenue and employee strength are associated with higher soft skill orientation, wherein Bank A expends a larger proportion of its revenue on soft skill training than Bank B. Oil A expends a larger proportion than Oil B, though oil companies put together require and are endowed with low soft skill levels. Higher employee productivity (Table 5.1) is associated with higher level of soft skill endowment, validating the human capital theory as mentioned in section 2.3.

The number of soft skill training programmes conducted by the institutions is associated with the expenditure and Bank A has the highest number followed by Bank B, Oil A and Oil B in that order. Also, the share of soft skill courses in the total training schedule is positioned in the same order. Customer care, effective communication, team building, business coaching, leadership and situational analysis have been the main programmes in Bank A, where 40 percent of the courses are meant mainly for the senior managers. In Bank B, courses on communication, customer care and team building have been conducted in larger numbers than others, with 44 percent of the courses mainly meant for senior managers. In Oil A, customer care is the main programme, whereas it is leadership training which leads others in Oil B. the proportion of courses meant for senior managers has been 45 percent in Oil A and 42 percent in Oil B. In the oil companies, courses on emotional intelligence and time management and also negotiation have not been conducted during the reference year.

The training policy relates to human resource development, adoption of best practices like e-learning, basic skills, needs analysis and personal development in the banks and human resource development and Omanisation in the oil companies. The coaching and mentoring policy aims at positive interaction and career development in the banks and is rather informal of experience sharing in the oil companies. Lack of demand for certain courses like emotional intelligence and funding for more number of courses in leadership are the main constraints in the banks. Also, there exist externalities like inadequate or lack of information on the opportunities for outside training and undue grabbing of opportunities by some of the trainees leading to dilution of human capital theory especially in Bank B. Because of this, those trainees who do not acquire the necessary know-how invariably get the promotions owing to their attending a large number of training courses, while the deserving managers are denied that owing to their not undergoing the courses. These constraints are visible in the oil companies also informally.

Soft skill recognition is given at the time of recruitment, performance appraisal, promotion, new assignments, interaction with customers and teamwork. The recognition of soft skills is rewarded with extra bonus, more responsibility, external training, increments, consultancy and mentoring opportunities. In all the instances, monitoring and performance appraisal, besides review meetings and market analysis assess the impact of soft skills.

The main objective of soft skill endowment in Bank A has been acquisition of knowledge, competency development and lifelong learning, while it is exposure to international markets, work plan development and lifelong learning in Bank B. In Oil A, the objectives have been integration with new technology and competence development, whereas in Oil B, they are integration with work plan and marketing besides competency development. In all the cases competence relates to acquisition of specialised competence in technical know-how; methodological competence requiring planning and problem solving procedures; social competence requiring individual social skills and interpersonal skills and participatory competence requiring decision making and leadership skills.

The soft skill endowment of those managers who have undergone training programmes during the reference period (50 percent of the sample) increases by 24 percent in Bank A for both senior and junior managers, 25 percent for seniors and 42 percent in juniors in Bank B, 16 percent for seniors and 37 percent for juniors in Oil A and 20 percent for seniors and 29 percent for juniors in Oil B, indicating a slower rate of increase in the scores of senior managers of the oil companies. The base period (pre-training) score positions the senior managers at a higher level than the junior managers (section 6.6). This is indicative of the different skill requirements and endowment between the senior and junior skill categories. Among the institutions, Bank A has higher scores in both the skill groups and among the soft skills, personal skills have higher scores followed by interpersonal and situational skills in all the cases.

Among the different soft skills, the rate of increase has been higher in the case of situational skills especially in junior managers, indicating their higher level of skill adaptation. When compared to the base, the overall scoring (post-training) for the entire sample shows an increase of 43 percent in Bank B juniors, 18 percent in Oil A and B juniors, 16 percent in Bank A juniors, 11 percent in Bank A seniors, eight percent in Bank B and Oil B seniors and four percent in Oil A seniors, indicating a higher rate of increase in the case of juniors (as indicated in Table 6.3). Innovativeness and enterprising skills belonging to personal skills show a larger gap in many skill groups. In interpersonal skills, analysis, creative thinking, decision making, negotiation and conflict management show a larger gap. In situational skills, the skills having a larger gap are goal setting, planning, negotiation, reliance, authority, problem solving and empathy. Punctuality is the main personal skill except in Oil B senior managers where it is positioned at third place; whereas leadership is the main interpersonal skill except in Bank A and Oil B junior managers where it is second. Cooperation is the main situational skill in junior managers, whereas in the case of senior managers, it is authority in all the institutions.

176

Distance travelled analysis (as explained in section 6.5.1) shows induction of lower score respondents before training into higher scores as a result of training, especially in the banks, indicating an improvement in soft outcomes. The soft outcomes in turn result in hard outcomes (better employability), though not in the same order, where the latter are equated with distance travelled to indicate how far the respondents have been able to realise improved performance as a result of skill enhancement. There seems to be no one-to-one relationship between hard and soft outcomes wherein hard outcomes is slightly lower than that of soft outcomes. Distance travelled has been considered in the scale 1-5 in correspondence with realisation of hard outcomes (as in Table 6.5). Distance travelled in Bank A is greater than in Bank B which is greater than in Oil A, which is greater than in Oil B. The junior managers, especially in Bank B and Oil A have been able to realise a higher rate of skill enhancement than the senior managers, the increase in skill endowment being 32 percent higher whereas it is only 21 percent in the case of the senior managers. Senior managers especially in oil companies have been able to travel a shorter distance when compared to those in the banks.

From the above, it is evident that the time gap between pre-training and post-training situations has been one year and the emphasis on soft skill is at a higher level in banks when compared to the oil companies, the emphasis being at a higher level in Bank A when compared to Bank B owing to better motivation and mentoring besides, increased number of training courses. Between the oil companies, Oil A places a greater emphasis on training and development, whereas in Oil B coaching and mentoring are as important as training, where Oil A has a higher number of courses and is slightly ahead of Oil B in soft skill endowment.

The regression analysis of senior and junior managers (discussed in section 6.7) shows that hard skill is still the dominant variable influencing performance, though soft skill has shown an increased level of contribution in the post-training scenario. Senior managers realise a rate of increase in soft skill much more than the rate of decline in hard skill. Junior managers realise an equal rate of increase in soft skill and decline in hard skill contribution, since they have not undergone many training and mentoring programmes. Also they have shorter periods of experience and hence the change in soft skill endowment is not substantial as in the case of senior managers, though the post-training scenario shows augmentation in soft skill in influencing productivity.

The analysis shows that not only the importance of soft skill vis-à-vis hard skills has improved in the post-training scenario and its contribution to performance enhancement is also visible. The increase in soft skill share has been 59 percent in the seniors, but only 24 percent in the case of junior managers. Decline in hard skills share is higher in the seniors (23 percent) when compared to the juniors (13 percent). It is evident that intervention programmes result in a greater distance travelled and a greater level of job satisfaction and organisational development.

177

The influence of family and school is marked in personal skill development and family influence, explained in section 7.4 is evident in development of personal skills like taking responsibility, being self-confident and punctuality. Interpersonal skills like recognition of merit in others, leadership qualities, respect to others and better communication and situational skills like goal setting, learning and empathy have an important role in skill enhancement. Development of situational skills has been the major objective of workplace training, mentoring and collaboration. The workplace is more focused on situational and interpersonal rather than personal skills. This shows that at least one third of the skill endowment of an employee is influenced by external forces, while the work environment accounts for the rest. The contribution of workplace learning is marked in the case of senior managers in all the institutions when compared to the junior managers. Hence, it can be concluded that the influence of family, school and higher education is relatively more on the junior managers.

In the workplace, training is major interaction programme in which the share of on-the-job training has been the highest followed by prior training and sponsored external training explained in section 7.5. The share of on-the-job training is very high in situational skill enhancement. Mentoring, experience, ideastorming sessions and publication and business reading are the other important intervention programmes. While the impact of mentoring is very high in personal and interpersonal skills, that of experience and ideastorming impact mostly situational skills. On-the-job training has a major impact in Bank A and Oil B seniors and Bank B juniors owing to better learning strategies.

Apart from academic qualification, training, leadership, motivation, planning, communication and team spirit are the major contributors to one's own development while qualification, training, planning, leadership and problem solving contribute most to company's development as mentioned in section 7.7. Though the junior managers originally were endowed with a lower level of soft skill development, they have been able to achieve a faster rate of enhancement, enabling narrowing down of the skill gaps between the seniors and juniors. The level of enhancement has been substantial in all the three soft skills in Bank B juniors, though in all the groups situational skills register the highest growth rate. The seniors have been able to achieve 27 percent increase in skill endowment when compared to the pre-training scores, the juniors have been able to achieve an increase of 48 percent. However, the banks have been able to a register a growth of 40 percent, whereas in oil companies it is only 35 percent. This suggests that the reference groups in the banks have been able to realise a higher level of skill enhancement.

8.4 The process of soft skill development

The findings of the study and the performance of HEIs in soft skill development show the necessity of developing crucial soft skills for better employability and performance. This section presents some cases relating to the application of experiential learning (as introduced in section 2.7) in respect of a few reference group members who exhibit special abilities when compared to others as exemplified by the cases narrated by them. The training programmes of the institutions and their impact can be interpreted through experiential learning as discussed by Eraut (2007a). The analysis centres on the following issues.

- senior managers exhibit higher soft skill score when compared to junior faculty, other things remaining equal
- higher education levels when combined with training and experience lead to better results especially in banks
- some skills have been developed faster than others due to experiential learning and
- skill wheel and distance travelled indicators are closely related to experience

8.4.1 Experiential learning

Since all learning experiences are personal and unique, each experience is influenced by the unique past of the learner. A senior trainer in Bank A who is familiar with workplace learning techniques has this story to tell about his experience with the training programmes and the opportunities created by them in the learning process.

> Once we become aware of a stimulus at a conscious or unconscious level, it is interpreted based on previous knowledge, previous experience, emotions, our concept of self, choice and the intensity of the stimulus, location and personal needs. The next stage involves making sense of the stimulus to assess whether it matches our existing mental constructs. If the experience happens as predicted there is no change to our mental schema and we assimilate it. If the experience is different to our expectations we may choose to modify our mental frameworks and accommodate the new information and experience. Alternatively, if the experience is so alien to our expectations and ways of seeing the world, we may reject it as being atypical, biased or incorrect (Senior Trainer, Bank A).

The crux of the problem lies in matching past experience with expectations and making the skill endowment amenable to the absorption of new information and knowledge. To that manager, learning style (Kolb, 1984) describes the attitudes and behaviours which determine an individual's preferred way of learning (Honey and Mumford, 1992). Two managers of similar intelligence and background who underwent a learning opportunity have been affected in different ways, where one becomes enthusiastic while the other is disaffected. The reason for this is that people have particular styles of learning that influence their attitudes and abilities toward learning opportunities. According to Honey and Mumford (1992), people learn in two ways. The first is through teaching and the second is through experience. While learning styles can alter when they change jobs and are therefore not fixed, the preferred learning style of a person assumes importance.

179

Based on learning styles, an attempt has been made wherein the learners can be grouped (following Kolb as mentioned in section 2.6) into activists, reflectors, theorists and pragmatists. Activists prefer to involve themselves in an experience and do so in an open-minded manner with the activity first and then weigh up the implications of their actions later. The narrative in case 6.2 is an example of taking action regarding the starting of e-banking which characterises the Bank B junior manager's learning style and its application. Reflectors gather information and carefully consider it before reaching a conclusion and are thoughtful and cautious, tending to reserve judgement until they are reasonably sure about their conclusions. The narrative in case 7.1 illustrating the augmentation of knowledge in the post-intervention stage showcases that the participants are able to demonstrate their capabilities in observation, understanding information and predicting consequences in new situations. This may be due to reflective learning.

Theorists gather information and attempt to develop a coherent theory about the experience. They are logical and prefer to analyse information and produce an encompassing theory. The experience as a football captain and how a team has to be run enables a junior manger in Bank B to improve his team's performance based on the logic of match playing. Pragmatists prefer to apply theories and techniques to investigate if they work and they are realistic people who seek out improved methods of operating. Taking a pragmatic decision on opening up of a new filling station (case 6.5) illustrates the oil manager's initiative in successfully applying what he had learnt. When we experience an event it is possible to learn from that experience at different times, learning from an event at the time it occurs; learning from the past event when reflecting on it later; learning more about a past event when thinking about it further and reinterpreting the past event differently in the light of further experience (Beard, 2006). This aspect makes experiential learning and skill development as the cornerstone of intervention programmes aimed at personal and institutional development (as mentioned in the regression analysis in Table 6.7). In addition to the narratives mentioned above in justifying the prevalence of experiential learning among the reference group members, a few more cases are presented to characterise the situation more methodically. The following narrative exemplifies understanding versus knowledge as expressed by a senior manager in Oil B:

> We may think about how we respond to what our colleagues might say (cognitive). We may decide that we like or do not like the pressure we are being put under at work (affective). We may physically respond by stepping back on to the pavement when we notice the truck speeding towards us (behavioural). Two people may look at the same object and receive the same stimuli but the sensations may be very different owing to differences caused by education and experience. For example, I am carrying a full mug of coffee. My senses are continually giving me feedback about how close to the brim of the mug the coffee is and thus adjust how quickly I walk, how I control the muscles in my arm and what attention I pay to other people walking nearby. My awareness that the colour of the mug is white represents a very temporary learning experience. I may possess an understanding of what 'white' means and thus respond to the visual stimulus of the mug. Learning relates to what has gone before. New ideas and new experience have to link to previous experience (Senior manager, Oil B).

The manager talks of cognitive, affective and behavioural qualities that are critical in the workplace learning process and certainly, new experience has to link with previous experience. Since educational planning (section 2.3) has the objective of realising not only knowledge-based goals but also skill-based and affective goals (Bloom, 1984), soft skills not only empower the workforce in advancing career development and personal growth, they create new opportunities and go beyond money motivation. The narratives illustrate the essentials of knowledge base that have to be fulfilled where the participants have to learn facts and concepts say about principles of leadership or negotiation as the case may be. Skill base requires that the trainees learn how to lead or negotiate and the affective goal implies that the trainees care about the practices of leadership essential for own and organisational development. Acquisition of soft skills influences the affective goals through changes in values and attitudes and play crucial role in experiential learning. When the skill base and affective goals undergo changes, the workplace will be in a position to register improvements in the quality of human capital stock as opined by a reference group member in Bank A:

> People learn from their mistakes- those who make a mistake once and learn from it so as not to make the mistake again; those who make a mistake once and are so obsessed with it they do not venture to that territory again and those people who continue to make the same mistake over and over again and never learn from previous experiences. The workplace is a learning environment that enhances formal education and foster personal development through meaningful work and career opportunities. It stresses the role of hard skill in lifelong learning and the development of individuals to their full potential (Reference group member, Bank A).

To learn from mistakes is not to repeat them. Regarding too much dependence on expatriate labour in the region, the Seventh Plan document of the Government of Oman (MONE, 2008b) discusses the importance of skill development of local labour in not only replacing expatriate labour but also in becoming self-reliant in skill endowment and competitiveness. Since small and medium enterprises dominate the industrial scene in the country, productivity increase could be realised not only by adoption of new processes, products or market technology but also by improvement in human resource as emphasised by Bank B below:

> Employers focus on soft skill enhancement along with improved technology, product development and market linkage. For this, hard outcomes have to be improved through soft skills. Hence, soft skill development assumes importance in any activity and discipline as the case may be. In other words, soft skills affect knowledge development and innovativeness so crucial for competitive advantage. In so far as soft skills complement hard skills, they cannot be treated in isolation and have to be considered in connection with particular education levels (HR manager, Bank B).

In short, the need of the hour is to develop soft skills not only at the workplace but also at the school and college levels. Development of oral communication, team work and listening skills identified as core skills by UK employers (TMPWR, 1998) may be appropriate for personal development here also. When training is front-loaded with an emphasis on initial education and training, the need arises for upskilling. In this way, education and training are being made more responsive not only to the society but also to the local labour market. The purpose of skill training is to make it more accessible to those who require it and to promote better adaptability and employability, at the same time maintaining employee retention which is essential for continuous skill development. Since the employer represents demand and the employees supply the required skills, whenever skill gaps are noticed, orientation, training and coaching are provided to balance between skill requirement and endowment. Customised and individualised training courses are also offered to suit individual needs and upgrade the skills to international standards. As was pointed out in narrative 7.2, simulated training and e-learning programmes are encouraged especially in the banks to equip the managers in not only basic skills but also in advanced technical and business skills.

The technical and vocational education and training programmes have been integral part of higher institutes of technology in Oman (section 8.2) to meet the skill requirement needs of local labour market. Private training and SANAD, development institutes and the training courses conducted by Shell Oman, Petroleum Development Oman, Khimji Ramdas, Bahwan training and others enable the Omani youth to acquire the required workplace skills and compete in the labour market. All these indicate that the institutions are aware of the importance of soft skills and that the education system has been geared to inculcate the skills required by the workplace. There may be differences in approaches to soft skill development by different institutions depending on not only budget provisions but also on the attitude of the top management in focusing on competitive advantage. While the universities and colleges consider soft skill development in their curriculum and exhibit concern for its propagation, some colleges such as HEI 2 go one step farther in incorporating its development as a special case so that the engineering students would acquire the core skills in the college before they are able to enter into the job market.

As explained by UNESCO (2007), performance to the extent of 60 percent of the target may be termed as a benchmark. In our case, a score of three would indicate that level. Table 8.1 lists the number of soft skills that have high scores (skills where the numerical score is more than three in the 5-point scale) in the sample institutions so as to identify which skills could be considered for development at the HEI level.

Table 8.1: High and low scoring skills in the reference groups (N=40)

Reference Group	No of high score (>3) skills			No of low score (<3) skills		
	Personal	Interpersonal	Situational	Personal	Interpersonal	Situational
Bank A SM	9	8	12	0	2	0
JM	7	3	3	2	7	9
Bank B SM	9	8	10	0	2	2
JM	5	3	2	4	7	10
Oil A SM	6	5	7	3	5	5
JM	6	5	1	3	7	11
Oil B SM	6	5	4	3	5	8
JM	6	3	1	3	7	11

When the number of soft skills (out of total 31) that are mastered by senior and junior managers in the sample institutions and their scores are assessed (as in table 8.1), it can be seen that senior managers in virtue of their long experience are able to realise competency in many soft skills and score high as contrasted to the juniors. We have taken 60 percent of the target score as necessary to establish some competency in any skill and by this norm, the skill deficiency occurs more so for juniors and the oil companies. From the table, age and experience, education level and the nature of the institution turn out to be the variables contributing to high soft skill scores. However, innovativeness and enterprise in personal skills; analysis, creative thinking, recognition, diverse capacity, decision making and conflict management in interpersonal skills and planning, effectiveness and problem solving in situational skills contribute more than experience, since it may be difficult to acquire these skills solely owing to experience. Therefore, the HEIs have to focus on the inculcation of these skills in their teaching and training programmes.

Section 6.3 showed the score differences according to different education levels and intervention scenarios. As the level of education improves, the soft skill scores rise; so also when there is training and mentoring, indicating positive association of education level and intervention with scores. However, experience delivers a higher score in the case of high schoolers when compared to graduates. In Bank B high school scores are higher than graduates scores and also in Oil A indicating the contribution of experience.

Oil companies place a lower emphasis on soft skill development when compared to the banks owing to higher level of technical requirements in them and less direct contact with mass clients. But they need soft skills to work together in addition to skills needed to deal with the clients. For this, they have to conduct training courses to equip their employees in essential skills. The capacity of the employees in the oil companies to absorb the outcomes of the intervention programmes is lower when compared to those of bank employees as seen by the post-training scores especially in the case of senior managers. When the requirement pattern differs, role of soft skills becomes rather subdued in institutions like oil companies. In the case of reference groups also, the scores of oil companies are lower when compared to those of banks.

When the skill difference in the case of junior managers is assessed as pre or post-training, it is lower by six percent in the pre-training and four percent during training period as indicated in section 7.2. Within the banks or the oil companies also the difference seems to be lower. The impact of intervention including that of experience has been greater in the case of senior managers especially in the banks. It appears that the approach to soft skill enhancement is biased toward senior managers in the banks who appear to utilise the intervention facilities to the maximum extent possible when compared to the junior managers.

In respect of improvement in human capital stock index, the bank senior managers realise higher scores in soft skill (31 percent) when compared to hard skills (20 percent), accounting for a higher contribution by experience whereas in the oil companies, the contribution of soft skill to the index has been only 16 percent but 23 percent in the hard skills. The bank junior managers are able to realise 16 percent in the soft but 126 percent in hard skills whereas the scores in the oil companies have been 114 and 121 respectively as per Table 6.8. Though soft skills are important, the analysis shows that hard skills dominate in all the institutions and it is only in Bank A that senior managers realise a higher contribution of soft skill than hard skills.

Soft skill enhancement leads to new learning processes as evidenced by the narratives 6.1 and 6.7 on facilitation; 7.2 on best practices; 7.8 on coaching and 7.3 on assessment. The learning process showcases what the employee thinks is the right principle and observe the results. Klabbers (2000) summarises this as a shift in focus from "learning as acquisition" to "learning by interaction". The employee learns leadership qualities by leading and not by reading about it. Such a learning process involves improvement in competency levels of the employees either as a watcher or doer.

> Learning requires abilities that grasp experience. Some of us perceive new information through experiencing the tangible qualities of the world, relying on our senses and immersing ourselves in concrete reality. We also tend to perceive, grasp and take hold of new information through symbolic representation or abstract conceptualisation of thinking about, analysing or systematically planning, rather than using sensation as a guide. In transforming or processing experience, we tend to watch others who are involved in the experience and reflect on what happens, while others choose to jump right in and start doing things. The watchers favour reflective observation, while the doers favour active experimentation. Each dimension of the learning process presents us with a choice (Training manager, Bank A).

8.4.2 The learning process

General training like communication raises productivity in the company where it is provided, besides having spillover effect to other institutions, specific training like business coaching raises productivity only in the institution where it is provided (Becker, 1993). We find this as evidenced in the sample institutions in establishing positive links between training and productivity (Holzer et al., 1993). Effective workplace learning establishes a direct link between training and productivity as has been reported in a survey of 215 Irish firms by Bartel (1994). Osberg et al. (1986) observe that the impact of training on the individual depended upon the labour market segment of the individual as indicated by soft skill demand. Employees who receive training in soft skills are relatively unlikely to quit their present job as pointed out by Levine (1998). This phenomenon has been explained both in terms of increased job satisfaction as a result of training and by an increased feeling of employee commitment to the employer due to the employer's investment in the employee (*a la* human capital theory). In our study, most of the reference group members in the banks subscribe to this viewpoint. As Gunderson and Riddell (2001) point out, gains are greater for individuals who already have higher skill levels.

The process of learning at the workplace especially by the reference group members is presented from the perspective of the learners. The reference group members feel competence improvement is required to relate theory and practice and use instruments to find out alternative ways to their future professional career (as indicated in case 7.2). It enables them to interpret, to find the main points, to understand, to evaluate, to deal with information, to critically evaluate, to apply theory and practice, to organise information, to understand, to place in context, to develop objectivity, to combine, to formulate, not just reproduce, to apply, to describe, to conclude, to think, to compare, to select and to differentiate and put themselves into the position to achieve this competence. The competence is directly related to the ability to solve problems and see the problem as a starting point to reach a certain level as indicated by the group. The problem may be at the core and all the activities to follow are part of the analysis and synthesis. In this way the capacity for analysis and synthesis is developed through reading and formulating ideas on a concept as a result of the reading, ideastorming and discussing focused work (discussed in section 7.5). Taking challenges reveals links between contemporary concepts quantifying information, applying relevant theory to source material, incorporating new conclusions into existing knowledge and placing specific problems into wider contexts. The members learn to analyse their own personality and their own options as to ask what type of persons they are and what have been their weaknesses and strengths at workplace. Trainees learn to analyse textbooks, media and internet being available for training, coaching and mentoring.

The members feel that different employees have different abilities and these have to be reflected in the learning process in the way in which the competence has to be developed. This may be done through group meetings and discussions. The assessment may be based on how the participants analyse textbooks or information from different sources. The methods of assessment may include discussions, questioning, observation, evidence of personal and professional engagement, supervision of reports and assignments, extending the already existing workplace interventions.

Table 7.3 showed that experience has been a major source of soft skill acquisition and there seems to be a link between training and experiential learning.

Learning process at the workplace involves formal, informal and situational learning opportunities (Watkins and Cervero, 2000). We can relate how some of the reference group members in our study make themselves amenable to such a learning process. Elaborating on section 2.6 to facilitate informal learning, the banks have established a library equipped with professional journals and books. For them, the library is not merely a learning resources centre, but a learning centre *per se*. In Table 7.3, it was shown that business reading contributes to 10 percent of soft skill acquisition. Periodical mentoring by senior managers have helped the juniors in performance planning and personal development. Intentional learning has resulted in effective team functioning purposes like membership roles and decision making. As one member put it:

> Our goal here is to learn from our experience as a group and thereby create the group we want to be. We do this by sharing experiences together and reflecting on the meaning of these experiences for each of us. We use these observations and reflections to create a collective understanding of our group, which serves to guide us in acting to create the kind of group experience that we desire (Reference group member, Bank A).

Apart from informal learning, incidental learning is another process wherein the employees observe their seniors in the process of performing tasks and seek out best practices. Working with new customers and jointly with other employees gives them an opportunity to learn and improve their competence. Formal learning is obtained by attending conferences and workshops, learning through the internet and participating in training programmes. In all these, past experience is responsible in showcasing the learning capacity and competency as illustrated by narratives 6.1, 6.2, 6.7, 7.3 and 7.6. Informal learning takes place due to both experience and learning from others as indicated by a manager in Bank B.

> Interpersonal roles deal with building relationships, working with others or maintaining good working relationships, team leading, inspiring and motivating others, selling ideas, negotiating and building team spirit. Relationship building: establishes trusting relationships with others facilitating communication and cooperation by helping others gain opportunities to grow (Junior manager, Bank B).

Eraut (2004) specifies the increasing awareness to particular soft skills increases the chances for informal learning between the workers. Narratives 5.1, 5.3, 6.4, 7.3 and 7.5 stress how past memories are linked with current experience. The managers reflect on past episodes, events, incidents and experiences and how these help them to solve the current problems. Some of the managers who have already undergone training course have acquired soft skills through informal learning from others.

Discussing the past events with colleagues enables the managers to recount the gains made from such experience and engage in a decision making process and solve problems as in setting up a new

186

filling station. The manager underwent 'implicit learning' along with deliberative learning during the course of training sessions and after and in the workplace due to interaction with others as in case 5.3. The interaction process involves participation in group activities, working alongside others, challenging difficult tasks and working with customers (Eraut, 2004) and through these, the managers are able to learn new knowledge and skills. The learning process depends not only on formal business reading, mentoring and ideastorming (Table 7.3) but also experience. According to that table, experience contributes 18 percent of skill development, next only to training. Its share is higher for situational skills and senior managers, indicating the crucial role of experience in the workplace as illustrated by Kolb's learning cycle.

> To learn from its experience, the bank must have employees a) who can be involved and committed to the bank and its purpose (concrete experience); b) who can engage in reflection and conversation about their experiences (reflective observation); c) who can engage in critical thinking about the bank's performance (abstract conceptualisation) and d) who can make decisions and take action (active experimentation). The employees have to experience, reflect, think and act that is responsive to the learning situation. Institutional development is a process in which the employees recreate themselves by learning from their experience (Senior manager, Bank A).

The above narrative pinpoints the crucial elements of learning cycles and how the bank employees have to experience that. According to a senior manager in a bank, taking responsibility and being committed to the job enable the learning process to fructify in its entirety Self-management assumes centre stage in facing the challenges and to manage critical moments (such as dealing with talkative manager or an irate customer by the reference groups as in section 7.7). Eraut (2007a) explains the growth in professional learning by improving planning, delegation of responsibility, listening to the customers and utilising new learning opportunities. The grouping of skills into personal, interpersonal and situational has been specifically intended to distinguish the characteristics of the learning process not only at the individual level, but also at the organisation and interactive levels. The reference group members feel that workplace learning is more strategic to the competitive advantage of both individuals and employers. A major development in workplace learning is simulation and e-learning (as in case 7.1). The following narrative lists out the different stages in experiential learning relating to a particular reference group, which is similar to Maslow's hierarchy of goals of fulfilling individual goals first, then achieving the collective and institutional goals for their gratification and self esteem.

> In the first stage, members of the group seek to fulfil individual needs. They come together to meet some immediate individual need such as attending a workshop on personal development. There is no sustained effort at gratification. In the second stage, individuals come together for gratification but develop ways to sustain the gratification. When the group decides to attend workshops regularly, this effort to sustain gratification requires individual learning because it involves developing informal strategies and implementing mechanisms to maintain the gratification over time. The third objective is developing a collective goal where the group becomes a team. This stage requires development of more formal strategies and structures to meet the group purpose. Here the members of the group transform from individual learning to group learning. They develop methods of coordination, develop adaptation

mechanisms and respond to changing external demands. In the fourth stage, the group no longer simply adapts to changes in the environment but makes self-directed changes directed by its stated desires. While external constraints are not completely eliminated, the group develops the freedom to set and pursue its own goals. At the fifth level the group can follow multiple goals, create high levels of innovation and manage diverse and conflicting types of issues. Any advance to the next stage may not be automatic and depends on the initiative of the members in conceiving new purposes and acting according to it (Senior manager, Oil A).

New purposes result in new learning processes and the rapidly growing interest in new knowledge as the source of competitive advantage enables an organisation's knowledge to grow in terms of the competency of its employees, their know-how, the processes and the need to capture what employees learn. Some managers feel that employees require benchmarking as a way of finding best learning practices to meet their changing needs. After the employees acquire the requisite knowledge and skills, they assess their workplace learning by rating one's performance and that of the institution. As a reference group member in Bank B put:

> The tasks for learning include getting to know one another and understanding individual member needs and goals and gaining a shared clarity and consensus. Matching between individual goals and institutional goals and developing specific skills enable the members to redefine and refine goals to respond to the business (Reference group member, Bank B).

To sum up the above discussion, the job of learning is to devise innovative ways to help learners find and assemble information and to offer them guidelines to make self-management more effective. Learning from others centre on allocation of work by seniors. In situational learning (Eraut, 2007b), understanding is developed though experience leading to intuitive decision making and deliberations with other employees. Professional learning involves transfer of knowledge into practice such that it is applied to problem solving and to identify which skill is required for which task and so on. Once the required competency is achieved, proper delegation of authority can be made. As explained by Eraut (2007c), learning at workplace involves situational assessment, coaching, mentoring and training to identify the problems arising out of them and solving through effective decision making and team work. Learning and working require blending of education levels, experience and the different intervention programmes.

8.5 Which soft skills have to be developed?

The International Institute of Educational Planning (UNESCO, 2004) has initiated a programme to support skills development strategy in many countries including Oman with a focus on policy analysis planning and capacity building. This strategy is being followed in Oman wherein soft skill development is an integral part of the strategy. The challenges of soft skill development are manifold and involve the following as indicated by the training programmes of the sample bank and oil companies (sections 5.5 and 8.2).

- Adequate capacity building owing to competitive nature of soft skills in leading to productivity enhancement (human capital theory) and changes in value system towards more amiable work and enterprise cultures just fit for purpose.
- Equitable access to all employees so that mismatch between supply of and demand for soft skills is eliminated.
- Diversification of training programmes to meet the changing requirements of knowledge-based economy.
- Building competency levels and lifelong learning rather than mere education qualifications and credentialism.
- Promoting private partnership in establishing soft skills training institutes and other innovative initiatives.
- The necessity of pooling adequate resources, both financial and human for implementing the different intervention programmes in order to define an appropriate national policy on soft skills.
- Development of soft skills in the higher education institutions and the workplace has to be monitored by a soft skill development agency so that the core skills required for recruitment may be standardised at the college level so that the workplace skills may be developed later. However, the students may be initiated in situational skills in a more practical way at the teaching level.

Effective coordination among different training programmes offered by different agencies enables standardisation of practices to be followed in each training course. Specific sectoral and local needs strategies have to be identified to diversify the training programme with active participation by the industry and the workers through appropriate partnership programmes. Over the years, the courses may be subject to accreditation, assessment and certification mechanisms. Since the programmes have to be inclusive of all categories of employees according to their needs, quality assurance will enable international standards to be achieved in which case the institutions can reduce their expenditure on the training programmes by outsourcing to the specialised institutions. UNESCO has envisaged fund allocation of two to five percent of GDP for skill development which will require a substantial expansion and deepening of the programme.

Since soft skill training has the objective of enhancing employability and ability of a person to adapt to changing technologies and labour market demands, opportunities have to be created to acquire the essential skills throughout life especially for new entrants to workforce and promotions. Development of highly skilled workforce becomes essential to meet the growing labour market demands and to be globally competitive which has become the main strategy of higher education. In other words, with proper workplace planning the training programmes in the HEIs and workplaces have to focus on skill mapping, enterprise development, integration of skills in the normal development process. Best practices include incorporation of soft skills in all aspects of curriculum, assigning the employees to teams to work together in completing the tasks and allowing the trainees to act as managers and leaders once in a while so that they can learn how to manage and be managed by managing others. The soft skill development agency to be established at the national level can identify the select colleges and universities where soft skill enhancement modules may be incorporated with the permission of the affiliated universities so that the students are equipped with the necessary job skills.

Insistence on appropriate workplace discipline and emulation of workplace environment in training (simulated trainings) programmes will have to be adopted by the institutions in order to improve the status of soft skills. The trainees have to be provided with opportunities in case studying successful people and also in acquainting with them which will go a long way in improving the effect of simulation.

8.5.1 Specific soft skills

Personal skills enable the employees to be more innovative and enterprising. There seem to be no specific training courses intended to develop these skills. While other personal skills could be developed through family, educational institutions and workplace, this deficient skill seem to have the characteristic of being developed not only in the workplace but also externally as opined by a bank manager.

> Behavioural attributes are required in deciding, taking action, completing the tasks and carrying out the goals. Goal-setting establishes standards to monitor and evaluate progress toward goals and making decisions committing to objectives and meeting deadlines. They are also required for taking initiative and of opportunities, besides taking risks (Training manager, Bank B).

The reference group respondents have slight improvement in personal skills (explained in Table 7.1), yet the bank juniors do not reach the threshold score of three in mentoring and innovativeness while the oil seniors and juniors do not reach the threshold score in these besides enterprise skill. Hence special programmes (individualised ideastorming workshops) are required to develop these skills in the deficient cases. Incorporation of these skills in the curriculum and imparting of special entrepreneurial development programmes could also be undertaken in HEIs.

Another skill which is of utmost importance is leadership quality as opined by an Oil manager wherein the leader is seen as a role model:

> Employees learn from experience by emulating leaders who are committed to the institution and its vision and who are creating new knowledge and identifying challenges. These managers engage in reflection and conversation about their experiences and making observations to ensure that all available knowledge has been addressed. Thinking critically about how the institution works and coming up with new theories, they devise plans for placing abstract events into coherent and simple explanations. They make decisions by taking action, at the same time experimenting with various approaches and strategies for problem solving (Junior Manager, Oil B).

In respect of interpersonal skills, in spite of intervention, low scores are seen in analysis (bank juniors), creative thinking (all groups), recognition (Bank B and Oil B juniors), diverse capacity (all groups), decision making (Bank B and Oil juniors) and conflict management (all juniors). The reference group scores high in analysis but in critical thinking, decision making and conflict

190

management especially in the oil companies, the threshold score is not obtained. Development of these skills appears to be associated with the nature of interpersonal relationship not only in the workplace but elsewhere also. The reference group in the banks fares better in analysis, decision making and also conflict management owing to better participation in ideastorming sessions, mentoring and experience-oriented business reading activities. At the time of recruitment itself, attention has to be given to the endowment of these skills in the prospective candidates.

The oil juniors score less than the threshold level in most of the situational skills while the bank juniors are not able to reach the threshold in respect of planning, negotiation, effectiveness, problem solving and empathy. As discussed in the general and reference group analysis, situational skills are mostly developed in the workplace especially through the training programmes which calls for specialised and intensive intervention programmes to rectify the deficiency. The budget allocation for soft skill training, especially in the oil companies has to be increased to make the programmes more intensive and productive.

The initiatives of higher education institutions (section 5.5) in infusing core soft skills in the curriculum and equipping the students (especially business and engineering) to the needs of the job market have been complemented by the training and development policy of the employers at the workplace. Not only the participation level has to be increased, programmes like team management, time management and problem solving have to be made more intensive and high scoring.

Our study has shown that technical and business skills are important; so are the soft skills in enabling the employees in effectively communicating with co-workers, management, clients and the employers. To succeed in business, one should have definitely hard skills with a good grasp of the fundamentals and one has to be fortified with latest technology in the concerned field of operation. In this, the various intervention programmes together with certification, experience, the internet and books are instruments toward lifelong learning. Soft skills are needed to create career and life opportunities. Since the essence of education and technical ability is opportunity, soft skills enable to utilise the opportunities. To bring value to the institutions and the customers, bank and other staff have to be involved in many non-technical activities to carry out the goals of the institutions. Motivating others, interpersonal relationships, team work and networking enable the managers to attend to the spot problems. No matter how 'good' one thinks, efficiency will not be obtained unless one knows how to communicate well with co-workers and customers. When the managers interact better with the people they work with, their performance tends to improve and they go away with a positive impression, where the meaning of positive impression is more opportunity and more responsibility.

Acquisition of soft skills empowers the managers by allowing them to build flexibility into their future career plans. Since soft skills such as communication, project management and team work

191

are transferable, they are needed in nearly all aspects of life, not just for career alone. Having the required interpersonal skills provides a must-have foundation for career growth. Technical expertise does not stop from developing leadership and motivational skills where one can be self-motivated and motivate others. Developing hard skills but cultivating poor soft skills at the same time tantamount to moving one step forward, two steps backward.

8.6 Conclusion

Though the reference groups are able to realise improved scores when compared to the pre-training scores except in Bank B seniors in respect of motivation skills, all the groups have to perform better to reach the maximum score. The additional scores (indicating the skill gap) required to reach the maximum level range from 14 to 54 percent, the oil companies requiring a higher score. Therefore, each of the sample institution has to have its own soft skill development cell and learning centre to assess the soft skill index of its employees periodically and to devise strategies to reduce the skill gap if found, over a period of time.

The impact of the intervention programmes not only has empowered the respondents, but also resulted in organisational development and experiential learning as illustrated by the narratives. Among the soft skills, leadership, motivation, communication, team spirit, problem solving and decision making have higher contribution in Bank A seniors as regards own development; for company's development, the critical soft skills have been planning, leadership, problem solving, decision making, team spirit, communication and motivation. Creative thinking, negotiation, enterprising and time management have lower levels of contribution which require rectification. Experiential learning has the capacity to improve soft skill endowment of the employees better than other methods.

The next chapter summarises the study by answering the research questions and concludes by giving an overview of its contribution and recommendations for future research.

9.1 Introduction

Structural changes in countries like Oman have caused increased demand for up-to-date skills and competencies in the workplace. The contribution of knowledge in production has been on the increase which necessitates the continual upgrading of the skills and competencies of the workforce toward achieving increased productivity. OECD (2001b) has argued that the growth of the knowledge economy, prompted by demand for new types of goods and services and increasing globalisation of economic activities and technological changes have necessitated new workplace competencies which are complementary to technical skills. We have seen that personal, interpersonal and situational skills are essential for personal and organisational development. These skills materialise through training, coaching, mentoring and experiential learning.

Soft skills not only empower the workforce in advancing career development and personal growth, also they create new opportunities and go beyond money motivation. When the skill base and affective goals undergo changes, the workplace registers improvements in the quality of human capital stock as mentioned in the sixth chapter. Hence, employers focus on soft skill enhancement along with improved technology, product development and market linkage. For the latter to improve, the hard outcomes have to be improved through soft outcomes. The purpose of soft skill training is to make it more accessible to those who require it and to promote adaptability and employability, at the same time maintaining employee retention. This chapter presents an overview of the findings of the study and discusses the lessons learned from the research and the contribution made to knowledge.

Section 9.2 recapitulates the research questions put forward in the fourth chapter and provides answers to them. Section 9.3 presents the chapter summaries, while section 9.4 summarises the major findings of the study and presents an overview and contribution of the study to knowledge. Section 9.5 critiques the limitations of the study while section 9.6 discusses some of the implications of the study and presents recommendations for soft skill development in HEIs and the workplace. Section 9.7 concludes, describing the process of development of the study, suggesting issues that can be considered for future research in the soft skill arena.

9.2 Research questions revisited

This section intends to provide the answers for the research questions posed in the third section of the fourth chapter.

1. What is meant by human capital and what are its components?

In section 2.2 on educational planning, it was shown that human capital approach to educational development (on the lines of Becker, 1993) was the appropriate strategy to be followed, wherein socio-economic development becomes a function of investment in human capital. Human capital, like physical capital is a factor in the production process and consists of both soft and hard skills. In that chapter, soft skills were defined as the soft component of human capital, which includes generic and transferable personal, interpersonal and situational skills that are essential to complement hard skills toward better employability. Employability indicates the achievement, understanding and personal attributes of individuals that make them more likely to gain employment and be successful in their chosen careers. Not only gaining better employment opportunities, but more importantly, succeeding in one's career and achieving competitive advantage in the labour market are the objectives of employability. This can be realised only with the enhancement of soft skills. Empirical analysis suggests a strong correlation between ability and education. Whereas hard skills are cognisable and easily measurable, soft skills are intangible and difficult to measure since they involve personal and subjective attributes.

2. What is meant by soft skill and how soft skill grouping may be accomplished?

The second and third chapters provide answers to the second research question. Soft skill is an ability or competence and can be either inherent or acquired which can be repeatedly performed. It can be verified and assessed through its performance only and can be demonstrated, learnt, taught, trained or coached but acquired only by performing them and improved through learning. Simpson (2006) and Hillmer (2007) speak of the criticality of soft skills in any teaching and training programme toward achievement of lifelong learning.

As discussed in section 3.3 and based on studies by ECOTEC (1998) on life, attitudinal and transferable skills; European Social Fund projects (Balgobin et al., 2004) on skills wheel and distance travelled; Moss and Tilly's (1995) study on interaction and motivation skills in black men's employment in the US; Heckman and Rubenstein (2001) study on general education development programme and measurement of soft skills in the US and studies by Motah (2007) and McMurtrey et al. (2008) on the necessity of soft skills in the workplace in any profession validate the importance of soft skills. Competency levels of employees would improve when

194

they are able to acquire interpersonal skills, intrapersonal attitudes, business understanding and technical skills to complement workplace learning (section 3.2). In section 3.3, soft skills were grouped into personal, interpersonal and situational skills, wherein personal skills include punctuality, language, enterprise and motivation (abilities which help in personal development), while innovativeness, mentoring and taking responsibility develop the competence of the individual toward organisational development. In interpersonal skills, recognising the worth of others and respecting them, communicating effectively with team members, conflict management and decision making enable the individual to be creatively thinking under diverse capacities and aid in team excellence and organisational competency. Situational skills are developed when both personal and interpersonal skills become critical, wherein learning, planning, goal setting, negotiations, empathy, time management and reliance assume utmost importance in any situation.

3. What type of treatment the higher education institutions in the region give to soft skill development?

The different training programmes conducted by the sample institutions on leadership, communication, negotiation, team building, emotional intelligence and customer care explain the significance of the intervention programmes. The training and development policies of the institutions capture the vital differences in soft skill orientation and development.

4. How may soft skills be measured and an index constructed?

5. How is distance travelled measured and assessed?

Soft skill measurement has been accomplished through the concepts of skill wheel and distance travelled in the third chapter, indicating how much progress an employee is able to make in achieving hard outcomes through accomplishing soft outcomes (Balgobin et al., 2004; Dewson et al., 2000a). Hard outcomes include transfer to a preferred place or position, promotion, foreign visits, participation in seminars, publication of papers, appointment as coach or mentor, awards, incentives, membership in committees, obtaining new qualifications and being given more responsibility and accountability, which are easily quantifiable. Soft outcomes are qualitative and indicative of the progress made toward achievement of the hard outcomes and signify improved time keeping, effective team building, improved communication and presentation skills, low sickness and absence from work, positive attitude and so on. These indicators will in turn improve the hard outcomes of the employee in achieving better employability and integration into the labour market. When this is accomplished, what is called 'distance travelled' occurs, being a measure of value-added success for both the individual and the institution.

In a skill wheel which consists of five circles pinpointing scores in a 5-point scale, if an employee scores nil in all the skills (which is not likely), then his score will be at the centre of the circle meaning nil. When the score is on the first inner circle line, it is equal to one. When the performance is evaluated as on the second inner circle line, it equals two and so on. An employee who performs such that is awarded a score of five in all the skills, then the scoring will be positioned on the outer circle line.

6. How soft skills are acquired and what are the different sources of their acquisition?

7. What is the relative contribution of various soft skill enhancement sources across different categories?

Discussion on the sources of soft skill acquisition is undertaken in the seventh chapter on reference group analysis, wherein workplace emerges as the main source, followed by higher education institutions, school and family in that order. Regarding the different intervention programmes contributing to soft skill enhancement, mentoring occupies the first place, followed by experience, on-the-job training, prior training, ideastorming, business reading and sponsored external training. When these programmes are delivered in terms of training, coaching or mentoring, experiential learning plays a critical role in skill enhancement. The outcomes of these intervention programmes include personality development, leadership, effective decision making and overall improvement in competence. This aspect has been brought to light by the various narratives of the participants.

8. What is the impact of various intervention programmes to enhance soft skills?

The impact can also be looked in terms of experiential learning exercises which enable the sample respondents to enhance their soft skills and contribute to personal and institutional development. Learning at the workplace, which stems out of soft skill endowment and results in its enhancement in turn takes place through work processes and is motivated by challenges and by consulting or working alongside others (Eraut, 2007a). Learning styles depend on the nature of intervention programmes and reflect how far personal development and group actions would be effective in achieving the required level of competence (Fidler, 2008). Competence represents the totality of knowledge, skills and abilities that are essential for professional work. Kolb's (1984) typology of learning styles is based on the concept of experiential learning, which is derived from the manner in which an employee tends to grasp new information and the methods that he or she tends to use when processing new ideas. Experience leads to observation and reflection, followed by concept formation, wherein new ideas and concepts may guide choices for new experiences. In all these courses of events, soft skills play a crucial role as illustrated by the case studies and narratives.

9. What is the nature of relationship between soft skill endowment and performance/productivity?

The regression analysis in the sixth chapter compares the pre and post training scenarios in respect of different categories to assess the relative contribution of soft skills relative to hard skills in respect of performance (proxy for productivity) of the respondents. Narratives in the fifth, sixth, seventh and eighth chapters on the training programmes express not only the individual opinion and assessment of various soft skills that have been imparted, but also their impact on individual performance and improvement in the quality of human capital.

With these answers, the objectives of the study are being probed into and before looking into the implications of soft skill development and experiential learning in terms of differences in importance and acquisition types and the relative contribution of different intervention methods in policy analysis, an overview of the study is presented in the next section, summarising the eight chapters.

9.3 The chapters in a nutshell

The chapter summaries are intended to highlight the contribution of each chapter to the overall argument on soft skill acquisition and development. The first chapter discusses different typologies wherein education is treated as investment in human capital resulting in economic growth, wherein its soft component complements hard skills and in modern workplaces has become an essential requirement.

The second chapter discusses the different approaches (human capital, willingness to pay, screening and manpower requirement) and showcases that the human capital approach has the advantages of developing the economy by investing in education and training to improve skills and competency of individuals. Human capital may be measured as a ratio of aggregate labour income to the wage of the uneducated worker according to foregone earnings or expected future stream of cash income flows or cost of mean years of schooling The human capital theory predicts that training results in progress at the workplace. In this, experiential learning is shown as a mechanism of human capital development, especially in the acquisition and enhancement of soft skills.

The third chapter defines soft skills and establishes their presence at the workplace. The grouping into personal, interpersonal and situational skills is accomplished based on literature survey and the concept of skill wheel is developed, the changes therein over a period of time explaining soft skill augmentation. Construction of soft skill index by averaging all the 31 sub-skills and presenting as scores in 5-point numerical scale would show how soft skills may be empirically tested at the workplace.

The fourth chapter identifies the research areas and poses the research questions as mentioned in the previous section. The questions relate to the components of human capital, grouping of the soft skills, skill endowment in different skill groups, measurement of distance travelled to indicate improvement in employability, sources of acquisition of soft skills, impact of different intervention programmes like training, coaching and mentoring, contribution of soft skill to performance and the role of reference groups. The objective of the study pertains to the interaction between hard and soft skills, the measurement of soft skill index across different institutions and skill groups and impact of training programmes in Oman. The various predictions specify soft skill variation in the skill groups, improvement in soft skills after intervention, hard outcomes depending on distance travelled, changing importance in soft skill groupings and the major soft skills and the intervention programmes. The research design consists of construction of the skill wheel, measurement of distance travelled, assessment of soft skill index, assessment of human capital index and reference group analysis, besides discussing qualitative case studies and narratives to complement the quantitative analysis. Soft skills are developed not only at the workplace, but also in family, schools and higher education institutions besides experiential learning and hence the focus of this study is on soft skills and their development.

Sampling has been so designed as to bring out the differences in soft skill practice not only in respect of different institutions but also in different skill groups. Banks and oil companies exhibit different emphasis on soft skills and between the banks or oil companies there could be further differences depending on the job and skill requirements. In order to represent the institutional and skill differences, senior and junior managers in two banks and two oil companies have been interviewed. Of 250 managers contacted in the four institutions, about 60 percent of them were willing to be interviewed and 120 respondents (15 in each skill group) were finally selected and among them, 40 most willingly to be in-depth interviewed have been selected for the reference group analysis. The reference period has been 2006 and soft skill practice is compared in terms of different interventions, 2005 being the base year. The study is quasi-experimental since it compares the post-intervention situation with the pre-training scenario for the same number of respondents who had undergone the training. In addition to questionnaires and personal observation, in-depth interviews and case studies have been undertaken to bring out the soft skill performance of the reference groups. Data analysis has been undertaken both quantitatively and qualitatively, the former indicating tabular and regression analyses and the latter comprising of case studies and narratives. The assessment of soft skills has been accomplished through scoring in the 1-5 Likert scale and the regression analysis brings out the relative contribution of hard and soft skills.

Chapter five analyses the soft skill orientation of the four sample institutions in respect of various intervention programmes conducted. After outlining the structure of the sample institutions in respect of productivity and profitability (to be juxtaposed to soft skill endowment), the different training programmes on leadership, communication, negotiation, team building, emotional intelligence and customer care are explained as to their significance. The training and development policies of the institutions are summarised to capture the vital differences in soft skill orientation and development. To substantiate the critical role of different training programmes, narratives by trainers and trainees have been illustrated.

The sixth chapter examines the nature of distance travelled and improvement in the quality of employability of the sample respondents through the analysis of skill wheel, soft skill index and improvement in human capital stock. Soft skills have been self assessed with appropriate triangulation based on cross assessment and author's own. Based on the scores of individual soft skills, ranking has been done and analysis accomplished as to which skill requires further enhancement. Comparing the post-intervention soft skill index with that of pre-training, the endowment of the intervention group (those who had undergone training during the reference year) is distinguished contrasting with that of the pre-training score in respect of both senior and junior managers in the institutions. While the intervention group (60) is characterised by soft skill enhancement owing to various intervention programmes, the non-intervention group is assumed to have the pre-training skill scores. The confidence limit analysis shows the differences in overall and the individual spreads. The regression analysis compares the pre and post training scenarios in respect of senior and junior managers to assess the relative growth in the importance of soft skills over hard skills in respect of performance (proxy for productivity) of the respondents. Narratives by the participants in the training programmes express the individual opinion and assessment of various soft skills that have been imparted.

The seventh chapter concentrates on the reference group analysis wherein the soft skill performance of that group is to be considered as the benchmark for other employees to follow. The different sources of soft skill acquisition (family, school, higher education institutions and workplace) are analysed. The share of different intervention tools (prior, on-the-job and sponsored training, experience, business reading, mentoring and ideastorming) in the workplace is assessed in respect of different reference groups. The outcome of the different programmes in enhancing the soft skills is analysed besides their impact resulting in the soft outcomes which determine the nature of distance travelled. The impact of the soft skills along with hard skills on own and company's development is evaluated so as to bring in the relative contribution of hard and soft skills. The various narratives pinpoint the views of the reference groups which can form as benchmarks for other groups to follow.

The eighth chapter provides major findings of the study and its implications in terms of experiential learning. After describing the four select higher education institutions in their treatment of soft skills in teaching and training, the overall relevance and importance of soft skills is established through the institutional case studies. The chapter extends the soft skill experience at the sample banks and oil companies to juxtapose to that of select higher education institutions to draw some lessons on experiential learning. Programmes like personal development planning, foundation courses and focus on language and communication have in-built mechanism for reflective learning and development of personal, creative and leadership skills of the students. A firm foundation in soft skills and work ethics at the HEI level prepares the employees at the workplace to be more like reference group members with high productivity. Toward this end, the narratives are replete in cases of effective workplace learning and development.

9.4 An overview of the study

The primary function of this section is to indicate the nature of contribution of the present study to the body of knowledge on soft skill evaluation. There are general studies on human resource development in Oman covering labour market situations (Al Dhahab, 1997; Goodliffe, 2004), higher education and Omanisation programme (Al-Lamki, 2000, 2002) and education development (ESCWA, 2003; Rassekh, 2004; Murphy, 2005), but there are no specific studies that deal with learning and soft skill development that are so essential at the workplaces. A study of this nature on soft skill development as applied to regional economies like Oman not only showcases the relevance of soft skills but also their contribution in personal and institutional development. Specific studies on the contribution of soft skills and their measurement are confined mainly to workplace evaluation where the employees are evaluated through multiple choice questions and rated based on their scores (Simpson, 2006). Human capital works concentrate on the productivity issues more than the implications of soft skills in its measure. Our analysis develops the concept of soft skill besides constructing the skill wheel and distance travelled as a result of changes in the wheel. Having grouped soft skills in terms of personal, interpersonal and situational skills and aggregating the scores facilitates comparison between different employee groups and institutions.

The analysis of soft skill acquisition and development attempts to capture the essence of soft skills, the sources of their acquisition, measurement and their impact on personal and institutional development. The division into three skill groups and how higher education and the sample institutions account for the development of soft skill profiles of their employees form the basis for this presentation. The overview relates to the four sample institutions, two each in banking and oil and hence the findings are indicative and not definitive. The main objective of soft skill development in Bank A has been acquisition of knowledge, competency development and lifelong learning, while it is exposure to international markets, work plan development and lifelong learning in Bank B. In Oil A, the objectives have been integration with new technology and competence development, whereas in Oil B, integration with work plan and marketing determine competency development. The narratives highlight the nature of trainings undergone, skill acquisition by employees, resource management, mentoring, team and communication skill development, presentation and leadership, emotional intelligence, peer relationship, management style, empowerment of local youth and importance of soft skills in the recruitment process.

According to the base period (pre-training) score in respect of overall 120 sample managers, seniors have higher scores than the juniors, indicating experience and positions are closely related to soft skill acquisition. Among the institutions, Bank A has higher scores in both the skill groups and, personal skills have higher scores followed by interpersonal and situational skills in all the cases. The soft skill endowment of those managers who have undergone training programmes during the reference period increases by 24 percent in Bank A for both senior and junior managers, 25 percent for seniors and 42 percent for juniors in Bank B, 16 percent for seniors and 37 percent for juniors in Oil A and 20 percent for seniors and 29 percent for juniors in Oil B, indicating a slower rate of increase in the scores of senior managers of the oil companies. This proves that intervention programmes serve the purpose of skill improvement in the employees and that whatever be the institution, training (on-the-job or otherwise), coaching and mentoring techniques besides business reading and ideastorming benefit contributing to skill enhancement.

When different soft skills are assessed, the rate of increase is higher in situational skills especially in juniors, showing their higher level of skill adaptation. Innovativeness and enterprising skills in the context of personal skills show a larger gap in all the groups. In interpersonal skills, analysis, creative thinking, decision making, negotiation and conflict management show a large gap. In situational skills, skills having large gap are goal setting, planning, negotiation, reliance, authority, problem solving and empathy. The skill wheels of senior and junior managers of both banks and the oil companies complement the distance travelled in the case of those who have been subject to intervention programmes, wherein the scores before and after training scenarios point out skill index increase in the post-intervention period.

Distance travelled in skill and performance analysis shows improvement in soft outcomes resulting in hard outcomes (better prospects for employment and career growth). Distance travelled in Bank A is greater than in Bank B which is greater than in Oil A, which is greater than in Oil B. The junior managers, especially in Bank B and Oil A have been able to realise a higher rate of skill enhancement than the senior managers, the increase in skill endowment being 32 percent higher, whereas it is only 21 percent in the case of the senior managers.

The regression analysis shows that hard skill is still the dominant variable influencing performance, though soft skill has shown an increased level of contribution in the post-training scenario. As a result of intervention, the shares of both hard and soft skills undergo a change. The

201

trend noticed has been one of declining share of hard skills and increasing share of soft skills in all the categories. By this account, senior managers realise a higher rate of increase in soft skill which is much more than the rate of decline in the share of hard skill. For example, if hard skill share show a decline of say 10 percent in the post-scenario, for status quo, at least 10 percent increase in soft skill share has to take place. In this case, the rate of increase in soft skills more than compensates the decline in the share of hard skills, indicating an overall improvement due to intervention. However, the rate of improvement in the case of juniors is lower since they have been able to realise only that rate of increase in soft skill which more or less equals the declined share of hard skills, showing no radical change. This is owing to the fact that they have not undergone many training and mentoring programmes. Also, they have shorter periods of experience and hence the change in soft skill endowment is not substantial as in the case of senior managers, though the post-training scenario shows augmentation in soft skill in influencing productivity. It is evident that intervention programmes result in a greater distance travelled and a greater level of job satisfaction and organisational development.

In-depth analysis of five respondents in each group shows that the reference groups have three to 12 percent higher level of performance when compared to the general groups, especially in the juniors in the banks. The influence of family and school is marked in personal skill development. Development of situational skills has been the major objective of workplace training, mentoring and collaboration. Workplace is more focused on situational and interpersonal skills. At least one third of the skill endowment of an employee is influenced by external forces (family, school and higher education institutions), while work environment accounts for the rest. In the workplace, training is major interaction programme in which the share of on-the-job training has been the highest followed by prior training and sponsored external training. Mentoring, experience, ideastorming sessions and publication and business reading are the other important intervention programmes. While the impact of mentoring is very high in personal and interpersonal skills, that of experience and ideastorming impact mostly situational skills.

The contribution of reference groups on own and company's development shows that the score is very high in Bank A seniors followed by Bank B seniors, Oil B seniors and the rest. In the case of Bank A seniors, qualification, training, leadership, motivation, planning, communication and team spirit are the major contributors to one's own development while qualification, training, planning, leadership and problem solving contribute to company's development. In Bank B, academic qualifications contribute to own and company development at a higher level, followed by training, motivation and leadership. In Oil A, the contribution of qualification is still higher followed by training and planning in both own and company development. In Oil B also, a similar trend is noticeable while planning and enterprising traits assume importance in the juniors.

Case studies of four higher education institutions in Oman as to their treatment of soft skills reveals that the universities and colleges accord importance to the teaching and imparting of soft skills in the curriculum of general, business and engineering studies; besides they conduct specialised training and orientation programmes through summer internships and workshops. The core skills that are being developed through teaching are literary skills, communication skills, critical thinking and problem solving skills. The contribution of the study rests on the exposition of soft component of human capital, its categorisation and development across leading sectors enabling better understanding of human capital theory and its application to an emerging economy like Oman.

9.5 Evaluation of methodology and limitations

The study concentrates on a mixed mode of data collection and analysis where both quantitative and qualitative data have been collected and quantitative and qualitative data analyses have been attempted. Comparison of different institutions has different orientation to soft skill development. Where soft skills would be very essential for organisational development and global competitiveness, the educational planners may focus on core skill development not only at HEI level but also at the workplace. Comparison of pre and post-intervention scenarios has resulted in the adoption of a quasi-experimental research design. However, the non-intervention group is assumed not to have acquired any soft skill during the reference period, though in practice, even they would have acquired some owing to experience or other factors like interaction and listening. While the regression technique brings out the relative strength of hard and soft skills of the senior versus junior managers in the workplace, the case studies and narratives of both general and reference group respondents showcase the advantage of personal observation and interview methods in eliciting personal and subjective data and information in a holistic way. Triangulation of data has resulted in cross-checking of different sources of data collection and putting them in an objective way for comparison across different categories. In addition to individual surveys, case studies of select HEIs have also been carried out to present a holistic view of soft skill development not only at the workplace but also at the education institution level.

In the collection of data, several hurdles were faced and owing to the novelty of the topic, except for the few plan documents, very little relevant information was obtained from the various ministries. In spite of these deficiencies, the researcher has taken pain to contact the institutions and respondents frequently and in convincing them to provide whatever information they had for the study. The different narratives have not only highlighted the importance of soft skills but also how they have been acquired and put into use. Encouraging case study approaches in the intervention programmes would give first hand information of the nuances of different soft skills. The contribution of the study rests on the exposition of soft component of human capital, its categorisation and development across leading sectors enabling better understanding of human capital theory and its application to an emerging economy like Oman. The concepts of assessment of soft skills and construction of skill wheel and soft skill index along with distance travelled can be adopted in workplaces so as to evaluate the quality of human capital stock and how it can be improved through various intervention programmes. Future studies can dwell on identifying the soft skill stock in different sectors across different skill groups so that the quality of that country's human capital stock and its contribution to socio-economic development can be assessed.

When the field survey was initiated, many managers could not tell exactly what they meant by 'soft' skills. They were able to identify skills like motivation, leadership, communication, presentation, customer relationship and business coaching as complementing hard skills and in improving not only their employability, but also their personal development. The author encountered lack of secondary data on skill development in the region. The reluctance of the respondents in answering questions related to earnings, monetary benefits and the detailed accounting of soft skills and their case studies were the other obstacles experienced. Many respondents at first refused to provide any information and it was only after persuasive discussion that some response was obtained. Even otherwise the response rate has been 48 percent only. In spite of these, the study purports to lead a way unto the building up of database for soft skill endowment under the broad umbrella of human capital.

Apart from problems encountered in data collection and convincing the employees to provide confidential information in such a new field as that of soft skills, it has been a difficult task to obtain the required information owing to the non-exposure of employees to such field surveys. The pilot survey was quite useful in convincing the respondents about the utility of such studies and training them to answer questions relevant to it. Classification of soft skills as personal, interpersonal and situational has proved a convenient tool to assess the essential workplace skills and their impact. The skill wheel and distance travelled measures have a wider area of application and pinpoint the efficacy of soft skill acquisition and development. This type of evaluation of methodology would bring up concerns about self-assessment on a subjective scale of such criteria as skills and productivity. The regression analysis documents the critical role of soft skills and their contribution as contrasted to hard skills. In tune with the quasi-experimental nature of the study, comparison of pre and post-intervention situations and the different narratives and cases show the attitudinal changes brought out by the intervention programmes and their impact on the personal and company development. The case studies of select higher education institutions in the region describe the type of treatment meted out to soft skills by them and how the institutions purport to deal with the issue.

9.6 Policy implications

Following Eraut (2007c), it can be said that the sources of learning in the sample banks and oil companies include challenge of the work itself, talking with other members of the team and discussions outside the group. Learning has become a by-product of work (as illustrated in the narratives of eighth chapter), resulting in group participation, working alongside others, role analysis and problem solving. Learning processes have occurred as a result of direct supervision, mentoring, coaching, meetings and conferences and independent study as evidenced by the narratives. Asking questions, locating resource persons, listening and observing, learning from mistakes, giving and receiving feedbacks and proactive social skills have enabled the managers to learn effectively (Eraut, 2007c). Evidence from experience has been followed with review so that the learning process becomes systematised.

As has been pointed out in the general and reference group analyses, soft skill development improves the employability assets of both senior and junior managers. These assets include enhancement of knowledge in banking and oil sectors, besides skill enhancement and having positive attitudes in career management. These have been embedded in better job search and job getting skills like CV writing, work experience and interview techniques and personal factors (family responsibilities) and external influences (current level of opportunity in the labour market). Given the type of skill development practised by the sample institutions (for example, personal development planning of HEI 2), HEIs in the region has to concentrate on disciplinarily content knowledge as applicable to different workplace situations and generic skills. With guidance, the junior managers have learned from their experiences in the banks and oil companies to develop their key competences and skills and enhance their employability (cases 5.5 and 7.1). From this perspective, it can be said that employers value people who have work experience and have been able to reflect upon that experience and then go on to articulate and apply what they have learned and hence association between employers and HEIs has to promote work-related learning experiences. Cases 5.6 and 5.9 illustrate the soft skill orientation of the sample institutions in hiring employees. The personal development planning exercises adopted by HEI 2 help the staff to plan, record and reflect upon their experiences in a way that develops their skills and self-awareness and understand how their transferable skills might be applied in new settings. Complementing this, training programmes of the sample institutions bridge the skill gap and enhance soft skills so that through upskilling, technical competency could be improved. It was shown by Table 5.2 that courses on leadership, communication, customer care and presentation are valued much more than others. It is not that these soft skills are more important than hard skills but they make an engineer a better engineer and a banker a better banker. As the conclusions of the study specifically relate to banks and oil companies, their application to other sectors or countries is subject to empirical testing of the model.

Since learning is necessary for the development of hard skills and employability, higher education institutions in the region have to improve teaching, changing the formal curriculum toward development of soft skills. Not only banks and oil companies, but other employers also demand graduates who present evidence that they have both personal qualities and complex achievements for workplace performance, as shown by their orientation to soft skill development in the fifth chapter. Employability quotient can be improved through competitive workplace experience and entrepreneurship. Support is focused through a clear, shared analysis of development needs, frequent review and feedback as in cases 5.1 and 7.2. The senior managers have to engage in informal coaching (Table 5.2), make good use of formal training and focus on finding the right kinds of experience within and outside their job. Table 5.3 shows the importance of all types of training followed by mentoring and experience. They have to offer active career development and work to help juniors have a realistic sense of their own potential and readiness for possible job moves, since the post-intervention skill enhancement rate is higher for the juniors. They have to see the juniors in the context of their previous work experiences and their interests and obligations outside work. The implication of this analysis for any kind of teamwork is creation of a climate of mutual trust essential for the sharing of practice and opportunities as evidenced by the reference group analysis. Cooperation in different situations requires that those involved have mutually developed understandings and collaboration besides having expertise that enable their problem solving capability.

Majority of employees work within a group and when their work is mainly individual, the group provides an important context for their identity and learning (cases 5.11 and 6.3). These factors interact in training to ensure that employees receive critical information and orientation courses have a social and cultural function providing opportunities for the employees to network outside their own function. In this, coaching and mentoring enhance the skill capability of the junior managers (Table 5.2). This is corroborated by Chartered Institute of Personnel and Development (2005) survey which found that 88 percent of UK respondents reported using internal coaching, 72 percent mentoring and 64 per cent external coaching. Mentoring has been derived from the relationship between an older or more experienced manager and a younger or less experienced employee. In such relationships the mentor has a personal interest in helping their mentees develop their potential (Bolden, 2005; Clutterbuck, 1998). As mentoring has focused on longer-term personal and career issues often helping the juniors, the same has to be mandated in every institution.

Experience is at the root of learning and it is seen as an interaction between the employee and the given situation, where abstract thinking becomes a product of concrete experience rather than knowledge that can be learned from books and lectures. The employees reflect on and observe their experiences from many perspectives and create concepts that integrate their observations into logically sound theories, utilising these theories to make decisions and solve problems following Kolb's learning theory as illustrated in the eighth chapter. Barriers to learning have been eliminated (as shown by the narratives) through changing attitudes and behaviours, addressing disincentives such as aspects of current superannuation and retirement income policies, tailoring skill development activities to suit the specific institutions and improving the adjustment mechanism to the labour market.

Factors affecting learning include appropriate degree of challenge in work, frequent and constructive feedback on job performance, time to learn at work, especially through talking to others, besides unnecessarily restrictive job design and excessive work pressure and stress. Supportive relationships with others, based on mutual respect and frequent informal discussions of work with colleagues, team meetings, attention to learning opportunities have facilitated allocating and designing work processes, work issues discussion with others and supportive relationships. Acquisition of soft skills (Table 7.3) has empowered the managers by allowing them to build flexibility into their future career plans. Since soft skills such as communication, project management and team work are transferable, they are required in all aspects of career in any institution. Technical expertise does not stop from developing leadership and motivational skills where one can be self-motivated and motivate others. Training programmes in the banks for example, have been diversified to meet the changing requirements of knowledge-based economy.

Learning by doing (emphasis on active involvement through role-plays, simulations, use of games and workplace visits) and working in groups (involving interactive project-based work, peer tutoring and assessment of performance) have to be developed not only in the banks and oil companies, but also in the HEIs to promote learning skills (providing employees with a sense of purpose and an awareness of task demands and feasibility). These skills have to be developed in an integrated and holistic way, through relevant and motivating learning tasks and activities. When government implements the process of assessing experiential learning derived from previous work and life experiences, this may provide greater access to higher education and a starting point for diagnosing an individual's continuing educational and professional development. Different institutions have different orientation to soft skill development. Whereas in some, soft skills would be very essential for organisational development and global competitiveness, the educational planners may focus on core skill development not only at HEI level but also at the workplace.

As soft skill development activities lead to improved labour market outcomes in terms of higher employment rates and wages (following the regression results), changes in attitudes, learning new skills and knowledge and personal circumstances play important roles. The concepts of assessment of soft skills and construction of skill wheel and soft skill index along with distance travelled as developed by this study can be adopted not only by HEIs but also industry and business establishments so as to evaluate the quality of human capital stock and how it can be improved through various intervention programmes. Insistence on appropriate workplace discipline and simulated training programmes will have to be adopted by the HEIs and industry in order to improve the status of soft skills. Workplace learning has to be performance or task-related, problem-based or team-based learning from work activities concerned with performance. Encouraging case study approaches in the intervention programmes as contemplated by the banks would give first hand information of the nuances of different soft skills.

The training departments of banks, oil companies in particular and industry and HEIs in general may be transformed into soft skill development cells to deliberate on the methodology of training and assessing its impact on the overall human resource management in the organisations. Regular exchange of ideas and discussions among the HEIs and companies would improve the soft skill component of human capital and hence frequent swaps between hard and soft skills becomes necessary. In the process, rewards and incentives have to be provided by companies for those employees who exhibit increased competency in their professions. Competency-based training has to be developed by them to deliver skills related to pre-employment and work maturity, basic skills, job specific skills, on-the-job training and customised training.

HEIs have to be responsive to changing labour market and working life demands and assist diverse range of learners seeking to develop their skills for employment. Apart from focus on learning and its assessment, HEIs have to encourage independent learning systems involving greater control over subject matter choice, learning styles, the pace of study and the assessment of learning outcomes. Wherever skill gap was noticed (evidenced by the skill wheel) it can be bridged by suitable curriculum changes and training and development programmes, focusing on employable and transferable skills. Support to personal skill development involving learner motivation leads the workers to learn through feelings as well as through intellect and solving problems through reflection (learning diaries, reflective journals, participant observation and videos). Since the factors enhancing or constraining learning at work tend to focus on specific factors or on the overall work culture, specific motivators in the companies have to include effective communication and feedback, work design, industrial relations, participation, continuity and training. The necessity arises for pooling adequate resources, both financial and human at the firm level for implementing the different intervention programmes in order to define an appropriate national policy on soft skills. Future studies can dwell on upon identifying the soft skill stock in different sectors across different skill groups so that the quality of that country's human capital stock and its contribution to socio-economic development can be assessed.

Soft skill development strategies by employers may concentrate on adequate capacity building owing to competitive nature of productivity enhancement (human capital theory) and changes in value system toward more amiable work and enterprise cultures. Equitable access to all employees has to be provided so that mismatch between supply of and demand for soft skills is eliminated. Diversification of training programmes has to take place especially in oil companies to meet the changing requirements of knowledge-based economy. Building global competency levels and lifelong learning rather than focusing merely on education qualifications and credentialism may be promoted by public-private partnership programmes in establishing soft skills training and accreditation institutes. Further, the necessity arises of pooling adequate resources, both financial and human by the government for implementing different intervention strategies in order to define an appropriate national policy on soft skills. Lastly, development of soft skills in the HEIs and the workplace has to be monitored by the soft skill development agency so that the core skills required for recruitment may be standardised at the college level so that the workplace skills may be developed.

The study has attempted not only to classify soft skills into three groups, but also in measuring them through the employment of skill wheel and soft skill index. Further, the impact of soft skills has been shown to result from various intervention programmes, the impact resulting in distance travelled. As the study is based on a small sample survey, the findings are to be viewed with caution as to generalisation. However, the concept of skill wheel, distance travelled and skill index can be applied to any situation irrespective of the work environment as they are deemed to be already established and empirically testable entities. In complementing qualitative analysis of narratives and case studies with quantitative analysis of regression and descriptive statistics, the study pinpoints as to the growing awareness on soft skills in emerging countries like Oman and how they could be developed at the workplace and at the higher education institution level. This study shows that intervention results in skill enhancement and that there are different ways of skill enhancement techniques. The classification of soft skills in terms of personal, interpersonal and situational contexts can be a methodological way to decipher their conceptualisation and application. Discussion on the different sources of soft skill acquisition like family, school, higher education institutions and workplace illustrates the major sources of skill acquisition and their relative importance. Further, the measurement of soft skills through skill wheel and assessment through distance travelled as a result of intervention provides a skill assessment methodology. The case studies and narratives illustrate the importance of qualitative assessment techniques with an emphasis on workplace learning. The focus of government policy has to strengthen the criticality of capacity building and provide equal access to training facilities to all the deserving employees. Further, public-private partnership in the diversification of training programmes may be encouraged to achieve increased competency levels toward competitive advantage The contribution of the study to policy issues on skill development, learning methods, employability and the employers' perspective also needs to be considered.

9.7 Conclusion

The study besides highlighting the importance of soft skills at the workplace, presents a mechanism through which soft skill development can be attempted by institutions that show interest in soft skill orientation. The findings reveal that the banks have a better soft skill orientation than the oil companies, where higher levels of capital investment, revenue and employee strength are associated with higher soft skill orientation. To keep employees motivated and productive they have to be motivated by the management through various incentives and intervention programmes. The skills gap is not limited just to banks or oil companies. Effective skills development depends on opportunities to practise soft skills with support and guidance, encouraging reflection and subsequently development-oriented learning. This study has been undertaken to specify the factors that have crucial role to play in the training and development programmes of banks and oil companies in Oman with reference to motivating the employees toward better employability and productivity in lines with human capital theory.

Training on leadership, time management, team work and negotiations have enhanced not only personal, but also interpersonal and situational skills areas, but the main focus in the sample institutions has been on effective personal development and problem solving aspects. Courses on communication, presentation and customer care have enhanced principally the interpersonal skills, while courses on situational analysis, emotional intelligence and time management have augmented situational skills. Business coaching sessions have led to development of coaching and mentoring capabilities and also enhancement of hard skills. Acquisition of leadership qualities has given an insight into the understanding of intricacies of management. Conflict avoidance facilitates difficult coping mechanisms and learning from others. Teamwork has enabled observation and motivation leads to critical thinking and enterprise capability. Overall, the impact of the intervention programmes indicates a mix of learning and experience wherein posing questions relate to response behaviour and communication relates to adaptation to different types of persons and statuses.

The author as dean of a college has been experimenting with the likes of personal development planning and other tools to improve the soft skill endowments of his students so that their employability skills may improve. However, he has not achieved much success in the matter. As long as the soft skill curriculum remains informal and outside the credit-based system, the chances are that the students may not devote much attention to their learning. If on the other hand, learning of soft skills are incorporated into the credit system, then there may be the required interest in the subject, paving the way for a better treatment on soft skills both at the HEI level and at the workplace in the region.

We have traversed into a new area where literature on soft skill development in the region is very scarce and not wholesome. An attempt has been made to develop a methodology pertaining to skill enhancement in sample banks and oil companies in the form of skill index and distance travelled which may be applied in circumstances requiring skill enhancement in organisations and where there is skill gap. Future research has to dwell on the standardisation of soft skill endowment and competency levels thereon in workplaces according to different work categories and positions so as to yield a soft skill measure such that like intelligence quotient or emotional intelligence quotient, soft skill quotient may be assessed not only at the time of recruitment, but also during promotion, transfer or any other hard skill demonstration. If this is achieved, the purpose of this research study will amply be justified.

References

Abegaz, B. (1994). *Manpower Development Planning: Theory and an African case study*. Aldershot: Avibury Press for the University of Warwick.

Al Lamki, S. (2000). Omanisation: A Three Tier Strategic Framework for Human Resource Management and Training in the Sultanate of Oman. *Journal of Comparative International Management*, 3(1), 36-48.

Al Lamki, S. (2002). Higher education in the Sultanate of Oman: the challenge of access, equity and privatisation. *Journal of Higher Education policy and Management*, 24(1), 75-86.

Al-Dhahab, M. (1997). The National labour force: self-sufficiency and development: role of technical and vocational training - The experience of the Sultanate of Oman. Paper presented at the conference on National Building in the Modern World: Technological Education and National Development, Abu Dhabi, 6-8 April.

Alstadsaeter, A. (2004). Measuring the Consumption Value of Higher Education. Discussion Paper No. SAM 04. Bergen: Norwegian School of Economics and Business Administration (NHH). Department of Economics.

Altbach, P. G. (2002). Perspectives on internationalising higher education. *International Higher Education*, 27(Spring), 6-8.

Anderson, K. H. & Hyneman, S. P. (2005). Education and Social Policy in Central Asia: The Next Stage of the Transition. *Journal of Social Policy and Administration,* 39(4), 361- 380.

Anderson, K., Butler, J. & Sloan, F. (1987). Labour market segmentation: a cluster analysis of job groupings and barriers to entry, *Southern Economic Journal,* 53(1987), 571–590.

Anderson, T. (2008). Towards a theory of online learning. In T. Anderson (Ed.), *Theory and Practice of Online Learning*, 2nd edition. (pp. 45–74). Edmonton, AB: AU Press.

Anon, (2007). Annual Report of Bank A. Muscat: Bank A.

Anon, (2008). Annual Report of Bank A. Muscat: Bank A.

Arab Regional Conference on Higher Education, (1998). Beirut Declaration on Higher Education in the Arab States for the XXIst Century. Arab Regional Conference on Higher Education, Bierut 2-5 March, 1998, Bierut: UNESCO.

Arrow, K. J. (1973). Higher education as a filter. *Journal of Public Economics*, 2(3), 193- 216.

Atkinson, J. & Williams, M. (2003). Employer Perspectives on the Recruitment, Retention and Advancement of Low-Pay, Low-Status Employees. Occasional Paper Series no. 2 Brighton: Government Chief Social Researcher's Office.

Avicenna, (1993). Thinkers on Education, *Prospects – Quarterly Journal of Education*, 23(1- 2), Geneva: UNESCO-International Bureau of Education.

Balgobin, E., Hutton, C., Rees, G. & Weinstock, W. (2004). *Unqualified Success. A Report on the Development of a Soft Skills Measurement Tool for Employment Projects.* London: Hackney Training and Employment Network.

Ball, S. J. (1999). Big Policies/Small World: An Introduction to International Perspectives in Education Policy. *Comparative education,* 34(2), 157-175.

Bardo, J & Evans, P. (Eds.) (2006). Towards a Policy Framework for Higher Education in the Knowledge Economy. Cullowhee, NC: Western Carolina University and Institute for the Economy and the Future.

Barnett, R. (2000). *Realising the University in an Age of Super Complexity.* Buckingham: Society for Research into Higher Education & Open University Press.

Bartel, A. (1994). Productivity gains from the implementation of employee training programmes. *Industrial Relations*, 33(4), 411-425.

Bassanini, A. & Scarpetta, S. (2001). Does human capital matter for growth in OECD countries? Evidence from pooled mean-group estimates. *Economics Department Working Papers* No. 282 ECO/WKP(2001)8, Paris: OECD.

Beard, C (2006). Keynote. Artificial learning environments - the implications for outdoor learning community. Northern Regional Conference of the Institute for Outdoor Learning, University College Lancaster, Penrith, 20 January, 2006.

Becker, G. S. (1962). Investment in Human Capital: A theoretical analysis. *Journal of Political Economy,* 70, 9-49.

Becker, G. S. (1964). *Human Capital.* New York: Columbia University Press.

Becker, G. S. (1975). *Human Capital.* Chicago state: Chicago University Press.

Becker, G. S. (1993). *Human Capital - A Theoretical and Empirical Analysis with special reference to education.* (3rd Edn.), Chicago state: Chicago University Press.

Becker, G. S & Nigel, T. (1986). Human Capital and the Rise and Fall of Families. *Journal of Labour Economics*, 4(3), 1-39.

Bedard, K. (2001). Human capital vs signalling models: University access and high school dropouts. *Journal of Political Economy*, 109, 749-775.

Bell, D. (1973). *The coming of the post-industrial society. A venture in social forecasting.* New York: Basic Books.

Berg, B. L. (2003). *Qualitative research methods for the social sciences* 5th edition, Boston: Allyn & Bacon.

Beryl, P. (2001). Assessment: Central to Learning. *New Zealand Journal of Applied Computing and Information Technology*, 5(2), 58-61.

Bloom, B. (1984). *Taxonomy of educational objectives.* Boston, MA: Allyn and Bacon, Pearson Education.

Blundell, R. L., Dearden, C. M. & Sianesi, B. (1999). Human Capital Investment: The Returns from Education and Training to the Individual, the Firm and the Economy. *Fiscal Studies,* 20(1), 1-23.

Bolden, R. (Ed.) (2005). What is Leadership Development: Purpose and Practice. Leadership South West Research Report, Exeter: Centre for Leadership Studies.

Boyatzis, R.E. (1982). *The competent manager: A model for effective performance.* New York: John Wiley & Sons.

Brannen, J. (2005). Mixed Methods Research: A discussion paper. Swindon. UK: Economic and Social Research Council (ESRC).

Brey, P. (2001). Disclosive Computer Ethics. In Spinello, Richard A. & Tavani, Herman T. (Eds.). *Readings in Cyberethics.* Sudbury, MA: Jones and Bartlett publishers. (pp.51-62).

Bryman, A. (2004). *Social Research Methods.* 2nd edition, Oxford: Oxford University Press.

Bryman, A. (2008). Of methods and methodology. *Qualitative Research in Organisation Management: An International Journal,* 3(2), 159-168.

Bryman, A., Bresnen, M., Beardsworth, A. & Keil, T. (1988). Qualitative research and the study of leadership. *Human Relations*, 41, 13-30.

Buck, S., Lees, R. & Cook, F. (2002). The Influence of Family History of Stuttering on the Onset of Stuttering in Young Children. *International Journal of Phoniatics, Speech Therapy and Communication Pathology,* 54(3), 117-124.

Bunker, K., & Wakefield, M. (2004). In search of authenticity: Now more than ever, soft skills are needed. *Leadership in Action*, 24(1), 17-21.

Business Wire, (2001). Reynolds & Reynolds. June 6, 2001.

Butcher, B. & Marsden, L. (2004). Measuring soft outcomes: A literature review. *The Research and Development Bulletin, 2*(3), 31-36. Norwich: The Research Centre, City College, Norwich.

Carneiro, P. & Heckman, J. (2003). Human capital policy. Working paper: 9495, Cambridge, MA: National Bureau of Economic Research, Inc.

Carneiro, P., Crawford C. & Goodman, A. (2006). Which skills matter? London: Institute for Fiscal Studies.

Chartered Institute of Personnel and Development, (2005). Performance Management. Survey report. London: Chartered Institute of Personnel Development.

CIA, (2009). World Fact book - Country: Oman. Washington, DC.: Central Intelligence Agency.

Clark, R. M. (1993). Homework-focused parenting practices that positively affect student achievement. In N. F. Chavkin (Ed.), *Families and schools in a pluralistic society* (pp. 85- 105). Albany, NY: State University of New York.

Clutterbuck, D. (1998). *Learning Alliances: tapping into talent.* London: Institute of Personnel & Development.

Cohen, L. & Manion, L. (1994). *Research Methods in Education*, London: Routledge.

Collins, R. (1971). Functional and Conflict Theories of Educational Stratification. *American Sociological Review*, 36, 1002-1019.

Cortright, J. (2001). New Growth Theory, Technology and Learning A Practitioners Guide. Reviews of Economic Development Literature and Practice: No. 4, Portland: Impresa, Inc.

Cunha, F., Heckman J., Lochner L., & Masterov, D. (2005). Interpreting the evidence on life cycle skill formation. Working paper No. 11331, Cambridge, MA: National Bureau of Economic Research, Inc.

Dash, J. (2001). Schools push soft skills for info security majors. *Computer world,* 35(6), 24.

De Grip, A. & Heijke, H. (1998). Beyond Manpower Planning: Labour Market Model and its Forecasts to 2002 ROA-W-1998/6E Maastricht: Research Centre for Education and the Labour Market

De la Fuente, A. & Ciccone A. (2002). Human Capital in a Global and Knowledge-based Economy. Final Report, Brussels: European Commission.

De Pinto, R & Deal, J. (2004). Differences in the Developmental Needs of Managers at Multiple Levels. Research Project, Brussels: Centre for Creative Leadership®

Dekker, R., De Grip, A. & Heijke, H. (1993). Indicating the Future Labour Market Prospects of Occupational Groups and Types of Education in the Netherlands. In Heijke, H. (Ed.), *Forecasting the Labour Market by Occupation and Education.* Boston, MA: Kluwer Academic Publishers.

Denzin, N.K. & Lincoln, Y.S. (2000). Introduction: the discipline and practice of qualitative research. In Denzin, N.K. & Lincoln, Y.S. (Eds.), *Handbook of Qualitative Research*, (pp.1-28), London: Sage Publications.

Denzin, N.K. (1989). *Interpretive Interactionism.* London: Sage Publications.

Dettori, G. & Paiva, A. (2009). *Narrative Learning in Technology-Enhanced Environments.* Dordretch: Springer Netherlands.

Dewson, S., Eccles, J., Tackey, N. & Jackson, A. (2000a). *Measuring Soft Outcomes and Distance Travelled: A Review of Current Practice,* (Research Report No.219), Brighton: The Institute for Employment Studies for DfEE.

Dewson, S., Eccles, J., Tackey, N. & Jackson, A. (2000b). *Guide to Measuring Soft Outcomes and Distance Travelled*, Brighton: The Institute for Employment Studies.

215

Dhuey, E & Lipscomb, S. (2008). What Makes a Leader? Relative Age and High School Leadership. *Economics of Education Review*, 27(2), 173-183.

Diener, E. & Crandall, R. (1978). *Ethics in Social and Behavioural Research*, Chicago State: University of Chicago Press, Chicago.

Doheny-Farina, S. (1993). Research as rhetoric: Confronting the methodological and ethical problems of research on writing in non-academic settings. In R. Spilka (Ed.), *Writing in the workplace: New research perspectives* (pp. 253-268), Carbondale: Southern Illinois University Press.

Drucker, P. (1969). *The age of discontinuity: guidelines to our changing society*. London: Heinemann.

Du, F., Yang, J. & Dong, X. (2007). Why do women have longer unemployment durations than men in post re-structuring urban China? Working Paper 2007-23. Gender Challenge Fund of the Poverty and Economic Policy, Ottawa: International Development Research Centre of Canada.

ECOTEC, (1998). *Soft Indicators: Demonstrating Progress and recognising Achievement,* ESF Employer Initiative Support Unit, http://www.employment.ecotec.co.uk

Edwards, R. & Usher, R. (2000). *Globalisation and Pedagogy: space, place and identity*. London: Routledge.

Eraut, M. (2000). Non-formal Learning, Implicit Learning and Tacit Knowledge in Professional Work. In Coffield, F. (Ed.) *The Necessity of Informal Learning*, London: Policy Press.

Eraut, M. (2004). Informal Learning in the Workplace. *Studies in Continuing Education*, 26(2), 247-74.

Eraut, M. (2007a). Professional knowledge and learning at work, *Knowledge, Work and Society*, 45-62.

Eraut, M. (2007b). *Theoretical and Practical Knowledge Revisited.* Proceedings of European Association for Research on Learning and Instruction 12th Biennial Conference for Research on Learning and Instruction, August 28th – September 1[st,] Budapest.

Eraut, M. (2007c). Learning from other people in the workplace. *Oxford Review of Education,* 33(4), 403-422.

Eraut, M. & Hirsh, W. (2007). The Significance of Work-based Learning for Understanding Groups and Organisations. Swindon, UK: ESRC.

ESCWA, (2003). Responding to Globalisation: Skill Formation and Unemployment Reduction Policies. New York: United Nations.

European Commission, (1995). Teaching and Learning. Towards the Learning Society. White Paper, Brussels: European Commission.

European Commission, (2003). Implementation of "Education & Training 2010" Work Programme Progress Report, Directorate-General for Education and Culture, Brussels: European Commission.

Evans, K. & Kersh, N. (2004). Recognition of tacit skills and knowledge: Sustaining learning outcomes in workplace environments, *Journal of Workplace Learning*, 16(1), 63-74.

Fan, S.C. Xiangdong, W. Junsen Z. (2005). "Soft" Skills, "Hard" Skills, and the Black/White Earnings Gap. Discussion paper no.1804, Bonn: IZA (The Institute for the Study of Labour).

Federico, R. (2008). Performance competition in local media markets. *Journal of Public Economics*, Elsevier, 92(7), 1585-1594.

Fidler, B. (2008). Teachers' Professional Development. Paper presented in the Conference on Enhancing Teachers Professionalism Towards the National Education System For The 21st Century, held at Brunei October 21 to 23rd 2008 Bandar Seri Begawan, Brunei Darussalam.

Fleischer, W. & Dressner, J. (2002). Providing the Missing Link: A Model for a Neighborhood-Focused Employment Program. Baltimore, MD: Annie E. Casey Foundation.

Ford, J.K. (1990). Understanding training transfer: The water remains murky. *Human Resource Development Quarterly*, 1, 225-229.

Forojalla, S. B. (1993). *Educational Planning for Development*. London: Macmillan Press.

Foss, N. (2008). Human capital and transaction cost economics. Centre for Strategic Management and Globalisation Working Paper No. SMG WP 2/2008 Copenhagen: Copenhagen Business School

Gewirtz, S. (2002). *The Managerial School: post-welfarism and social justice in education*. London: Routledge.

Gibbons, M., Limoges, C., Nowotny, H., Schwartzman, S., Scott, P., Trow, M. (1994). *The New Production of Knowledge: the dynamics of science and research in contemporary societies*. London: Sage Publications.

Goldstein, I. L. & Ford, J. K. (2002). *Training in Organisations*. (4th Edn.). Belmont, CA: Wadsworth.

Goleman, D. (1995). *Emotional intelligence*. New York: Bantam Books.

Goodliffe, T. (2004). Personal Development Planning: Addressing the skills gap for engineers in Oman. *Global Journal of Engineering Education,* 8(2), 147-152.

Gorman, H. (2000). Winning hearts and minds? - Emotional labour and learning for care management. *Journal of Social Work Practice*, 14(2), 149-158.

Gribbons, B. & Herman, J. (1997). True and quasi-experimental designs, *Practical Assessment Research & Evaluation*, [online], 5(14), available from: http://PAREonline.net/getvn.asp?v=5&n=14.

217

Grossman, G. M. & Helpman, E. (1991). Quality leaders and product cycles. *Quarterly Journal of Economics,* MIT Press, 106(2), 557-86.

Gubrium, J. F., & Holstein, J. A. (1997). *The new language of qualitative method.* Oxford: Oxford University Press.

Gullason, E.T. (1989). The consumption value of schooling: An empirical estimate of one aspect. *Journal of Human Resources,* 24(2), 287-98.

Gunderson, M., & Riddell, C. (2001). Training in Canada. In A. Berry (Ed.), *Labour Market Politics in Canada and Latin America* (pp.243-265). Boston: Kluwer Academic Publishers.

Gundlach, E. (2001). Interpreting Productivity Growth in the New Economy: Some Agnostic Notes. Kiel Working Papers 1020, Kiel: Kiel Institute for the World Economy.

Guzman, L. & Jekielek, S. (2004). Indicators of the Social Context of Families: Family Time In Indicators of Child, Family and Community Connections: Companion Volume of Related Papers (pp. 23-43). Washington, DC: Office of the Assistant Secretary for Planning and Evaluation, U.S. Department of Health and Human Services.

Hargreaves, D. (2000). Knowledge management in the learning society. Paris: OECD.

Härkönen, E. (2008). Integrating transferable skills into academic curricula Employability, Employer Involvement and Student Work Placement Finland: University of Turku.

Heckman, J. & Lochner, L. (2000). Rethinking Education and Training Policy: Understanding the Sources of Skill Formation in a Modern Economy. In Sheldon H. Danziger & Jane Waldfogel (Eds.), *Securing the Future: Investing in Children from Birth to College* (pp. 47–83). New York: Russell Sage Foundation.

Heckman, J. & Rubinstein, Y. (2001). The Importance of Non-cognitive Skills: Lessons from the GED Testing Program. *American Economic Review*, 91(2), 145-149.

Heckman, J., Stixrud, J. & Urzua, S. (2006). The Effects of Cognitive and Noncognitive Abilities on Labour Market Outcomes and Social Behaviour, *Journal of Labour Economics*, 24(3), 411-482.

Hillmer, G. (2007). Social and Soft Skills Training Concept in Engineering Education. International Conference on Engineering Education - ICEE 2007, September 3-7, 2007, Coimbra, Portugal.

Holzer, H., Block, R., Cheatham, M. & Knott, J. (1993). Are training subsidies for firms effective? The Michigan experience. *Industrial and Labour Relations Review*, 46(4), 625-636.

Honey, P. & Mumford, A. (1992). *The Manual of Learning Styles*. Maidenhead: Honey, Ardingly House

UNESCO, (2004). Promoting Skills Development: Report of an Interregional Seminar Paris, 22-23 January 2004, Paris: UNESCO-International Institute for Educational Planning.

ILO (1972). Employment, incomes and equality, Geneva: International Labour Organisation.

ILO, (2006). Implementing the Global Employment Agenda: Employment strategies in support of decent work, "Vision" document, Geneva: International Labour Organisation.

Jeong, B. (2002). Measurement of human capital input across countries: a method based on the labourer's income. *Journal of Development Economics*, 67(2), 333-349.

Johnes, J. (2006). Efficiency and productivity change in the English higher education sector from 1996/97 to 2002/03. Working Papers 004051, Lancaster: Lancaster University Management School, Economics Department.

Jorgenson, D. W. & Fraumeni, B.M. (1992). The output of the education sector. In Griliches Z. (Eds.), *Output measurement in the Services Sector*. Chicago state: The University of Chicago press, (pp.303-338).

Kay, T. (2004). The family factor in sport: A review of family factors affecting sports participation. Loughborough: Institute of sport and leisure research, Loughborough University

Kelly, C., Kocourek, P., McGaw, N. & Samuelson, J. (2005). Deriving Value from Corporate Values. Queenstown, MD: The Aspen Institute and Booz, Allen, Hamilton.

Kenney, S. J. (2004). Gender, the Public Policy Enterprise and Case Teaching. *Journal of Policy Analysis and Management,* 23(1), 159-178.

Kirkpatrick, D.L. (1994). *Evaluating Training Programs: The Four Levels.* San Francisco, CA: Berrett-Koehler.

Klabbers, J. H. G. (2000). Learning to handle complexity in social systems. In I. P. McCarthy & T. Rakotobe-Joel (Eds.), Proceedings of the International Conference on Complexity and Complex Systems in Industry (pp. 616-638). Warwick,: University of Warwick.

Klein, R, Richard S. & Weiss, A. (1991). Factors Affecting the Output and Quit Propensities of Production Workers. *Review of Economic Studies*, 58(2), 929-954.

Kodde, D. A. & Ritzen, J. M. (1984). Integrating consumption and investment motives in a neoclassical model of demand for education. *Kyklos,* 37(4), 598-605.

Kolb, D. A. (1984). *Experiential Learning: experience as the source of learning and development.* Englewood Cliffs, NJ: Prentice-Hall.

Konting, M., Khatijah, Y. & Sidek A. (2005). Human Capital Development: Soft Skill Initiatives at Universiti Putra Malaysia. *Journal of the World Universities Forum*, 1(4), 89-98.

Krathwohl, D. R. (1998). *Methods of educational and social science research: An integrated approach.* 2nd edition, New York: Addison-Wesley Educational Publisher, Inc.

Krueger, R. A. (1994). *Focus groups: A practical guide for applied research*. Thousand Oaks, CA: Sage publications.

Lane, R. E. (1966). The Decline of Politics and Ideology in Knowledgeable Society. *American Sociological Review*, 31(5), 649-62.

Lazear, E. (1977). Academic achievement and job performance. *American Economic Review*, 67(2), 252-254.

Le, T. Gibson, J. & Oxley, L. (2005). Measures of Human Capital: A Review of the Literature. Wellington: New Zealand Treasury.

Leedy, P. & Ormrod, J. (2001). *Practical Research Planning and Design*, 7th edition, Englewood Cliffs, NJ: Prentice-Hall.

Levine, D. I. (1998). *Working in the twenty-first century: policies for economic growth through training, opportunity and education.* Armonk, N.Y.: M.E. Sharpe.

Lleras, M. P. (2004). *Investing in Human Capital – A Capital Market Approach to Student Funding.* Cambridge: Cambridge University Press.

Lloyd, R. & O'Sullivan, F. (2003). *Measuring Soft Outcomes and Distance Travelled: A Methodology for Developing a Guidance Document.* London: Department of Work and Pensions.

Lucas, R.E. (1988). On the Mechanics of Economic Development. *Journal of Monetary Economics*, 22(1), 3-42.

Lucas, R.E. (1993). Making a miracle. *Econometrica*, 61(2), 251-272.

Maguire, T. & Hogan, D. (2004). *The Competencies for Next Generation Employability.* Report produced by The Programme for University Industry Interface, Limerick: University of Limerick.

Malhotra, N.K. (2004). *Marketing Research An Applied Orientation.* 4th edition, Upper Saddle River, NJ: Pearson.

Mantle, G., Modules, T., Johnson, K., Leslie, J., Parsons, S. & Shaffer, R. (2007). Whose Wishes and Feelings? Children's Autonomy and Parental Influence in Family Court Enquiries. *British Journal of Social Work,* 37(5), 785-805.

Martin, E. & Polivka A. (1995). Diagnostics for redesigning questionnaires. *Public Opinion Quarterly*, 59(4), 547-567.

McMillan, J. H., & Schumacher, S. (2001). *Research in education: A conceptual introduction.* 5th edition, New York, NY: Longman.

McMurtrey, M., Downey, J., Zeltmann, S. & Friedman, W. (2008). Critical skill sets of entry level IT professionals: An empirical examination of perceptions from field personnel. *Journal of Information Technology Education*, 7, 101-120.

Merriam, S. B. (2001). *Qualitative research and case study applications in education.* San Francisco: Jossey Bass.

Michael, R. T. (2004). Family Influences on Children's Verbal Ability. In Ariel Kalil & Thomas DeLeire, (Eds.) *Family Investments in Children: Resources and Behaviours that Promote Success.* (pp. 49-84), Mahwah, NJ: L. Erlbaum Assoc. Inc.

Mincer, J. (1958). Investment in Human Capital and Personal Income Distribution. *Journal of Political Economy,* 66, 281-302.

Ministry of Manpower, (2000). Occupation Segregation: A Gender Perspective. PAPER NO. 1/00, Singapore: Manpower Research and Statistics Department.

MONE, (2008). Seventh Five Year Development Plan 2006 – 2010, Muscat: Ministry of National Economy (MONE).

Moja, T. (2002). *Globalisation Apartheid-The Role of Higher Education in Development.* New York: Steinhardt School of Education.

MONE, (2003). General Census of Population, Housing and Establishments, Muscat: Ministry of National Economy.

MONE, (2008a). Statistical Year Book, Muscat: Ministry of National Economy.

MONE, (2008b). Seventh Five Year Plan document, Muscat: Ministry of National Economy.

MONE, (2009). Population and Development Bulletin - Second Issue, January 2009 A Quarterly Bulletin Issued by the Technical Office of the National Committee for Population, Muscat: Ministry of National Economy

Moss, P. & Tilly, C. (1995). Skills and Race in Hiring: Quantitative Findings from Face- to-Face Interviews *Eastern Economic Journal.* 21(3), 357-374.

Moss, P. & Tilly, C. (2001). *Stories Employers Tell. Race, Skill and Hiring in America.* New York: Russell Sage Foundation.

Motah, M. (2007). Study of the Influence of Multiple Intelligences and the use of Soft Skills in Project Write-up among IT and Non-IT Students: A Research Paper. Proceedings of the (2007) Informing Science and IT Education Joint Conference University of Technology, Mauritius Pointe aux Sables, Mauritius.

Motah, M. (2008). The Influence of Intelligence and Personality on the Use of Soft Skills in Research Projects among Final Year University Students: A Case Study. Proceedings of the Informing Science & IT Education Conference (InSITE) 2008 University of Technology, La Tour Koenig, Pointe aux Sables, Mauritius.

Mulligan, C. B., & X. Sala-i-Martin (1995). Measuring Aggregate Human Capital. *Journal of Economic Growth,* 5 (3), 215-252.

Murphy, R. & Salehi-Isfahani, D. (2003). Labour market flexibility and investment in human capital. 10th Annual Conference of Economic Research Forum, Morocco, December 16- 18, 2003.

Murphy, R. (2005). Evaluating new priorities for assessment in higher education. In: C. Bryan & K. Clegg (Eds.) *Innovative Assessment in Higher Education,* (pp. 37-47), London: Taylor & Francis.

Murray, T. S. (2005). Aspects of Human Capital and the Knowledge Economy: Challenges for Measurement. Luxembourg: Eurostat.

National Committee of Inquiry into Higher Education in UK, (1997). Report of the National Committee of Inquiry into Higher Education. London: The Stationery Office.

NESS, (2003). National Employers Skills Survey (2003) Key Findings, Learning and Skills Council, Institute for Employment Research. Coventry: University of Warwick.

NFQ, (2003). Determinations for the Outline National Framework of Qualifications. Dublin: The National Qualifications Authority of Ireland.

Nonaka, I. & Johansson, J. (1985). Japanese Management: What about the Hard Skills? *Academy of Management Review*, 10(4), 181-91.

NZME, (2005). Effective family engagement in children's literacy skills development, New Zealand - The best evidence. Wellington: Ministry of Education.

O'Donoghue, J. & Maguire, T. (2005). The individual learner, employability and the workplace A reappraisal of relationships and prophecies. *Journal of European Industrial Training*, 29(6), 436-446.

OECD, (1980). *Educational Planning: The historical overview of OECD work.* Paris: OECD

OECD, (1994). *The OECD Jobs Study: Facts, Analysis and strategies.* Paris: OECD

OECD, (1998). *Human Capital investment: an international comparison*. Paris: OECD.

OECD, (2000). *Investing in Education: Analysis of the 1999 World Education Indicators*. Paris: OECD.

OECD, (2001a). *The Well-being of Nations: The Role of Human and Social Capital.* Paris: OECD.

OECD, (2001b). *Human Capital Investment: An International Comparison*. Paris: OECD.

OECD, (2006). Education at a Glance: OECD Indicators, Paris: OECD

Onisk, M. (2006). Is measuring soft-skills training really possible? *Element K Training Newsletter.* Rochester, NY: element k.

Oosterbeek, H. & van Ophem, H. (2000). Schooling Choices: Preferences, Discount rates, and rates of return. *Empirical Economics,* 25(1), 15-34.

Osberg, L., Richard, A. & Clairmont, D. (1986). The Incidence and Duration of Individual Unemployment: Supply Side or Demand Side?, *Cambridge Journal of Economics*, Oxford University Press, 10(1), 13-33.

Ospina, S., Dodge, J., Godsoe, B., Minieri, J., Reza, S. & Schall, E. (2004). From consent to mutual inquiry: Balancing democracy and authority in action research. *Action Research* 2(1), 47–69.

Peters, R. (2007). Effective Practices in Early Childhood Learning. Montreal: Early Childhood Learning Knowledge Centre.

Porter, M. (1990). *The Competitive Advantage of Nations.* London: MacMillan.

Power, N. C. (2000). Global trends in education. *International Education Journal,* 1(3), 152-163.

Proctor, R. & Dutta, A. (1995). *Skill Acquisition and Human Performance.* Thousand Oaks, CA: Sage Publications.

Psacharopoulos, G. & Patrinos, H.A. (2002). Returns to Investment in Education: A Further Update. World Bank Policy Research Working Paper Series No.2881, Washington, DC: The World Bank.

Psacharopoulus, G. & Woodhall, M. (1985). *Education for Development.* New York: Oxford University Press.

Quiggin, J. (1999). Human Capital Theory and Education Policy in Australia. *Australian Economic Review,* 32(2), 130-44.

Rassekh, S. (2004). Education as a Motor for Development –Recent Education reforms in Oman with particular reference to the status of women and girls. Geneva: International Bureau of Education. UNESCO.

Rausch, E., Sherman, H. & Washbush, J. (2002). Defining and assessing competency-based, outcome-focused management development, *Journal of Management Development,* 21(2002), 184–200.

Rich, E., Burke, W., Heaton, C., Haga, S., Pinsky, L., Short, P. & Acheson, L. (2004). Reconsidering the family history in primary care. *Journal of General Internal Medicine,* 19 (3), 273-280.

Robeyns, I. (2006). Three models of education: rights, capabilities and human capital. *Theory and Research in Education,* 4(1), 69-84.

Romer, P. (1990). Human Capital and Growth: Theory and Evidence. *Carnegie- Rochester Conference Series on Public Policy* 32, 251-286.

Sakamoto, A. & Kim, C. (2006). Estimating the Human Capital and Screening Effects of Schooling on Productivity in U.S. Manufacturing Industries, 1979-1996. Paper presented at the Population Association of America, 2006 Annual Meeting Program, Los Angeles, CA. March 30 – April 1, 2006.

Salganik, L., Rychen, D., Moser, U. & Konstant, J. (1999). Projects on Competencies in the OECD Context: Analysis of Theoretical and Conceptual Foundations, Neuchâtel: Swiss Federal Statistical Office.

Sanders, J.R. (1981). Case study methodology: A critique. In W.W. Welsh (Ed.), *Case study methodology in educational evaluation.* Proceedings of the 1981 Minnesota Evaluation Conference. Minneapolis: Minnesota Research and Evaluation Centre.

SCANS, (1991). What work requires of schools. Washington, DC: Secretary's Commission on Achieving Necessary Skills, U.S. Department of Labor.

Schick, S. (2000). Hard truth about soft skills. *IT Training & Careers*, p.25.

Schneider, C. & Holman, D. (2005). *A Profile of Migrant Workers in the Breckland Area: Summary Report*, Norfolk: Keystone Development Trust.

Schultz, T. (1961). Investment in Human Capital. *American Economic Review,* LI, 1- 17.

Schurink, W., Krüger, C., Bergh, A., Van Staden, C., Roos, J., Pickworth, G., Joubert, P., Du Preez, R., Grey, S., Lindeque, B. (2006). Medical students' perceptions of their development of 'soft skills' Part II: The development of 'soft skills' through 'guiding and growing' *South African Family Practice,* 48(8), 14-14d.

SCQF, (2003). *An introduction to the Scottish credit and qualifications framework,* 2nd edition, Glasgow: Scottish Qualifications Authority.

SELD, (2006). FAQ: Soft Indicators, Spring. [online] Available from: http://www.regenwm.org/rWmImages/selddocs/Soft%20Indicators%2006-04-06.doc

Shank, G. (2002). *Qualitative research: A personal skills approach.* Upper Saddle River, N.J.: Prentice Hall.

Sianesi, B. & van Reenen, J. (2000). *The returns to education: A review of the Macro- economic literature.* London: Centre for the Economics of Education, London School of Economics.

Simpson, J.A. (2006). The measurement and recognition of soft skills Developing a Common Standard? Brussels: European Union.

Skinner, C. (2002). High School Graduate Earnings in New York City: The effects of Skill, Gender, Race and Ethnicity. *Journal of Urban Affairs*, 24 (2), 219-238.

Spence, M. (1973). Job market signalling. *Quarterly Journal of Economics*, 87(3), 355-374.

Spence, M. (1974). *Market Signalling: Informational Transfer in Hiring and Related Screening Processes.* Cambridge state: Harvard University Press.

Stasz, C., Ramsey, K., Eden, R., Melamid, E. & Kaganoff, T. (1996). Workplace skills in practice: Case studies of technical work. MDS-773. Berkeley, CA: RAND and the National Centre for Research in Vocational Education.

Stehr, N. (2001). Modern Societies as Knowledge Societies. In George Ritzer and Barry Smart, (Eds.), *Hand Book of Social Theory.* London: Sage. (pp.494-508).

Stephen, G. & Weimerskirch, A. (2007). *Total Quality Management.* Narrated by Lloyd Bochner, Beverly Hills, CA: Phoenix Books.

Stephens, D, & Hamblin, Y. (2006). Employability skills: are UK LIM departments meeting employment needs? *New Library World*, 107(5/6), 218-227.

Thomas, J. R. (2002). Community Development as Human Development: A New Paradigm. Paper presented at the 2002 International Community Development Conference. Cleveland, Mississippi, July 20-24, 2002.

Thurow, L. (1996). *The future of capitalism: how today's economic forces will shape tomorrow's world.* New York: William Morrow.

Tinto, V. (1993). Leaving college: rethinking the causes and cures of student attrition, 2nd edition, Chicago state: University of Chicago Press.

Tissot, P. (2000). Glossary on identification, assessment and recognition of qualifications and competences and transparency and transferability of qualifications. In Bjornavold, J. (Ed.) *Making learning visible: identification, assessment and recognition of non-formal learning in Europe.* Luxembourg: Office for Official Publications of the European Communities.

TMP Worldwide Research, (1998). *Soft Skills: Employers' Desirability and Actual Incidence.* London: TMP Worldwide Research (1998).

Turner, D. (1992). Game Theory in Comparative Education: Prospects and propositions. In J. Schriewer and B. Holmes (Eds.), *Theories and Methods in comparative education.* Bern: Peter Lang.

UNDP, (2005). *Human Development Report 2005.* New York: Oxford University Press.

UNDP, (2008). *Human Development Report 2007/2008.* New York: Oxford University Press.

UNESCO, (2000). *The Right to Education: Towards Education for All Throughout Life.* World Education Report (2000) Paris: UNESCO publishing.

UNESCO, (2003). Higher education in the Arab Region, 1998-2003. meeting of higher education partners, Paris: UNESCO.

UNESCO, (2007). Results-Based Programming, Management and Monitoring (RBM) at UNESCO. Paris: UNESCO.

van Eijs, P. (1994). *Manpower Forecasting in the Western World: The Current State of the Art.* Maastricht: Research Centre for Education and Labour market.

Von Seggern, M. & Young, N.J. (2003). The Focus Group Method in Libraries: Issues Relating to Process and Data and Analysis. *References Services Review*, 31(3), 272-284.

Wagiran, (2008). The importance of developing soft skills in preparing vocational high school graduates. Paper presented in the inaugural VTE Research and Networking Conference, 7-8 July 2008 Bali, Indonesia.

Watkins, K.E., & Cervero, R.M. (2000). Organisations as contexts for learning: A case study in certified public accountancy. *Journal of Workplace Learning*, 12, 187-194.

Webster, M. (1970). Three approaches to Educational Planning. A Review and Appraisal of the Demand-for-Places, Manpower-Requirements and Rate-of-Return Approaches to Educational Planning. *ERIC* #: (ED044769), Washington, DC: Education Resources Information Centre.

Weitzman, M. (1998). Recombinant Growth. *Quarterly Journal of Economics,* 113(2), 331-60.

Wenger, E., McDermott, R. & Snyder, W. (2002). *Cultivating communities of practice: a guide to managing knowledge.* Cambridge, MA: Harvard Business School Press.

Williams, D. T. Jr. (1973). A Conceptual Framework for Theories in Higher Education. *ERIC* #: ED078727 Washington, DC: Education Resources Information Centre.

Williams, G. (1974). The Events of 1973-74 in a long-term Planning Perspective. *Higher Education Bulletin*, 3(1), 8-17.

Winter, J. (2004). Best Practices in Workforce Development. Grand Rapids, MI: Community Research Institute.

Woodhall, M. (2001). Human capital: educational aspects. In: Smelser, N.J., Baltes, P.B. (Eds.), *International Encyclopaedia of the Social and Behavioural Sciences*, vol. 10. (pp. 6951–6955) New York: Elsevier.

World Conference on Higher Education, (1998). World Declaration on Higher Education for the Twenty First Century: Vision and Action. World Conference on Higher Education, Paris, 5-9 October 1998, Paris: UNESCO.

Yang, K. & El-Haik, B. (2003). *Design for Six Sigma: A Roadmap for Product Development* 1st edition, Hightstown, NJ: McGraw-Hill Publishing Company.

Other sources

Executive, (2007). [Personal communication]. 2 June.

HR Manager, (2007). [Personal communication]. 11 June

HR Manager, (2007). [Personal communication]. 20 September

Junior Manager, (2007). [Personal communication]. 25 June

Junior Manager, (2007). [Personal communication]. 26 June

Junior Manager, (2007). [Personal communication]. 4 June

Junior Manager, (2007). [Personal communication]. 5 June

Junior Manager, (2007). [Personal communication]. 20 September

Junior Manager, (2007). [Personal communication]. 15 October

Participants, (2007). [Personal communication]. 30 June

Participants, (2007). [Personal communication]. 1 July

Participants, (2007). [Personal communication]. 13 June

Reference group member, (2007). [Personal communication]. 5 November

Reference group member, (2007). [Personal communication]. 12 November

Reference group member, (2007). [Personal communication]. 12 November

Senior Engineer, (2007). [Personal communication]. 3 July

Senior Executive, (2007). [Personal communication]. 10 June

Senior Manager, (2007). [Personal communication]. 17 June

Senior Manager, (2007). [Personal communication]. 23 June

Senior Manager, (2007). [Personal communication]. 23 June

Senior Manager, (2007). [Personal communication]. 13 June

Senior Manager, (2007). [Personal communication]. 14 June

Senior Manager, (2007). [Personal communication]. 15 August

Senior Manager, (2007). [Personal communication]. 16 August

Senior Manager, (2007). [Personal communication]. 18 August

Senior Manager, (2007). [Personal communication]. 1 September

Senior Manager, (2007). [Personal communication]. 3 September

Senior Manager, (2007). [Personal communication]. 8 September

Senior Manager, (2007). [Personal communication]. 20 October

Senior Manager, (2007). [Personal communication]. 2 November

Senior Manager, (2007). [Personal communication]. 10 November

Senior Trainer, (2007). [Personal communication]. 20 October

Technical Manager, (2007). [Personal communication]. 1 July

Training Manager, (2007). [Personal communication]. 26 May

Training Manager, (2007). [Personal communication]. 28 May

Training Manager, (2007). [Personal communication]. 29 May

Training Manager, (2007). [Personal communication]. 30 May

Training Manager, (2007). [Personal communication]. 17 October

Training Manager, (2007). [Personal communication]. 10 September

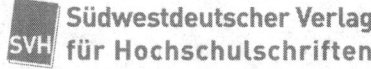